970
.011
Wil

Wilson, Ian, 1941-
   The Columbus myth : did men of Bristol reach
America before Columbus? / Ian Wilson. -- London ;
Toronto : Simon & Schuster, 1991.
   xvi, 240 p. : ill.

Includes bibliographical references (p. 229-234) and
index.
04937953   ISBN:0671710672

1. Columbus, Christopher - Journeys. 2. Explorers -
Spain - Biography. 3. Explorers - England - Bristol -
                    (SEE NEXT CARD)
2859   92FEB10   30/rh   1-00568099

THE COLUMBUS MYTH

The Columbus Myth

Did men of Bristol reach America before Columbus?

IAN WILSON

SIMON & SCHUSTER

LONDON·SYDNEY·NEW YORK·TOKYO·SINGAPORE·TORONTO

First published in Great Britain by
Simon & Schuster Ltd in 1991
A Paramount Communications Company

Simon & Schuster Ltd
West Garden Place
Kendal Street
London W2 2AQ

Simon & Schuster of Australia Pty Ltd
Sydney

A CIP catalogue record for this book is
available from the British Library
ISBN 0-671-71067-2

Typeset in Sabon by Selectmove Ltd
Printed and bound in Great Britain by
Butler & Tanner Ltd, Frome.

For the people of Bristol, England,
my home for more than two decades,
with much affection

Contents

Illustrations

Plates

Text Figures

An age will come after many years
when the Ocean will loose the chains of things,
and a huge land lie revealed;
when Tethys will disclose new worlds
and Thule no more be the ultimate

Prophecy from Seneca's *Medea*,
Written in the first century AD

Against this passage in his father's personal copy of Seneca's works, Columbus's son Fernando proudly wrote:

This prophecy was fulfilled by my father
the Admiral, in the year 1492

Author's Preface

This book really had its beginnings in 1973 when, while employed by the *Bristol Evening Post* newspaper group, I worked on a variety of publications and events celebrating Bristol's six hundredth anniversary as a city and county. At that time local journalist the late Max Barnes vividly rekindled many colourful episodes from the city's history, not least of these Bristol's long associations with the discovery of America. In that same year I met elderly Philip Cabot, who claimed to be a descendant of the John Cabot who sailed from Bristol to North America in 1497 (he certainly bore a striking resemblance to the only known portrait of John Cabot's son Sebastian). At the Bristol Council House staff brought to my attention the existence of little-known historical documents showing that John Cabot's paymaster had been one Richard Ameryk. More recently I happened to move to a house in which, from my study window, I can look out (in the winter months at least) on the very stretch of river along which the ships of Cabot and others had to pass when setting out and returning from their voyages of discovery.

It would have been remiss to write about America's discovery without direct experience of the continent, and although my first visit had been in the early 1970s it was in 1979, during my very first weeks as a full-time writer, that I explored the northern continent in proper depth, in the company of my family. During a memorable six weeks we zig-zagged from New York to the Great Lakes, south to the Smoky Mountains, west across the Mississippi valley to New Mexico and Colorado, then westwards again via the Grand Canyon, through Death Valley to the Pacific Coast. Not least of the insights gained from this, most noticeably in the dusty Arizona town of Kayenta, was just what the European incursion into America, the direct consequence of the discovery, had meant for the pride and culture of the true *native* American, a theme the reader will find reflected in this book. Further visits took us across Mexico and to Florida, and for more recent and specific research my wife and

I toured Newfoundland and Cape Breton Island in the autumn of 1990 and also southern Spain in early 1991.

Inevitably I am deeply indebted to those who have earlier written on the discovery of America, perhaps the most formidable of these having been the late US admiral and Harvard professor of history, Samuel Eliot Morison, whose volumes on Christopher Columbus, in particular, remain arguably the most definitive in the English language. Morison was always quick to accuse other writers of bias, and in this regard I have to plead utterly guilty to weighting this book's focus heavily towards my own home city's rôle in America's discovery. Accordingly I have differed from Morison in certain conclusions.

It is important to make clear, however, that many of the arguments advanced in this book are not so much new, as unfamiliar hitherto to any wide, non-specialist readership. One scholar to whom I am particularly indebted is Professor David Quinn, recently retired from the chair of history at the University of Liverpool, and author of *England and the Discovery of America, 1481–1620*, published in 1974; also a monumental five volume *New American World*, complete with exhaustive documentation, published in 1979. Particularly to Professor Quinn's 1974 work, out of print and now very hard to obtain, I owe the key arguments that men of Bristol reached Newfoundland as early as the 1480s. A similar debt is owed to eminent naval historian and former Hakluyt Society vice-president, the late Dr James Williamson, whose *The Cabot Voyages and Bristol Discovery under Henry VII*, published in 1962, essentially blazed the trail for my arguments that one or more ships from the lost Cabot voyage of 1498 may have reached the Caribbean coast of South America. A third major scholar upon whom I have heavily relied is Dr Alwyn Ruddock, former reader in history at Birkbeck College, University of London, and author of specialist papers on two of the most crucial documents to be discussed in this book.

Professor Quinn has been particularly kind in his help to me, both with answering individual queries and with reading the manuscript of this book, saving me from several inadvertent errors. I also owe a great debt to Mrs Caroline Forbes Taylor of Bristol who made available to me her late husband's exhaustive but unpublished researches into Bristol's customs accounts. On Newfoundland, Anne Hart, Head of the Centre for Newfoundland Studies at the Memorial University, St John's, guided me to certain scholarly papers that had not reached Britain; the staff of the Newfoundland Museum Historic Resources Division, St John's, very kindly provided me with complimentary copies of local archaeology reports; the Memorial University's Professor James Tuck and underwater archaeologist Janette Ginns helped me with my enquiries concerning land and underwater remains at the island's earliest English fishing harbours, and Bruce Bradbury, Superintendent of the L'Anse aux Meadows National Historic Park gave me every assistance during my study of the Norse remains at this location. Archaeologist Birgitta Wallace also kindly provided me with the latest available information concerning the significance of butternuts found among the most recent excavations. On Nova Scotia, archaeology collection supervisor Jim Campbell was equally helpful with my enquiries concerning the Louisbourg cannon.

Maps are one of the most important source materials for study of America's discovery, and because of their size and age those of the fifteenth and sixteenth centuries rarely reproduce well in book form (although a happy exception is Kenneth Nebenzahl's *Maps from the Age of Discovery*, published in 1990 just in time for my researches, and highly recommended as a companion to my own book). Accordingly I have been particularly grateful to the National Geographic Society of Washington and the Museo Naval, Madrid, Spain, for their providing me with excellent transparencies of the La Cosa map for research purposes; also Schuler Verlag of Stuttgart for superb prints of the Waldseemüller world maps of 1507 and 1516.

My thanks are also due to the patient help provided by the staff of the Round Room at the Public Record Office, London during my examination of the original documents of Bristol's customs accounts and other related source materials; to John Williams and staff of the Bristol Record Office for help with my studies of the Ricart *Kalendar* and Richard Ameryk's property transactions; to Anne Sutton, archivist of the Mercers' Company, London for her help with my study of the Balsall accounts; to former Bristol city archivist Mary Williams for her kindness in providing me with her careful transcription from the Bristol alien subsidy roll of 1484; to Lewis Cobb, former assistant verger at Bristol's St Mary Redcliffe church for his assistance with my studies of the John Jay and Joan Ameryk memorial brasses in that church; to the Hon. Diana Uhlman and Stephen Jelfs of Croft Castle, near Leominster for their help with my researches concerning Thomas Croft; to Dr Sheridan

Bowman and Janet Ambers of the British Museum Radiocarbon Laboratory for the latest information on radiocarbon dating of the Norse remains at L'Anse aux Meadows; to the staffs of the Bristol and Gloucester Record Offices; to the Cultural Affairs Division of the Canadian High Commission, London; to Jean Lester and Ron Simpson of Bristol United Press; to Mr and Mrs Weston of Lower Court Farm, Long Ashton; to Roy Avery and Eric Ginns; also, as always in my researches, to the staffs of the British Library, the Bristol University Library and the Bristol Central Library.

The writing of this book would never have been accomplished without the enthusiastic support of Nick Brealey, Claudia Shaffer and Brian Perman of my publishers Simon & Schuster. Equally valuable have been constructive criticisms of the manuscript made by Simon and Schuster's reader, Fenella Copplestone, to whom I am particularly indebted for some of the Hakluyt references incorporated into Chapter 13. By no means least, I have been indebted as ever to the long-term patience and encouragement of my literary agent Bill Hamilton, and also of my wife Judith, who was at my side throughout our explorations of Newfoundland, who took charge of the physical printing of the manuscript, and who spent hours making a careful rubbing of the memorial brass of the fifteenth-century Bristolians John and Joan Jay.

On a point of style, I have in general modernised the spellings and English of certain of the documents quoted, sacrificing quaintness for a greater readability. For exact sources of all quotations readers should consult the Notes and References section at the end of this book. For certain historical names there is no standardisation among scholars, some, for example, preferring to refer to Columbus's son as Ferdinand, others as Fernando. In these instances I have simply tried to follow the more generally accepted styling.

Bristol, England
May 1991

The Columbus Myth

Every day, in every country, even the very best newspapers present an unavoidably distorted view of world events. An entire front page and several inside ones may be devoted to the 'shock' resignation of one government minister. By contrast, the death of 20,000 by earthquake or flood in some distant and inaccessible foreign region may merit scarcely a paragraph. It is not wholly that a home politician's career crisis is more newsworthy than the loss of thousands of lives in some far-off country. Availability of on-the-spot reporting may also be of considerable relevance.

In the same light there has perhaps been no more distorted or mythologised 'fact' of history than that of Christopher Columbus's so-called 'discovery' of America five hundred years ago. On both sides of the Atlantic umpteen generations of schoolchildren have been taught to regard the continent of America as having been an island effectively cut off from the rest of the world until Columbus's out-of-the-blue arrival at the Bahaman island he named San Salvador on October 12, 1492.

Even the most authoritative textbooks have reinforced this view. In my personal library is the thirteenth edition of a massive compendium, the *Lincoln Library of Essential Information*, compressing into a little over two thousand pages everything that a well-informed US citizen ought to know on every conceivable subject. It incorporates a twelve-page chronological chart of the salient facts of American history commencing:

> 1492. Columbus sails from Palos, Spain, and discovers West India islands

It is as if up to that moment nothing of any consequence had ever happened on the American continent; as if (among many other of the continent's peoples) the histories of the mighty Incas, Toltecs, Aztecs and Mayas, all of them punctilious in the keeping of their own records, had never been. It is also as if before 1492 there had

1

been no form of contact between the Old World and the New.

As scarcely anyone is likely to have avoided becoming aware, 1992 of course marks the quincentenary of Columbus's historic arrival on San Salvador. The event is being commemorated both in Europe and on the American continent in innumerable ways, including commemorative voyages, an ambitious 'Expo' in Seville and the publication of dozens of books.

In this regard, this book is not especially an attempt to go against the tide of the 1992 celebrations, or to undermine what Columbus achieved. It is undeniable that October 12, 1492 was a breakthrough moment in the general European realisation that a huge, undiscovered new world was waiting to be reached by anyone with the temerity to venture westwards across the Atlantic.

Nor is it particularly my intention to subvert Columbus's claim to being 'first' to discover America. Effectively any such aim is quite unneccessary because it has already been achieved, and utterly convincingly. Thanks to comparatively recent archaeological discoveries it is now a well-established fact that Norsemen, if not Irishmen before them, reached Newfoundland and built homes there almost exactly five hundred years before Columbus arrived on San Salvador. We will in fact be briefly reviewing such evidence for Norse and related pre-Columbian transoceanic visitors to America, though predominantly to set the scene for what follows.

Rather, our prime concern is to try to put Columbus and his voyage of 1492 into proper perspective in what was happening generally among European seafarers at that time. This is particularly with regard to certain seafarers from England who, as we will be showing, may well have reached America's shores over a decade before Columbus found San Salvador, yet rather in the manner of newspapers' minimal reporting of certain far-off events, have simply failed to find their deserved niche in the pages of history.

An important consideration in this regard is the inevitably distorting effect of the far more abundant contemporaneous documentation for Columbus than for almost any other voyager of his period. For instance, there has survived, albeit in secondhand and partly truncated form, a transcript of the very journal he kept on his historic First Voyage of 1492–3.

Made back in the early-sixteenth century by the Spanish priest Bartolomé de Las Casas, who personally knew Columbus, this transcript was rediscovered early in the nineteenth century by Spanish scholar and former naval officer Martín Fernández de Navarrete. Today it is one of the most prized items in the collection of Madrid's National Library, and provides essential reading for anyone trying to come to a proper understanding both of Columbus's mentality and at least something of the circumstances which led him on his First Voyage.

Columbus also benefited from having a contemporary hero-worshipper in the person of his illegitimate son Fernando, a bookish individual who assembled a great collection of his father's papers after the latter's death, and wrote a biography from these. Others who directly knew Columbus, such as the historical scholar Peter Martyr and the official chronicler Gonzalo Fernández de Oviedo, who witnessed Columbus's reporting of the success of his First Voyage to Ferdinand and Isabella, also contributed useful biographical material. Additionally there have survived published copies of the official Letter describing his First Voyage, some 40 handwritten letters and other documents carrying Columbus's own signature, several portraits (though probably none absolutely contemporary), and also some of his collection of books, complete with his marginal jottings. Not least, three places, Seville, Havana and Santo Domingo, claim to possess Columbus's bones, and another eight his ashes.

By contrast, of Columbus's fellow-Genoese John Cabot, who under the flag of England's King Henry VII sailed from the West Country port of Bristol to 'discover' North America in 1497, there survives no journal, no biography, not a single document in his handwriting, nor even any remotely contemporary portrait. Nor does Cabot have any known grave. Arguably the only known physical relic of his existence is the rib of a cow whale, preserved in Bristol's St Mary Redcliffe church, that he is said to have brought back from his voyage of 1497. And even this is thought to be of doubtful authenticity.

Somewhat predictably, there is even less material evidence concerning the Bristol fishermen whom, as we will be trying to demonstrate, may well have preceded both Cabot and Columbus to the shores of America by over a decade. As far back as Biblical times fishermen have been regarded as among the very lowliest members of society, and the fifteenth century was no exception. But this is no justification for these individuals' arrival on American shores, if they genuinely preceded Columbus, being regarded as any the less noteworthy. Arguably our whole perspective on Columbus would be altered, and the significance of 1492 justifiably undermined, if

Fig. 1: The earliest datable portrait of Columbus, a late-sixteenth century woodcut made by Swiss artist Tobias Stimmer, who copied a collection of portraits of the famous made about 1550 by Paolo Giovio of Florence.

we were able to establish that these voyages definitely took place, that Columbus knew all about them but deliberately chose to ignore mentioning them in order not to undermine his own achievement.

Nor should the reader, brought up to regard Columbus as one of history's great discovering heroes, be disinclined to believe that he could have been capable of any unworthy suppression of information. It is important even at this early stage to set down a few salient facts.

Columbus was, for instance, as recognized by most leading historians, both suspiciously reticent and on occasion downright untruthful about his personal background. His own statements even concerning the age at which he first went to sea vary by as much as nine years. Late in his life he seems to have put about, certainly as relayed by Fernando, that he came from a distinguished family, that he had studied at the University of Pavia and was not the first member of his family to have been an Admiral. In reality, on the best available historical information, he was the son of a poor Genoese wool-weaver, received a fairly minimal education, and before his First Voyage had no known previous experience either in the command of a ship or as a navigator.

Even on his own admission Columbus was also more than ready to make a virtue out of blatant deception. It is well known that the Journal of his First Voyage, as transcribed by Las Casas, records how day after day he relayed to his crew a deliberate under-estimate of the distance travelled in order that they should not become over-alarmed at their distance from home. For example, on 10 September, 1492 he recorded:

> On that day and night we made 60 leagues [about 180 miles] . . . but I reported only 48 leagues [about 144 miles] so that the men would not be frightened if the voyage were long.

The next day he wrote:

> In the night we went nearly 20 leagues and I reported only 16 for the reason stated.

This he continued day after day until successfully sighting land.

In 1495 he bragged to the Spanish monarchs Ferdinand and Isabella of how when in Sardinia as a 'young captain' (and there is no evidence he ever held such a post), he secretly flipped his ship's compass card 180 degrees to trick an unwilling crew into believing that they were steering overnight north to Marseilles, whereas in reality they were heading south to Tunis, just as he wanted.

Similarly, trying to save face with his Spanish royal patrons, in 1494 Columbus forced all the crews of his Second Voyage to sign a sworn statement that Cuba was not an island but mainland, despite the island's natives having told him to the contrary. With regard to the latitude readings he recorded, he seems frequently deliberately to have falsified these, even in the reports prepared for the Spanish monarchs, so that only he would be able to find his way back to his discovery.

In such acts of deception Columbus was probably no worse than many others of his time. Late-fifteenth-century Europe was rife with tricksters and spies, and kings and princes had themselves become well practised in deception and double-dealing, as epitomised not least by Machiavelli's *The Prince*.

One of the most fundamental examples of Columbus's evasiveness was his non-disclosure to anyone, at any time of his life, of exactly what it was that impelled him to pursue so doggedly his idea of reaching 'Asia' by sailing westwards. This is all the more remarkable given that he spent at least eight humiliating and often penurious years having his ideas rebuffed by some of the most learned men of both Spain and Portugal. For a man known to have been proud, such repeated rejections must have hurt all the more deeply.

Nor, despite popular supposition, was it his belief that the world was round that attracted such opposition. This was accepted by most educated people. It was his estimates of the distance to 'Asia' that were so hotly derided. There has therefore to have been something very powerful that sustained him in his belief during his wilderness years, something rather more solid than mere geographical theory. So what was it? And who did he learn it from?

It should be made quite clear that Columbus himself never made any claim to have 'discovered' America. To his dying day he was convinced he had reached Asia. It was his snobbish biographer son Fernando who, in the light of the knowledge accrued after Columbus's death, made this particular claim, at one and the same time probably adding to whatever falsehoods had emanated from his father. But, mistaken destination notwithstanding, Columbus would undoubtedly have been more than concerned to secure his place in history.

It is against this highly complex scenario – one of on the one hand a superfluity of material of dubious trustworthiness, and on the other a desperate shortage of alternative information – that our quest is set. The story is an unavoidably tangled one in which we will be obliged to hunt among the merest scraps of historical material, contemporary maps, customs records, trading licences and the occasional chance-preserved letter, for possible clues.

At its heart lies the case for believing that Columbus, in setting out upon the ocean blue in 1492, was sailing by no means as blind as has hitherto been supposed. Our thesis will be that he knew something from others, most notably from men of Bristol, who had crossed the Atlantic before him, albeit on a more northerly route. Even they, as we will show, had by no means been the first. But first we will begin at the beginning.

CHAPTER 1

'America Had Often Been Discovered Before'

Of course America had often been discovered before, but it had always been hushed up

Oscar Wilde

When Oscar Wilde made the above-quoted remark he intended it as a flippant anti-American joke. Nonetheless it also deserves to be taken seriously. Whatever the fuss made about the quincentenary of Columbus's first landfall, quite incontrovertibly America had been discovered before 1492. And the first and most obvious of its discoverers were the ancestors of those already living there when Columbus arrived, the so-called American 'Indians'.

It has been not the least of the Old World's abominations practised upon these New World peoples that the very name popularly accorded to them derives directly from Columbus's colossal misidentification of what he had discovered. The 'Indies' was one of the vague terms used in Columbus's time to denote the more eastern parts of the Asian continent. Even after it became realised that America was not Asia, the nomenclature 'West Indies' stuck. And so too did the name 'Indians' for the inhabitants of the entire continent, its perpetuation symptomatic of an underlying European assumption that these people were somehow too insignificant to warrant any proper identity of their own. As at least some token of personal protest, wherever possible I will be using the still unsatisfactory term 'native Americans'.

But however we describe them, America's true discoverers must in all logic have been the ancestors of these native Americans, peoples generally agreed by anthropologists to have been hunters of Siberian origin who long ago followed migrating herds of musk-ox, mammoth and caribou across a land-bridge that joined Siberia and Alaska up to the end of the last Ice Age. According to generally accepted theory, when the ice melted the sea level became raised, covering the land-bridge with what is now the Bering Strait, and thus isolating the emigrants on the new continent.

Now as the same anthropologists stress, this Siberian ancestry of America's native peoples should not cause them to be dismissed as mere variants of Mongoloid Asiatics. Rather more accurately, they and the Mongoloids of Asia simply share the same ancestry, both populations having subsequently developed separate characteristics. In the case of the native American the more notable of these are dark eyes, coarse, straight head hair, a virtual absence of facial and body hair (both in men and women), and absence also of the blood types A^2, B, D and r. The homogeneity of these characteristics right across the native populations of the two halves of the continent is thought to have resulted from the comparatively narrow gene pool of original discoverers from whom they all descended.

The main uncertainty concerning the entry of these first peoples into the American continent, fifteen million square miles of mainland and islands hitherto quite empty of human occupants, is the precise date of their arrival. As part of the general down-grading of its native population, America has often been described as a 'young' continent in human terms. Almost incredibly, only as recently as 1930 professional anthropologists were still insisting that the original crossing of the Bering Strait was by boat and as little as three thousand years ago.

This thinking started to change, however, around 1928 when archaeologists and palaeontologists began excavating in the New Mexico part of the Great Plains. Here they came across skilfully made stone spear points in close association with more than twenty deeply buried skeletons of the extinct long-horned bison. Subsequently several similar sites were found in which, above older levels totally lacking in evidence of human occupancy, there came to light remains indicating the arrival of a people who were clearly successful hunters of big game animals such as the bison and mammoth. With the development of carbon dating, the earliest of these remains became dated to around 10,000 BC. For archaeologists such as the University of Arizona's Professor Vance Haynes, this date now represents the best approximation of when America's true first discoverers made their migration from Siberia.

However, within recent decades fresh finds have been made which suggest that the original discovery may have occurred considerably earlier still. At Monte Verde in Chile the archaeologist T. Dillehay and a Chilean team have found the remains of an encampment of mastodon hunters datable to 12,000 BC. A skin scraper made of caribou bone, found in the Yukon in 1966, has been radiocarbon dated to around 27,000 BC. Most notable of all have been the findings of a Franco-Brazilian archaeological team led by Parisian Professor Nìede Guidon, who since the 1970s has been investigating and excavating more than 300 prehistoric rock shelters set amidst spectacular red sandstone cliffs at São Raimundo Nonato, north-eastern Brazil. More than two-thirds of the region's prehistoric shelters are decorated with lively cave-paintings, and one indication of their antiquity has been that alongside some of the traces of the paintings' creators, Professor Guidon's team found the bones of long-extinct mammals such as the giant sloth, the mammoth and the sabre-toothed cat.

But the real surprise, and one still not accepted by all archaeologists, is that the carbon dating of some of the charcoal fires of these painters furnished dates of around 32,000 years ago. If human infiltration had reached this far south at such an early date, this suggests that the original discoverers must have made their first venture into the northern part of the continent earlier still. Since even Europe was only being peopled at about this time, the arguments for America being a 'young' continent have been wearing progressively more thin.

Certainly one important indication of the long-established nature of native settlement in the Americas is the sheer diversity of the peoples as they had developed throughout the length and breadth of the continent by the time of Columbus's arrival. With regard to language alone, for instance, it has been estimated that by 1492 there were some 200 different languages spoken on the northern part of the continent, 350 in its central region, and 1,450 in its southern part.

Equally remarkable was the diversity of life-style. Living closest to the original Siberian homeland were peoples such as the Tlingit and Haida of the Pacific north-west, who wore leather and fur garments, crafted large communal wooden houses for themselves, and subsisted mainly by hunting and fishing. Following a relatively similar life-style, except that their houses were mainly of skin, were the Beothuks of Newfoundland and Micmacs of Nova Scotia.

Quite different, however, were the tribes who lived south of the Great Lakes. These, such as the Iroquois and Delaware, were notable for their skills in agriculture and hand-crafted pottery, while to the south-east the Creeks, Choctaws and Seminole congregated in permanent villages and could weave their own cloth. Across the Great Plains the Sioux stalked their natural larder of the vast herds of bison who grazed on their doorstep. To the south-west, Pueblo peoples lived in well-constructed houses, wove brilliantly designed blankets and dug elaborate canals to irrigate their beans, maize, cotton and other crops. Further south, in what is now Mexico, the Aztecs designed elaborate temples and canals, and ordered their lives with the aid of a calendar and pictographic writing system.

On South America's western coast the Incas had developed an elaborate road network, developed metal-working, weaving factories, pottery industries, huge grain stores, and unmortared stone buildings especially designed to withstand earth tremors. By contrast, the Guarani and related peoples, spread from the Amazon to Paraguay, along with the Arawaks of South America's north-east coast and Caribbean islands (the ones first met by Columbus), lived mostly in the starkest of nakedness. Yet even these latter could craft pots, could hew 40-man canoes from treetrunks, and knew how to grow corn and yams.

While of necessity this represents only a thumbnail sketch of America's peoples at the time of Columbus's arrival, the very fact of such extraordinary diversity inevitably raises some fundamental questions. After the severing of the Bering land-bridge in the wake of the last Ice Age, did these peoples subsequently remain totally isolated, and therefore independent of any Old World influences up to the time of Columbus's arrival? Or were there continued further 'discoveries' of America by sea, either via the Atlantic or the Pacific coasts?

As is well known, this is an issue which has long fascinated Norwegian Thor Heyerdahl, leader of the famous *Kon-Tiki* expedition. For decades Heyerdahl has studied some of the striking cultural parallels between the pre-Columbian American peoples and those of the Old World.

He has pointed, for instance, to Ancient Egyptian and Assyrian relief sculptures on which can be seen detailed depictions of the making of reed boats by a method consisting of lashing bundles of reeds together in a manner still practised by the fishermen of Lake Chad in central Africa. When the Spaniards who followed Columbus began to push their way into America, they found identical boats built to a near identical design being made and used in Mexico and also in Inca Peru, both inland and on the coast. Indeed, such boats can still be seen to this day in use on Lake Titicaca between Bolivia and Peru.

So were the techniques of making such reed boats somehow passed down from the original Siberian migrants? Were they brought across the Atlantic by unknown voyagers in antiquity? Or were the methods independently developed by the native Americans in genuine isolation?

On its own, the making of reed boats might well be dismissed as an idea sufficiently simple that peoples totally isolated from each other could have thought it out quite independently. But as Thor Heyerdahl has stressed, there are many more Old World/New World parallels that are rather more difficult to explain away. These include pyramid building, sun worship, marriage between brothers and sisters in royal families, mummification of the dead, trepanning of the skull, irrigation and terrace agriculture, cotton cultivation, spinning and weaving, pottery, fitted megalithic masonry, musical wind instruments, paper manufacture, writing and calendar systems, the use of zero, and much else.

Several of these parallels are of a cultural order substantially higher than could conceivably have been reached by the last migrants across the Bering land-bridge. Furthermore, features like pyramids, mummification and paper manufacture suggest Ancient Egyptian links. Heyerdahl for one, therefore, has adopted the so-called Diffusionist argument that Ancient Egyptians and/or Phoenicians (as antiquity's most noted sailors) must have preceded Columbus across the Atlantic.

In order to demonstrate this he set up an Atlantic version of the *Kon-Tiki* expedition by the commissioning of a simple, single-sail boat, *Ra II*, built entirely according to Ancient Egyptian methods and materials, in which he and a five-man crew set sail westwards from Safi, Morocco, in May 1970. Fifty-seven days later they successfully reached Bridgetown, Barbados with *Ra II* having suffered no worse disaster than a broken steering oar. In fact this very calamity served to demonstrate that for anyone trying (or perhaps even not trying), to cross the Atlantic westwards at the right latitude, it would not even have been necessary to have any means of steering. The winds and current, acting as a giant conveyor belt, would do it all.

Independent evidence that someone could have strayed across the Atlantic as early as Phoenician times is indicated by the virtual certainty that a whole Phoenician fleet made a complete circumnavigation of Africa during the reign of the Egyptian Pharaoh Necho II (610–595 BC). The Greek historian Herodotus, in recounting this, mentioned the Phoenician sailors' incredulity at seeing the sun to their right on their westward rounding of Africa's southern tip, something they could only have observed if they had genuinely made a round trip of this kind. It needed only one of the fleet's vessels to have been blown off course for America to have been reached and at least some Old World knowledge imparted to the New.

It is also perhaps worth mentioning that Martin Alonso Pinzón, captain of the *Pinta* on Columbus's First Voyage, was said to have gone along with Columbus because he had been shown in the Vatican Library a document asserting that in the time of King Solomon, the Queen of Sheba had sailed westwards out into the Atlantic and found a vast new land 'fertile and abundant, and whose extent surpasses Africa and Europe.'

The problem, however, is the lack of truly hard evidence anywhere on the American continent demonstrating that any such voyages from the Old World happened during antiquity. Every now and again the finding of some 'Phoenician' inscription is reported, as in the case of the so-called Parahyba tablet found last century in north-east Brazil. Purporting to have been made by Phoenician sailors blown off course during a circumnavigation of Africa, one distinguished Near Eastern languages scholar, Professor Cyrus H. Gordon, has been persuaded of its authenticity. But most have concluded otherwise, on the grounds of linguistics, anachronisms, and the original tablet itself never having been made available for scholarly scrutiny.

Also, several of the Heyerdahl-type parallels between the Old World and the Americas might be more impressive were it not for seemingly irreconcilable time gaps between them. For instance, while the golden age of Egyptian pyramid building was around 3,000 BC and had greatly declined in fashion by 2,000 BC, in the Americas the most primitive pyramids did not begin until circa 600 BC, and the more impressive ones, such as the Toltec Teotihuacan in Mexico, date from several centuries *after* the birth of Christ.

Similarly at first sight there might seem to be a very striking parallel between an 'astronomical clock' built into the design of the megalithic tomb chamber at Newgrange, Ireland, and a near identical device to be found at the south entrance to the Chaco Canyon in New Mexico. Geographically some 5,000 miles apart, the two even exhibit near identical spiral decorations. Yet the harsh reality is that while the Newgrange 'clock' was made about 3,000 BC, as early as the earliest pyramids, the Chaco one was made about 1200 AD, only three centuries before Columbus. Such findings weigh heaviest in favour of the so-called Isolationist argument, that minds widely separated by time and space may and sometimes do come up with uncannily similar ideas, a fascinating phenomenon in its own right. Also in favour of the Isolationist argument is the fact that although some native Americans developed the making of pottery as early as 3,000 BC, none anywhere on the continent took up the use of a potter's wheel until after Columbus's arrival.

For the purposes of this book there is in fact no particularly pressing need to make any hard-and-fast choice between the Diffusionist and Isolationist arguments. On balance it simply seems more reasonable than unreasonable to believe that there might have been at least the occasional chance Old World/New World contact during the millennia of mankind's broadly parallel developments into full-scale civilisation.

It is important not to disregard the likelihood of occasional voyages across the Pacific as well as the Atlantic. In the north, of course, no great distance is involved; a relatively sustained contact is certainly suggested by parallels in funerary practice and language between the Mongolian and some of the north-west American peoples, not least of these a sharing in common of the name and function of the 'shaman'.

More spectacularly, an ancient Chinese manuscript seems to record a voyage from China to America by a Buddhist missionary monk, Hwui Shan, back in the fifth century AD. According to nineteenth-century translations of this manuscript, Hwui Shan and some companions voyaged to a country called Fusang that lay an immense distance east of China. His description of this has strongly suggested to some that he reached Mexico, at that time controlled by the Aztecs' highly developed predecessors, the Toltecs.

But perhaps the most intriguing evidence of all for early discoverers of America (and arguably ones who crossed the Atlantic), derives from the well-attested Aztec and Inca reaction to the bearded Spanish conquistadors immediately upon their arrival on American shores. As already described one of the most notable characteristics of native American males, as found virtually throughout the entire continent, is their lack of facial and body hair. Yet to the amazement of the Spanish, both the Incas and the Aztecs cherished a strong belief that they had been visited long before by white men with beards from across the ocean, men whom they still remembered and venerated as gods who had taught them the higher aspects of their culture.

Thus when Hernando Cortés and his Spanish conquistadors arrived among the Aztecs in 1519, the early Mexican chronicler Tezozomoc reported how the Emperor Montezuma's artists:

> ... showed him pictures of the bearded Spaniards ... the emperor could doubt no longer and exclaimed: 'Truly this is the Quetzalcoatl we expected, he who lived with us of old in Tula.'

Similarly, in his *Carta Segunda* for October 30, 1520 Cortés personally recorded the speech which Montezuma made to him through an interpreter, after welcoming him by sacrificing a human victim in his honour:

> We have known for a long time, by the writings handed down by our forefathers ... that we were led here by a ruler, whose subjects we all were, who returned to his country ... We have ever believed that those who were of his lineage would some time come and claim this land as his, and us as his vassals. From the direction whence you come, which is where the sun rises, and from what you tell me of this great lord who sent you, we believe and think it certain that he is our natural ruler ...

That this belief was not just confined to Central America is indicated by the fact that during the 1530s on the southern continent, in Inca Peru, Francisco Pizarro encountered similar reaction, with merely the names changed. No sooner had Pizarro and his men landed than Inca relay runners took word to their Emperor Huayna Capac and his son Atahualpa that their gods, the Viracochas or sea-foam people, had returned. Apparently again one of the reasons for this recognition was the Spaniards' beards. As Pizarro noted, the statues of the Incas' 'gods', the Viracochas, repeatedly showed these as with astonishingly European-style beards. The Spaniards were told that these 'Viracochas' were a pre-Inca people, responsible for some particularly spectacular architecture, such as at Vinaque, between Cuzco and the Pacific coast. As reported by the Spanish chronicler Cieza de Léon in 1553:

> When I questioned the neighbouring Indians as to who had made that monument of antiquity, they answered that it was another people, who had been bearded and white like ourselves, who, they say, came to these parts a long time before the Incas reigned ...

Now whatever the historical facts behind these legends – and the Mayans had similar, relating to a bearded visitor called Kukulcan, who taught them pyramid building – what is absolutely certain is that they were very, very real to those who believed in them. So much so, indeed, that they were arguably the key factor which enabled so few Spaniards to overthrow the most flourishing and militaristic of the American native peoples with such relative ease, enabling Cortés to conquer the whole Aztec people, along with its armies of tens of thousands of warriors, with just four hundred men, and Pizarro to subjugate the Incas with an even smaller force.

The root problem concerning these early 'discoverers', in particular their identity and date of arrival, relates to the paucity of surviving documentation. In the case of the Aztecs, this is not for any lack in their system of proper written records. In fact, Cortés and his men found books and related documents everywhere. The very moment of their landfall emissaries of Montezuma presented them with two elaborate codices. When they enquired about port facilities in the Gulf of Mexico they were given a map of the whole coast down to the Isthmus of Panama. Every city which they came upon had substantial archives – 'many paper books doubled together in folds like cloth of Castile' – attached to its temples and palaces. Because the Aztecs set great store by their calendar, and are reliably believed to have kept methodical records at least as far back as the sixth century AD, their archives would almost certainly have included exact details of the arrival of 'Quetzalcoatl' and any other similar transoceanic visitors.

The tragedy is that most of the Spanish regarded the Aztecs' written records, along with all other aspects of their culture, as works of the devil, deserving only of the most thorough destruction. In barely a generation they obliterated all the record offices and temple libraries that had previously been scattered across Aztec Mexico. Any remaining documents became sold as 'wrapping paper to apothecaries, shop-keepers, and rocket-makers'. Today all that is left is barely a handful of totally inadequate scraps.

The Incas, although lacking writing, almost certainly retained a highly developed oral system of record-keeping, aided by *quipus* or knotted strings which they used as a counting system. But any chronicles they kept by this means similarly perished in the destruction Pizarro's men meted out to their whole empire.

Overall then, while almost certainly America did have occasional overseas visitors after its original discovery by Ice Age Siberians, unquestionably most if not all hard evidence of these has been lost. Similarly, anyone who might inadvertently have strayed across the Atlantic by no means necessarily survived to return to tell the tale. There is no reason therefore to suppose that the mostly Mediterranean peoples among whom Columbus directly mixed had the slightest awareness in his time of any significant land-mass that might be reachable by sailing west.

But as we are about to show, this situation was markedly different among certain other peoples, most notably the Irish and Norse of Europe's north.

CHAPTER 2

Irish Monks and Icelandic Norse: 'America' Memories Preserved

Arguably at much at the same time that Hwui Shan and his Chinese Buddhist missionaries reached America's Pacific shores, Irish Christian monks probably reached its Atlantic ones, or at least those of its offshore island of Newfoundland.

Unquestionably a common phenomenon during the earliest centuries of Christianity was for those of more extremist religious inclinations to 'get away from it all' by finding places far from the stresses and temptations of the normal temporal world. In warmer climes the fashion was to seek out caves and pillars of rock in the desert. Irish monks, however, had no readily accessible desert, so their alternative was to cast themselves in tiny boats on to the empty ocean, in search of islands where they could live in similar isolation.

The founding of the monastery of Iona in the Inner Hebrides derived from one such venture, by St Columba, who arrived there in 563 AD. Another such location was Iceland. Although this had been known since the time of the Romans, who called it Thule, it stayed uninhabited until Irish monks found their way there about 795 AD. As recorded in the Icelandic *Landnámabók*, written in the thirteenth century:

> But before Iceland was settled from Norway, there were men there whom the Norse men style '*papar*'. These men were Christians, and people consider that they must have been from the British Isles, because there were found left behind them Irish books, bells and croziers, and other things besides, from which it might be deduced that they were Vestmenn, Irishmen.

We know that the Norse arrived on Iceland about 860 AD, inevitably shattering the peace and solitude that the Irish monks so earnestly sought. As the *Landnámabók* makes clear, they certainly moved on, and in such a hurry that they left behind much of the trappings of their religious life. No document explicitly reports where they ventured next, but if, as would seem logical, they chose to push further west then Greenland would have been the next obvious stepping stone.

Here, intriguingly, Scandinavian excavations during the 1920s at the easternmost of the two known Norse settlements on Greenland's ice-free western coast uncovered a building the archaeologists described as 'the earliest house known in Greenland'. This was of turf construction, with enormously thick walls, as much as twelve feet in places, and consisting of just a single room. In a variety of features, such as its lack of a central fireplace, its narrowness, and the provision of a crude but effective running water supply, the building substantially differed from any of the earliest indisputably Norse dwellings found on Greenland. Instead, in its floor plan, its side-entrance door location, and ratio of length to width, it closely resembled the design of Dark

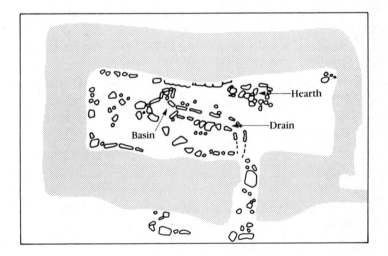

Fig. 2: Irish monks' house on Greenland? Floorplan of the earliest habitation found on Greenland, at the Eastern Settlement. In its exceptionally thick turf walls, off-centre hearth and lack of a raised bench area it more closely resembles Irish, rather than Norse, dwellings of the Dark Ages.

Age Irish farmhouses. The likelihood has to be therefore that it was a refuge built by those Irish monks who had fled Iceland.

If this was the case, and that Irish monks did indeed reach Greenland, then only the comparatively narrow width of the Davis Strait, a mere two days' sail, separated them from America.

But inevitably yet more closely associated with a possible pre-Columbian visit to America is the literary story of the Irish monk St Brandon or Brendan. A definite historical personage who was sixth-century abbot of the famous Irish monastery of Clonfert in County Galway, Brendan seems to have cultivated a reputation for himself as an inveterate voyager and 'navigator'. Reportedly, he customarily travelled by boat to visit other Christian communities from the Scottish Western Isles to Brittany. But most famous is the story, preserved in a mediaeval tale known as the *Navigatio Sancti Brendani Abbatis*, of how in traditional Irish fashion he cast himself upon the waters in search of a far-western and fog-enshrouded 'Promised Land of the Saints'.

Brendan was apparently in his seventies, and well established at Clonfert, when he was told of this western 'Promised Land' by a monk called Barrind, who had found it while on a typical solitude-seeking voyage with another abbot, St Mernoc. Inspired to visit it, Brendan reportedly built 'a wood-framed boat covered in oak-bark-tanned oxhides', smeared the joints of the hides with fat in order to seal them, and set sail westwards with 17 companions and 40 days' worth of provisions. After wandering to a variety of strange islands, they reportedly found the fog-enshrouded 'Promised Land' just as it had been described to them, following which they made a successful return to Ireland.

Somewhat predictably for a work of the Dark Ages, the *Navigatio* contains a number of dubious elements. One such is an incident in which, having landed on an 'island' and lit a fire, the monks found that this was in reality the back of a whale. The whale must have been a very forgiving creature, for even after having its back cooked it treated the monks with every kindness!

On the whole, however, the St Brendan story is creditably free of 'miracle' elements and contains an impressive amount of practical detail suggesting that it is based on one or more real voyages venturing far out into the North Atlantic. Furthermore it includes sufficient description of some of the locations for them to be identified with reasonable assurance.

Thus mentions at the voyage's beginning and end, of 'Islands of Sheep', strongly suggest the Faeroe Islands to the north of Scotland, which Brendan may well have called at both on his outward journey and his return. Another passage suggests the witnessing of an eruption by one of Iceland's volcanoes, possibly Hekla:

> . . . they saw through the clouds to the north a high smoky mountain . . . Before them was a coal-black cliff like a wall, so high they could not see the top of it . . . Then a favourable wind blew them clear, and looking back they saw that the smoke of the mountain had been replaced by flames which shot up and sucked back, so that the whole mountain glowed like a pyre.

Another intriguing passage suggests an encounter with a large, floating iceberg:

> . . . they saw a pillar in the sea . . . It was so high that Brendan could not see the top of it, and a wide-meshed net was wrapped around it. The boat could pass through an opening in the mesh which was the colour of silver but harder than marble, while the column itself was of bright crystal. Taking down the mast and shipping the oars, the monks pulled their boat through the mesh, which they could see extending down into the clear water, as did the foundations of the pillar. The water was clear as glass and the sunlight was as bright below as above . . .

Given the difficulty of interpreting this as anything other than a description of an iceberg, this passage particularly powerfully suggests that Brendan and his companions ventured a considerable distance westwards. The North Atlantic's large icebergs originate as broken-off portions of the glaciers of west Greenland that float southwards down the Davis Strait and although some can stray as far as the Azores, most are most usually found either around the island of Newfoundland off America's north-eastern coast, or at most a few hundred miles west of this, just as so fatefully encountered by the *Titanic* in 1912. Furthermore the description of the 'Promised Land' as being 'fog-enshrouded' is particularly evocative of Newfoundland, lying as this does at the confluence of the cold Labrador Current coming southwards from the Arctic Circle, and the warm Gulf Stream moving northwards from the tropical Caribbean.

So was Newfoundland St Brendan's 'Promised Land'? And could

Brendan indeed have reached it? One man who during the 1970s was certainly tempted by this possibility was the English author/adventurer Tim Severin. Studying the *Navigatio* alongside navigation charts of the north Atlantic, Severin became deeply impressed by the text's wealth of compass directions, days' sailing information, etc. From this he formed the idea that Brendan most likely followed the so-called Stepping Stone route, from Ireland to the Hebrides, to the Faeroes, to Iceland, to Greenland, and then arguably on to Labrador and/or Newfoundland. This would have minimised the amount of time spent in the open sea. It would have made use of all the best available winds and currents, and it would actually have been very nearly the shortest sailing distance, even though it does not look this way on maps drawn to the Mercator projection.

In the identical spirit of Thor Heyerdahl's *Kon-Tiki* and *Ra* expeditions, Severin therefore decided that the only proper way to test his hypothesis was to build a boat to a traditional Irish *curragh* design, and to try sailing this on the Stepping Stone route for himself. Using only the materials specified in the *Navigatio*, he and a team of helpers sewed together some four dozen oak-bark-tanned oxhides around an ashwood frame, sealed all the seams with three-quarters of a ton of sheep's grease, and then added a mast and a flax sail. In this scarcely sturdy-looking craft, which they could do no other than name *Brendan*, Severin and four companions set off into the chilly and blustery north Atlantic on St Brendan's Day, 1976, their destination Newfoundland.

Predictably, and even with a stop-over in Iceland, it was anything but an uneventful voyage, with fierce gales, swamping seas, and repeated encounters with whales, who, as in the case of the original voyage, seem to have regarded the *Brendan* with a sometimes uncomfortably fraternal curiosity. In fact, the worst danger came from ice floes which may well not have been around in the slightly warmer climatic conditions thought to have prevailed at the time of the original voyage. Even so, although one floe actually punctured the boat's skin, a patch of more ox-hide, sewed on in the midst of a heaving, freezing sea, saved the day and after encountering a true St Brendan-type sea-fog a relieved Severin and his companions made safe landfall on Peckford island, Newfoundland on June 26, 1977. Just as Heyerdahl's *Ra II* in respect of the Egyptians, they had effectively proved that a boat constructed from just the primitive materials described in the *Navigatio* could indeed have reached America.

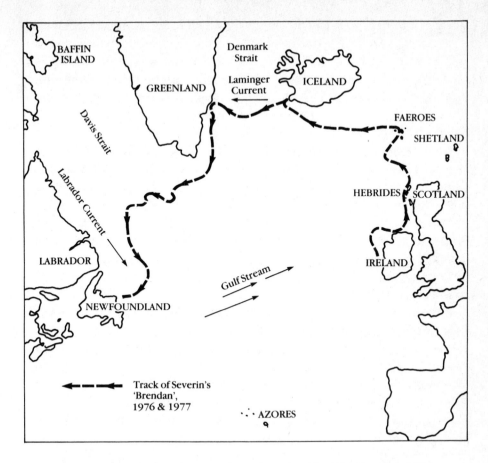

Fig. 3: The voyage of St Brendan, as retraced by Tim Severin, 1976 & 1977.

As will become clear later, whether St Brendan and his companions actually reached America at this time is not crucial to our argument. The important point is that his story was widely believed and well known in Europe during the Middle Ages, particularly in northern climes. Some indication of this is derived from the *Navigatio*'s survival in some 120 manuscripts dating from the eleventh century onwards. Fifteenth-century map-makers, even in Mediterranean countries, and even though they had no definite knowledge of the location of St Brendan's 'Promised Land', similarly felt obliged at least to mark it on their maps, showing it far out into the Atlantic, sometimes on the same latitude as Spain, sometimes far to the west of Ireland.

And of course, besides St Brendan and his Irish monks, there was one other group of European people yet more powerfully associated with possible pre-Columbian voyages to America: the Norse. As is well known, during the last two centuries of the first millennium AD the Norse were northern Europe's leading seapower, to the east threading their way down rivers leading to the Caspian and Black Seas, and to the west heading far out into the Atlantic.

In our account of these individuals it is important to explain why we are referring to them as Norse rather than as Vikings. 'Viking', the Old Norse word for a seafaring buccaneer, is most correctly applied as a pejorative term to those Norse who conducted the notorious terror raids on much of Europe during the ninth and tenth centuries AD. And undoubtedly there were many Norse – pagan, quarrelsome and sexually prolific – driven out of their country by the curious Norse laws by which only the eldest son could inherit his father's property, who deserved to be described as Vikings.

But there were many others who, although forced out of their homeland by the same pressures, had much less aggressive intentions. Some were peaceable free-born peasant farmers anxious to make a decent living from their grazing animals wherever they could do so with least friction. Others were simple deer and seal hunters, yet others fishermen. And it was mostly these latter groups who in the wake of the Irish monks followed the Stepping Stone route out into the Atlantic, arriving in Iceland about the 860s.

In fact, such was the vigour of the Norse thrust westwards at this time that it took no more than a couple of generations for Iceland's population to swell to 30,000, for its pasturage to become seriously over-grazed, and for feuding over land to become as violent as back in the homeland. As might be expected, those would-be settlers to arrive last on Iceland were the most troublesome, among these a fiery young man called Eirik the Red, who in 982 was sentenced to three years' exile for his part in a land-war murder.

It is for what happened next that historians are unavoidably indebted to the great Icelandic sagas that provided for expatriate Norsemen both their oral history and their banquet-hall entertainment. Some time about the 950s the Icelanders had discovered the existence of Greenland, but so far had taken little interest in it. It was to this still largely unknown island that Eirik the Red set sail to serve out his three-year sentence. Being already aware that Greenland's eastern coast was permanently ice-bound, Eirik made for its southernmost point, Cape Farewell, with the aim of exploring its western side. Even here, as he found, the terrain was mostly massively glaciered and icebound, and therefore quite unsuitable for any settlement. There were also virtually no trees. But in two locations he came across extensive pasturage for animals, and at one of these the only signs anywhere of human occupation (almost certainly that of the Irish monks), though it was now deserted. He also found caribou and polar bear for hunting, and plenty of cod in the sea.

Accordingly, on completing his exile and returning to a by now seriously famine-stricken Iceland, Eirik was able to paint such an enticing picture of 'Greenland' (the name derives directly from him), that in 986 he led from Iceland a full-scale migration of Exodus-style proportions. This comprised some 25 ships carrying perhaps 3–400 people, together with their horses, cattle, sheep, goats, pigs, and vital supplies and equipment, and although 11 vessels were either lost at sea, or driven back to Iceland, 14 successfully rounded Cape Farewell to settle in the two promising-looking locations that Eirik pointed out to them. Eirik himself settled at the more southerly of these, Eiriksfjord, later to be known as the Eastern Settlement, building there a farm which he called Brattahlid. Others ventured some 250 miles north to a mountain-protected and meadowed region today known as the Godthaab district to found what became known as the Western Settlement.

The historical evidence of these settlements, as described in the sagas, is firmly established from archaeological remains. The site of Eiriksfjord, the Eastern Settlement, has never been forgotten, and here during the 1920s Scandinavian archaeologists excavated the ruins of several farms, one of which has even been identified as that of Eirik the Red, complete with the outbuildings in which he and his retainers overwintered their animals. It was on this same site that the archaeologists also found the remains of the already mentioned thick-walled house thought to have been built by the earlier Irish monks.

But the fascination for us is that the sagas go on to describe episodes indicative that these Icelandic Norse, even in the very year they settled in Greenland, also reached as far as America, albeit initially quite inadvertently. As related in the *Greenlanders' Saga*, a trader called Bjarni Herjolfsson arrived in Iceland from an overwinter voyage only to find that his father Herjolf had departed for Greenland with Eirik the Red just a few weeks earlier.

Not even pausing to unload their ship, Bjarni and his men impetuously set off to follow, using directions that had been left behind for them, only to find themselves after three days caught in a storm which drove them south. Next they found themselves lost in a fog in which they drifted blindly for several days with sail furled. Only when the sky cleared were they able to take their bearings and set sail again, choosing a westward course.

As the saga relates, within a day they came upon a land that was 'not mountainous . . . covered with forest, with low hills'. Leaving this to port, i.e to their left, in another two days they came upon a land that was 'flat country . . . covered with woods'. Continuing further north, they came upon a third land 'high, mountainous and glaciered'. After following the coastline of this until it became evident it was an island, they then headed out to sea for four days, only at this point coming upon a land that accorded with what Bjarni had been told to expect of Greenland. Astonishingly, the very first human habitation they came across turned out to be Herjolfnes in

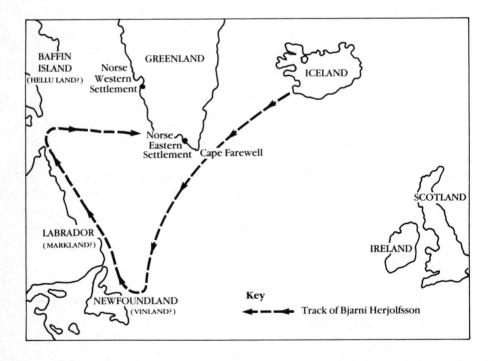

Fig. 4: The voyage of Bjarni Herjolfsson c.986 AD, as reconstructed from the *Greenlanders' Saga*.

the Eastern Settlement, precisely where Bjarni's father Herjolf was building his new homestead.

For those intent on determining who might have been the first European to discover America the saga account of Bjarni's voyage provides a fascinating 'where did he wander?' exercise in map deduction. Logically, Bjarni was most likely just off southern Greenland when he became caught in the storm. This was almost certainly one of the notorious polar north-easters which pushed him southwards into the equally notorious fog-belt east of Newfoundland.

On his heading westwards, Newfoundland would therefore have been the forested and low-hilled land he came across first, with the second 'flat country . . . covered with woods' southern Labrador, and the third land 'high, mountainous and glaciered' either northern Labrador's Kaumajet peninsula, or Baffin Island. At this latitude Bjarni would then have needed only a relatively simple crossing of the Davis Strait to his father's new homestead on Greenland, just as described.

But since Bjarni did not actually land at any of the three pre-Greenland locations he reported, the rôle of Norse discoverer of what seems to have been America is usually bestowed on Eirik the Red's son Leif Eiriksson who on hearing Bjarni's story set off with a crew of 35 to investigate each location in reverse order. The third, glaciered 'Baffin Island' location he named Helluland, literally 'Slab Country'. The flat, wooded one, thought to have been Labrador, he named 'Markland', or 'Forest Country'. And on landing at the one seen first by Bjarni, thought to have been Newfoundland, he not only decided to build 'big houses' in which to overwinter, he also seems to have found it sufficiently attractive to give it the name 'Vinland', or 'Wine Country', apparently on account of the finding by Tyrkir, a German member of the party, of vines with wild grapes.

The name of 'Vinland' is one that has long caused a hornet's nest of controversy. Today there are no wild grapes growing on Newfoundland, nor any further north than 45°N, the latitude of the US state of Maine. This has therefore seemed to suggest that Leif Eiriksson and his men must have wandered further to the south on the American continent.

To some the explanation is a climatic one: that since Newfoundland enjoyed the so-called Little Climatic Optimum at the time of the Norse voyages, it could possibly have supported grapes then. This view finds corroboration in the journal of a seventeenth-century English surgeon, James Yonge, who reported 'wild grapes incredible' at the time of a visit he made to southern Newfoundland in 1663. But present-day specialists in Newfoundland's flora strongly disagree that this could ever have been possible in the last few thousand years.

Others have suggested that there might have been an early confusion between the Norse word *vin* with a long 'i' meaning wine, and the Old Norse *vin* with a short 'i' meaning hay or pasturage. Arguably, when the sagas were composed in oral form the second meaning was the one intended, any territory carrying the name 'Pasture Country' inevitably being welcome news to the land-starved Norse of that time. But when after some centuries the sagas became committed to writing this second meaning had become obsolete, so that those who wrote the sagas genuinely thought that vines and grapes were being referred to, and embellished the story accordingly. This would make sense of an otherwise bizarre saga description that those who overwintered in Vinland filled a boat 'in the April' with 'vines/grapes' to take back to Greenland. It seems hardly likely that anyone would have wanted to take back a boat-load of the last season's rotted and withered grapes and vines. A cargo of cut hay for Greenland's overwintered cattle would be far more credible.

However, such have been the uncertainties associated with the Icelandic sagas, not least because of the problems associated with the Vinland name, that until comparatively recently the story was doubted by many scholars, including the eminent Norse explorer Fridtjof Nansen. In his two-volume *In Northern Mists*, published in 1911, Nansen dismissed the sagas as far too mythical to be taken seriously.

Nor were doubts resolved by the dramatic announcement, on Columbus Day 1965, of the discovery of the so-called Vinland Map. Purportedly datable to 1440, this map shows to the west of Iceland and Greenland a large irregularly shaped island clearly marked 'Island of Vinland, discovered by Bjarni and Leif in company'. At the time of the announcement of the map's discovery its authenticity was vouchsafed by some distinguished specialists, notably R.A.Skelton, Superintendent of the British Museum Map Room, George R.Painter, the British Museum's Assistant Keeper of Printed Books, and Thomas Marston, Curator of Mediaeval and Renaissance Literature at Yale University. A variety of clues, including matching wormholes to the paging, seemed to indicate that the map and an accompanying

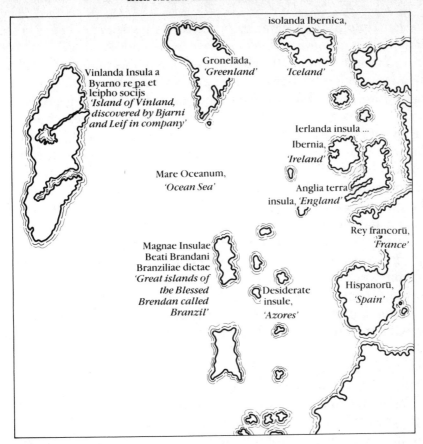

isolanda Ibernica,

Gronelāda,
'Greenland'   'Iceland'

Vinlanda Insula a
Byarno re pa et
leipho socijs
'Island of Vinland,
discovered by Bjarni
and Leif in company'

Ierlanda insula ...

Ibernia,
'Ireland'

Mare Oceanum,
'Ocean Sea'

Anglia terra
insula, 'England'

Rey francorū,
'France'

Magnae Insulae
Beati Brandani
Branziliae dictae
'Great islands of
the Blessed
Brendan called
Branzil'

Desiderate
insule,
'Azores'

Hispanorū,
'Spain'

Fig 5: Detail after Yale University's so-called Vinland Map, showing
what purports to be the 'Vinland' of the Norse sagas.

mediaeval text, the Tartar Relation, originally formed part of an
unquestionably genuine mid-fifteenth-century volume, Vincent de
Beauvais's *Speculum Historiale*.

But then in 1972 the Chicago microscopist Dr Walter McCrone was
invited to make a microanalytical study of the map and its ink. When
McCrone found the ink to contain traces of the modern commercial
product titanium dioxide he declared the map to be a modern forgery.
More recently, however, the proportions of titanium McCrone claimed
to be present have been challenged by analysts at the University of
California's Crocker Nuclear Laboratory. They have also reported
similar traces on several mediaeval manuscripts of unimpeachable
genuineness, leaving the question of the map's authenticity in an
unresolved limbo.

Thankfully, all these continuing uncertainties relating to the Vinland story and its accompanying map have been rendered largely obsolete thanks to indisputable findings of Norse remains on Newfoundland by a Norwegian husband and wife archaeological team, Helge and Anne Stine Ingstad. In 1960 barrister-turned-explorer Helge Ingstad arrived on Newfoundland on a needle-in-a-haystack search for any surviving remains of the sort of turf houses built by the Norse on Greenland, remains which he and his wife had studied at first hand a few years earlier. At L'Anse aux Meadows, on Newfoundland's north-western peninsula, Ingstad was shown faint depressions in the ground which seemed to indicate what had been several early rectangular-shaped dwellings, and when he and his wife began to excavate these they were revealed as unquestionably of turf, a type of construction typical neither of Newfoundland's original native inhabitants, nor of any post-Columbian settlers.

All over the site the Ingstads found slag as from the smelting and working of iron, a technique certainly unknown to any of America's pre-Columbian native inhabitants. But the houses were of such simple construction and so devoid of meaningful contents, that it was not until the fourth season of excavation, in 1964, that an artefact indisputably identifiable as Norse came to light.

Under the fingers of Canadian Tony Beardsley, one of several different nationalities of archaeologists helping the Ingstads, there emerged a small soapstone spindle whorl, as used for the flywheel of a handheld spindle. It was of a type well-known from Norse sites in Greenland, Iceland and Norway itself. Nearby was a quartzite whet-stone, of a type used to sharpen needles and small scissors.

Not only were both these finds very distinctively Norse, they also indicated that the inhabitants of the turf houses included women. Not long after there occurred the further find of a typically Norse ring-headed bronze pin, just under four inches long. Humble and unspectacular as these finds might seem, they effectively proved that Norse peoples unquestionably arrived and built houses on Newfoundland, just as described in the Vinland of the Icelandic sagas.

Whether, despite this evidence, Newfoundland was the Icelanders' 'Vinland' is a much more open question. Given the certainty of the Norse reaching of Newfoundland, it is a reasonable enough supposition that they may have wandered further south.

One indication of this, from post-Ingstad excavations sponsored

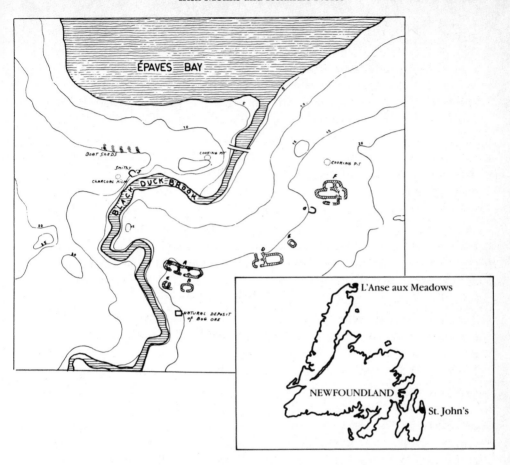

Fig 6: Plan of the Norse house-sites excavated at L'Anse aux Meadows, with inset of the location on Newfoundland's north-western promontory.

by the Canadian government, has been the finding, amongst Norse remains in three separate locations at L'Anse aux Meadows, of butternuts, that is, nuts of the native American butternut or white walnut tree. Since the butternut does not grow on Newfoundland, and, again so far as can be determined, did not grow there during the Norse era, arguably they were brought from further south. Because butternuts go rancid if kept for any period, it seems unlikely that they were brought by trading Indians, suggesting that the Norse themselves wandered further south, necessarily at least as far as Canada's St Lawrence valley and the inner reaches of the Miramichi river that are the butternut's northernmost limit. This happens, in fact, also to be the limit for the wild grape. Accordingly, while L'Anse aux Meadows remains the only absolutely certain Norse site found anywhere in America, arguably it was not necessarily the furthest extent of the Norse wanderings.

Equally clear, however, from both the sagas and archaeological findings in common, is that the Norse settlement in America/Vinland was very short-lived. The sagas relate how a party of Norse tried settling with their livestock in 'Vinland' but then, after a short while, were driven out by a native people whom they called *Skraelings*, a general term the Norse used for any people more primitive than themselves.

The archaeological findings corroborate this. The turf dwellings excavated at L'Anse aux Meadows show none of the signs of repeated rebuilding necessary in northern climes for houses of that type of construction; rebuilding evident from the Norse settlements on Greenland, and requisite also to this day for the wooden-box homes of modern Newfoundland. Another indication of L'Anse aux Meadows' short-term occupation is the fact that no burial ground has been found there, again unlike on Greenland. Yet another pointer derives from carbon dating of the charcoal in the fireplaces of the L'Anse aux Meadows houses. According to the latest reckonings the charcoal can be dated to the surprisingly narrow period of 975–1020 AD, precisely the period of the short-lived settlement in Vinland as described by the sagas.

But while the Icelandic Norse might not have settled on Newfoundland/the American mainland, this does not preclude Greenlanders in the subsequent centuries from having made occasional visits to the land just across the water from them, particularly the heavily wooded coastline of Labrador that they seem to have called Markland. Since, as already noted, Greenland was treeless, its only directly available timber being driftwood, regular expeditions to Markland would have been vital for their wood supplies for shipbuilding, house-supports, fuel, etc. Although unlike the Icelanders, the Greenlanders are not known to have kept any annals of their year-by-year activities, there do remain a few clues to such expeditions.

Thus the Icelandic Annals for 1347 recorded:

> There came also [to Iceland] a ship from Greenland . . . There were seventeen men on board, and they had sailed to Markland, but were afterwards driven hither.

This has been interpreted as a timber-gathering voyage from Greenland to Markland/Labrador badly blown off course on its return journey, thus inadvertently landing in Iceland.

The second derives from a lost account of an English (or Irish) Franciscan friar's voyage to Greenland in 1360, a work entitled *Inventio Fortunatae*, that is known fragmentarily mainly thanks to a summary made in 1577 by the famous sixteenth-century Dutch geographer Gerard Mercator for his English friend, Dr John Dee. Even the friar's name is uncertain, Nicholas of Lynn being one identification, and Hugh of Ireland another.

But quite definite from Mercator's information is that the friar was an Oxford mathematician who at some stage during his time in Greenland was taken to a location a little way inland with clearings in the woods where trees had been felled. 'Hugh' or 'Nicholas' also apparently mentioned seeing what he thought to be 'many trees of brazil-wood', a curious remark since the term 'brazil-wood' principally refers to the reddish wood of the East Indian sappan tree from which a red dye is derived. But whatever the exact species, the absence of any trees on Greenland strongly suggests that Hugh/Nicholas accompanied another timber-fetching run to Markland/Labrador or thereabouts, the 'brazil-wood' idea perhaps having been suggested by the liberal usage of red ochre on the part of north-east American native peoples such as the Beothuks of Newfoundland, after whom the term 'Red Indian' became derived.

In summary, therefore, there is absolute certainty that Icelandic Norse (if not the Irish before them) reached what we now know as north-eastern America. Equally definite is that the memory of this was well preserved in the subsequent centuries in the form of the Icelandic sagas. With the Icelanders' conversion to Christianity around 1000 AD their sagas, previously passed by memory from one bard to another, became set down in writing, the *Islendingabók* or *Book of the Icelanders* about 1127 AD, the *Grœnlendinga Saga*, or *Greenlanders' Saga* about 1190 AD, and the *Eiriks Saga Rauðva* or *Eirik the Red's Saga* about 1260 AD. These works, extensively copied in later centuries, became as much part of the Icelanders' heritage as the *Iliad* and *Odyssey* for the Greeks, and the *Ramayana* and *Mahabarata* for the Hindus.

Other indications derive from an Icelandic geography of the early-fifteenth century which clearly identifies Vinland, Helluland and

Markland as real locations – 'South from Greenland is Helluland, next to it is Markland, thence it is not far to Wineland the Good, which some men think is connected with Africa' – and also the Icelandic Skálholt map, which although it survives only from a seventeenth-century copy, again seems to have its origin in knowledge directly gained from the Vinland/Markland/Helluland voyages.

None of this is to suggest that the Icelandic and Greenlander Norse had any concept of America as the huge continent we now know today. Their interest would seem to have been confined solely to the extent to which the limited parts they touched on could or could not help supply their immediate practical needs.

But what is important to us is that both they and (arguably) the Irish remembered it in their different ways and under different names, and that even as late as the fifteenth century something of this memory might have rubbed off on those of other nationalities who became closest associated with them. Shortly we will be looking in detail at fifteenth-century individuals with precisely such associations: merchants and seamen from the English West Country seaport of Bristol.

But first we must set the scene for a Europe on the brink of when Columbus and others began contemplating sailing westward. . . .

CHAPTER 3

Europe on the Brink . . .

If we could take a spy satellite view of Europe in the year 1475, we would see whole countries shaking off their old mediaeval compartments of duchies and baronies, and assuming something of their present-day borders. By the marriage of the teenagers Ferdinand of Aragon and Isabella of Castile, there became created by 1479 what we now know as Spain. France, having almost completely chased out the English, took to itself in 1477 the formerly independent Duchy of Burgundy, followed a few years later by Provence and Brittany. England was within a few years of settling by battle and by marriage the old rivalries between the houses of York and Lancaster. Much earlier in the century, marriage alliances had caused Norway and Sweden to fall under the sway of Denmark.

As further benchmarks of the state of progress in the the year 1475, the first ever printed book was a mere twenty years old, William Caxton was within months of opening his Westminster publishing house, the newborn Michelangelo was still being weaned by his wet-nurse, and the first watches just about to be made at Nuremberg. Firearms, in the form of cannon and the like, were just beginning to assume ascendancy in the conduct of war.

But the people we are primarily interested in are the merchants – effectively, thanks to the power of the money they handled, the new great barons of the late-fifteenth century. They made their money in much the same way as the Onassises and Niarchoses of our own time, by owning ships in which they could carry people, troops, and most importantly goods for trading between one country and another. In an age in which road transport was difficult, dangerous and slow, and rail travel not even dreamt of, ships had something of the charisma of air travel in this. And although those who owned them stood great risks, both from natural disasters and from piracy, they also stood to earn great profits.

A typical success story at about the middle of the century had been that of French fleet owner Jacques Coeur. In his heyday, Coeur had been the second most powerful man in all of France. Granted a papal licence to 'trade with infidels', he sent his ships as far as Alexandria, Beirut and Cairo. His exchanges of French silver for Arab gold, and his dealings in Eastern cloths, jewels and spices, were said to double his capital investments with each voyage.

Similarly prosperous were the merchants of the Italian city-states of Venice and Genoa. Their oared galleys swept the Mediterranean, calling like Coeur's at the great ports of the East, and carrying spices, silks, wines and fruits as far as southern France and southern Spain. Beyond Gibraltar the Genoese formed a substantial colony in Lisbon. They and the Venetians also visited Bruges, Southampton and London, and at all these places set up agents of their own nationality.

Dominating the north were the great merchants of the Hanseatic League, an association of German cities that extended its net from Kiev in the east to the North Sea in the west, also south via Europe's land and river routes, even to the Mediterranean. By building a huge fleet of cogs – sturdy, rudder-steered vessels – they made themselves northern Europe's master cargo-transporters. At one and the same time they set up great master trading posts, or staples, one at Bergen for timber and fish, another at Novgorod for furs, a third at London for woollen cloth, and a fourth at Bruges, also for cloth. Having thereby achieved monopoly in both markets and transport, they were able to dictate the most advantageous trading and customs terms with Europe's kings, often far exceeding those of a country's nationals.

Merchants such as these, by their very competitiveness, watched each others' innovative successes, and matched them. This brought about major developments in shipping and navigational aids that made possible voyages over greater distances and against more adverse sailing conditions than had ever previously been contemplated.

Largely as a result of the Hanse's development of the cog, for instance, the clumsy old steering oar that ship's helmsmen had used for millennia became replaced by the modern-style rudder. Almost at a stroke the helmsman's job assumed greater status, further enhanced by the protection of his post with a 'castle', a built-up area aft that developed into officers' quarters. The decking-over of ships afforded greater protection for the cargo they carried. And from what had been single-masted ships with just a single square sail, there evolved two- and three-masters, the aftmost or mizzen sail often made to a triangular or lateen shape that enabled the keeping of a course to within six or seven points of the wind.

Fig. 7: Woodcut of late-fifteenth-century ship showing rudder, castle, and use of combination of square and lateen sails.

The lateen design sail had been copied from the Arabs, and another similar acquisition from Arab knowledge was the astrolabe which English scholars such as the Greenland-visiting Oxford friar who wrote the *Inventio Fortunatae* had been using as early as 1360. Pointed at the sun or at other heavenly bodies, the astrolabe enabled the calculation of latitude, though it was best used on land since readings taken on a heaving ship's deck had little chance of accuracy.

Also partly due to Arab mathematical skills, Mediterranean map-makers, particularly in Majorca and Portugal, began to produce maps that were vastly more sophisticated than previously. Earlier the earth had most commonly been depicted in maps as a largely land-filled circle with Asia in its upper part, Europe and Africa in its lower part, and Jerusalem in the middle, in a manner perhaps best typified by the famous Hereford Mappa Mundi. Now the known countries of the world began to be drawn on maps with outlines approximating commendably close to their actuality, as in the case of the great Catalan Atlas made in Majorca by Jewish map-maker Abraham Cresques about 1375. And just as each merchant worked to out-do his peers, so each map-maker tried likewise, each one striving to incorporate just that bit more geographical knowledge than had his predecessor.

Important in this regard had been the arrival from the east, brought by Byzantine scholars fleeing from the steadily encroaching Ottoman Turks, of classical manuscripts embodying knowledge of world geography that had been gathered by the Greeks and Romans. Prime among these were the works of the second-century AD geographer Claudius Ptolemy, who had listed the places of the world by their latitude and longitude as best he had been able to calculate them. In 1475 the first published edition of Ptolemy's *Geography* was already in preparation and only two years from publication.

By far the most informed source of knowledge of the world further east had been the Venetian traveller Marco Polo, who with his father and uncle had visited China back in the late-thirteenth century. In Marco Polo's time, China had been dominated by the great Mongol Khans, and although these had long been overthrown, the comparatively few fifteenth-century Europeans conversant with Marco Polo's works assumed that they were still in power.

And of course of equal importance to the map-makers were findings from the latest exploratory voyages. Foremost among the explorers were the Portuguese. Earlier in the century the Portuguese Infante Dom Henrique, better known as Prince Henry the Navigator, had founded what might best be described as an information centre for navigators at Sagres on Portugal's southernmost tip, with Abraham Cresques' young son Jehuda as his chief geographer.

Henry encouraged fresh discoveries. Up until 1434 it had been widely supposed that the sea boiled if one tried to sail further south than Morocco's Cape Nun. In 1434 Portuguese captain Gil Eanes disproved this notion, after which the Portuguese proceeded steadily to make their way southward down the coast of Africa.

When in 1459 Portugal's King Alfonso V commissioned a major
new world map from the great Venetian map-maker Fra Mauro, he
drew Africa as circumnavigable, anticipating by nearly thirty years
the actual rounding of the Cape of Good Hope by the Portuguese
Bartholomew Diaz in 1488. Theoretically the exact navigational
findings from such voyages were state secrets, Alfonso's successor
King John II being by nature particularly secretive and partial
to disinformation. But well-placed informers usually ensured new
navigational information's dissemination to other nations within a
few years.

One event that during the two decades preceding 1475 had the
most profound effect on many merchants' minds, particularly those of
Genoa and Venice, had been the fall of Constantinople to the Ottoman
Turks in 1453. For centuries, goods of the Orient had been laboriously
carried overland on great caravan routes via countless middlemen from
their places of origin much further east. These products, predominantly
silks, perfumes and spices, might seem relatively easy to forego. But
perfumes were regarded as near-essential by those rich enough to
be offended by the body odours of the world's great unwashed.
Cloves, only obtainable in the Moluccas, were highly valued both
medicinally and as meat preservatives. Other oriental spices such
as nutmeg, pepper, paprika and cinnamon could similarly only be
highly prized in an age anxious to disguise the flavour of food often
long past what for us would be its recommended sell-by date.

The disruption to this trade caused by the Turks inevitably turned
entrepreneurial men's minds to look to other routes by which they
might obtain the products of the east, routes that would be all the better
if they by-passed the hitherto obligatory chains of middlemen.

It was perhaps not inappropriate that around the very time of
Constantinople's fall there should have been born the two men
who later in life would become most identified with the idea of
finding an alternative route to the east: John Cabot and Christopher
Columbus.

As already remarked, all too little is known of the origins of John
Cabot, but like Columbus he is thought to have been born in Genoa.
Quite definitely some time between 1471 and 1473 Cabot was granted
Venetian citizenship, a privilege he could only have earned by having
been based in Venice for fifteen years. His interest in the oriental trade
would seem to have been long-established, for according to a later
report on him by Milan's Ambassador to England, he had travelled

on more than one occasion as far as Mecca, apparently in an attempt
to find out where the spices and other commodities of the east had
their origin. As at 1475, however, there is not the slightest evidence
for his having any idea of reaching the east by sailing westwards.

Columbus for his part would seem to have been still at home in
Genoa in 1475, but a year later would go to Lisbon to earn a living
as a map-maker. Here, because of Portugal's lead in geographical
exploration, he would have worked on charts showing the best
available knowledge of the Atlantic (or as it was then known, the
Ocean Sea). He would have seen various islands marked in mid-ocean,
some of these very definitely real, as in the case of the Canaries which
the Spanish had rediscovered in 1336. Also Madeira, first shown in
a sea atlas of the year 1351, and the Azores which the Portuguese
found, almost certainly accidentally, sometime around 1430.

He would also have seen marked on the same charts various
islands to us now mythical. Not least would have been the island
of St Brendan which some maps showed as part of a chain of islands
stretching northwards from the latitude of Tangier, others as west
of Ireland. To add to the confusion another island was shown from
1424 onwards in the middle of the Atlantic called Antillia, or the
Island of the Seven Cities. Yet another, sometimes shown as west
of the British Isles, and sometimes as due south of 'Isla Verde' or
Greenland, was called Brasil.

Exactly how the idea of an island named 'Brasil' arose is by no
means clear. One explanation is that it originated in the brazil-wood
trees which the author of the *Inventio Fortunatae* reported in what
seemed to be the Icelanders' Markland, or Labrador, and which we
have suggested to have been inspired by Beothuk Indians' red ochre.
Another is that it derived from the Celtic *breas-i*, big or fortunate isle,
i.e. Celtic St Brendan's 'Promised Land'. Yet another that it was simply
a shortening of '*Brandani Insulae*', St Brendan's isle, which became
corrupted to 'Branziliae', 'Braziliae' and then 'Brasil'. Interestingly,
the Vinland Map, if genuine, seems to show this half way 'Branziliae'
form (see fig.5). Certainly it had nothing to do with what we now
know as the South American country of Brazil, undiscovered until
1500, and unnamed as such until around 1511.

Also quite definite is that as at 1475, and indeed up to and including
the time of his First Voyage, Columbus had little or no interest in these
islands in the middle of the Ocean Sea. Even when actively en route to
the 'Indies' he gave specific instructions that if St Brendan's isle or its

like were sighted they were to be disregarded. Nor would it be for some years that he developed the idea of reaching the east by sailing west. To the best of available knowledge in 1475 he would have accepted the prevailing wisdom that the westward distance from Europe to Asia was so vast that it was far beyond the capabilities of any vessel of the time.

Ironically, just as in southern Europe no one was looking west, so in northern Europe all the westward-thrusting population pressures that had so motivated the Norse around 1000 AD had long since dissipated and begun to go into reverse. The Norse had been particularly badly hit by the Black Death in the middle of the fourteenth century, and whether directly or indirectly because of this, Greenland's Western Settlement, the more northerly of the two founded by Eric the Red, was mysteriously abandoned. One of the Eastern Settlement's priests, Ivar Bárdarson, on a visit to it around 1350, reported only untended cattle and sheep, with no indication of what had happened to the inhabitants.

Although the Eastern Settlement survived longer, it too was in serious decline, so badly neglected by the Danes in whose territory it fell by their union with Norway, that they had to send a Danish pilot, Johannes Scolvus, on an apparent voyage to rediscover it in 1476. Well-preserved clothing from corpses excavated from the cemetery at Herjolfnes, shows fashion trends from the second half of the fifteenth century, but from no later, the general explanation being that the remnants of the inhabitants simply became assimilated with the Eskimoes, who had begun to move south at about this time.

Iceland nearly suffered the same fate largely because for most of the first three-quarters of the fifteenth century the Hanse, exerting the tightest control on Norse/Danish trading activities, had little interest in such a far-flung outpost. Written into the Icelandic constitution was an understanding that Norway would send at least six ships to Iceland per year, but by the early-fifteenth century they were lucky if they received more than one. Indeed, for 1412 the Icelandic Annals sorrowfully recorded: 'no news from Norway to Iceland'.

However in this very same year there arrived a strange boat off their island of Dyrholm which, when they rowed out towards it, turned out to contain 'fishermen out of England'.

Whoever these Englishmen were they seem to have been well pleased with their mission, for the very next year some 30 more turned up, to be mostly welcomed by the Icelanders even though there was a language barrier. They brought useful commodities which the Icelanders could not make for themselves. They were followed the year after by another 30, this time accompanied by a proper merchant vessel whose captain carried letters of authority that had been obtained from the Norwegian King Eric, perhaps at the intercession of the latter's English wife.

Once the Hanseatic League heard about this, King Eric seems to have been very smartly told who was in charge. Almost certainly under orders from the Hanseatics, whose pawn he was, he sent totally contradictory letters directly to Iceland, now forbidding its people from trading with the 'outlandish men'. These were followed by a letter of complaint to England's King Henry V.

One curiosity is that there appears to have occurred at this time a mysterious change in the normal gathering places of the fishing shoals. We know that sometime between 1416 and 1425 the herring shoals of the Baltic, the very basis of the Scandinavian fishing industry so tightly controlled by the Hanseatics, very decisively moved from the Baltic to the North Sea. At about this same time the whales that had hitherto been prolific in the Bay of Biscay began to migrate to much further out in the North Sea, causing their traditional hunters, the Basques, to be obliged to follow them. With regard to Iceland, it is therefore of considerable interest that the English response to Eric of Norway's letter of complaint was to assert that the fishermen had moved to Iceland specifically since 'as is well known' the fish had changed their normal haunts to congregate in large numbers there. These fish we may assume were most likely to have been cod.

In the event, Norway rejected the English protests, and the English government, anxious not to offend Norway, ordered proclamations of the prohibition of ventures to Iceland. But there seems to have been too much of a mutual need between the Icelanders themselves and the English merchants and fishermen who came to them for such distantly issued decrees to have much effect, particularly given the neglect the Icelanders had been suffering from their political masters. In 1419 the Icelanders wrote to King Eric:

> Our laws provide that six ships should come hither from Norway every year, which has not happened for a long time, a cause from which Your Grace and our poor country has suffered most grievous

harm. Therefore, trusting in God's grace and your help, we have traded with foreigners who have come hither peacefully on legitimate business, but we have punished those fishermen and owners of fishing smacks who have robbed and caused disturbance on the sea.

This letter vividly conveys the Icelanders' resentment of their treatment by Norway, (whose ships were totally controlled by the Hanseatics) and their gratitude to the unidentified 'foreigners'. It also makes a clear distinction between those foreigners who simply helped themselves to the fish around Iceland's waters, and those who came legitimately to trade with the Icelanders by bringing them the utilitarian goods they needed, inevitably receiving in return Iceland's virtual sole export commodity, dried cod. As becomes more and more evident during the ensuing decades of the fifteenth century, these latter were not Englishmen in general, but more and more predominantly men of the westward-looking English city of Bristol. One indication of this derives from a political poem, *The Libelle of Englyshe Polycye*, written about 1436, referring to Bristol mariners navigating to Iceland 'by needle and by stone'.

And as we will now see, it was from this English city and its conflict with the Hanseatics, who by their domination of Norwegian affairs controlled Iceland's trading, that an all too little-known chapter in the history of America's discovery was to be born.

CHAPTER 4

Bristol: the Irish and Icelandic Connection

Of Iceland to write is little need,
Save of stock-fish [dried cod]:
Yet forsooth indeed,
Out of Bristol, and coasts many a one,
Men have practised by needle and by stone
Thitherwards within a little while
Within twelve years, and without peril
Gone and come . . .

Libelle of Englyshe Polycye, 1436

For anyone approaching Bristol from its seaward, or western, side even to this day there remain clues to its ancient Norse associations. All along the Bristol Channel's South Wales coastline, from Fishguard to the islands of Gateholm and Skokholm, to Milford, Tenby and on to the mid-Severn islands of Flat Holm and Steep Holm, the abundance of Norse place-names attest to a one-time frequenting of these waters by the Norse.

Having passed these landmarks, any fifteenth-century Bristol-bound sailing vessel would pause at Kingroad, a deepwater part of the Severn estuary just downriver of where it is joined by its tributary river Avon. When the tide was right, theoretically a vessel could then be floated by it the six miles up the Avon to Bristol, but the river's strong currents and winding bends made navigation dangerous for the uninitiated. Accordingly there lived at Crockern Pill, near the Avon's mouth, a community of river pilots and sturdies who made their living from guiding and hauling vessels along this stretch of river, taking them beneath the spectacular Avon Gorge cliffs that are little changed to this day.

Upon rounding the last of these, St Vincent's Rocks, the incoming vessel would then catch its first glimpse of a Bristol feature with the strongest Irish, and specifically Brendonian, associations, a green hill just outside the city well known to this day as Brandon Hill [see seventeenth-century view of Bristol, pl. 1]. Although now topped by a late Victorian tower commemorating John Cabot, on this same spot in the fifteenth century there stood a small, centuries-old chapel dedicated to St Brendan, at which many mariners, Irish and Bristolian, would call to give thanks for a safe voyage.

For any incoming mariner perhaps Bristol's most surprising feature, however, would have been its tides. Together with Nova Scotia's Bay of Fundy, Bristol has one of the highest tidal ranges in the world, the Avon's neaps (or lowest) tides having a rise and fall of 21 feet, and its springs (or highest) tides a spectacular 40. Since the early-nineteenth century an ingenious 'Floating Harbour' lock-gate system has served to keep the city-centre river-level to a constant high, but in the fifteenth century any unprepared ship's crew mooring at Bristol's Quay would suffer within hours the disconcerting experience of the water disappearing virtually completely from beneath their keel, leaving them high and dry on a bed of mud. As described by the eighteenth-century satirist Alexander Pope in a letter to his friend Martha Blount:

> . . . in the middle of the street, as far as you can see, hundreds of ships, their masts as thick as they can stand by on another, which is the oddest and most surprising sight imaginable. This street is fuller of them than the Thames from London Bridge to Deptford, and at certain times only, the water rises to carry them out; so that at other times, a long street, full of ships in the middle, and houses on both sides, looks like a dream.

The origins of the city of Bristol itself are lost in the mist of history, but certainly by the eleventh century it was important enough to have a powerful castle built for it by William the Conqueror and to have its own mint. In the Domesday survey it was noted as next in size after London, York and Winchester, and by the reign of the mid-twelfth-century Norman King Stephen reported as:

> nearly the richest of all cities of the country, receiving merchandise by sailing vessels from foreign countries; placed in the most fruitful part

of England, and by the very situation of the place the best defended of all the cities of England.

Even so, at about this time Bristol was still sufficiently small as to be virtually totally protected by its castle to the east, by the water of the rivers Avon and Frome, and by its sturdy walls that were penetrable through just three gateways. Each was topped by a church, one

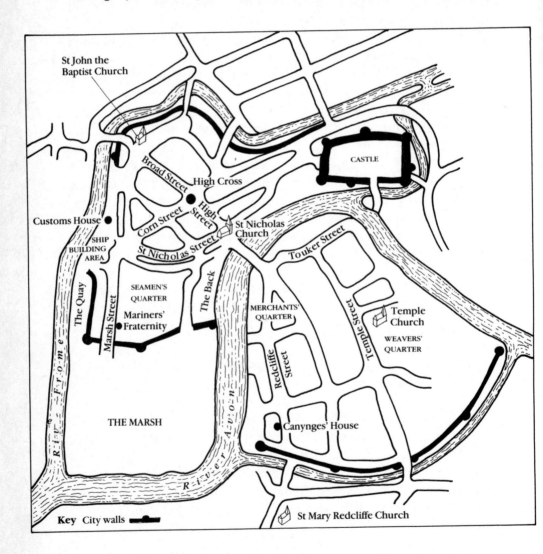

Fig. 8: Plan of Bristol circa 1475, showing its main streets, port area, merchants' and seamens' districts, etc.

(St John's) still extant in this form, and it is still possible to walk some of the original streets, Broad Street, High Street, Corn Street, etc, their names largely unchanged, even though the mediaeval buildings have been mostly obliterated by redevelopment and Hitler's Luftwaffe.

By the fifteenth century, however, Bristol had already begun to over-spill its original confines. South of the Avon a whole new suburb had grown up to process the wool from Bristol's prolific sheep-farming hinterland, with communities of tuckers (in Touker Street) to clean and beat the wool, dyers to transform it into saleable colours, and weavers to turn it into cloth. In the same area lived a colony of linen workers; also many tanners, saddlers, girdlers, glovers, etc, making readily marketable products from the hides of Welsh cattle.

Another over-spill area was a low-lying and in parts marshy area of land just south of the main city, close to where the tributary river Frome joined the Avon. This became the seamen's quarter, a Fraternity for Mariners being formed in 1445 in still-extant Marsh Street. Nearby was also a foundry, second only to London, for the making of bells and also for the manufacture of that up-and-coming instrument of war, the cannon.

By far the most superior quarter of the city, however, was that of its effective princes, its richest merchants and ship-owners, their favoured residential quarter, Redcliffe Street, fronting the Avon. From the fine and spacious houses they had built here, some of them several storeys high, they could look out on all the to-ing and fro-ing of river traffic to the Back where ships loaded and unloaded much of the merchandise by which they made their wealth.

In the year 1475 few would have disagreed that one of the most illustrious of these merchants, though he had died just the previous year, had been William Canynges the Younger, five times Mayor of Bristol and twice its Member of Parliament. One of a dynasty who had been steadily passing on the business from father to son for the best part of a century, Canynges in his hey-day reportedly owned no fewer than ten ships, employing 800 men on these, together with another 100 or so workmen, carpenters, masons, etc. When King Edward IV made an inspection visit to Bristol in 1461, it was Canynges who entertained the King and his entourage to a sumptuous banquet at his Redcliffe Street mansion. And when in 1446 a violent electrical storm sent the tower of Bristol's fine St Mary Redcliffe church toppling through its roof, it was Canynges again who financed the church's restoration, even adding a clerestory, an extra level of windows, to give it greater magnificence than before.

Canynges was by no means unusual in such civic-mindedness, Bristol's merchant clans in general showing a commendable readiness to band together to provide amenities and utilities that could often put other bigger ports to shame. Typical of this was the proper building up of the Quay and Back with piles, and the facing of them with freestone to provide an ease and cleanliness of loading and unloading a far cry from the tidal mud that characterised so many foreign ports and harbours. Even merchant's widow Alice Chester, who carried on her husband's business after his death in 1470, personally provided for the Back a crane 'for the saving of merchants' goods of the town and of strangers'. And the city's streets were well paved and maintained.

But what particularly gave Canynges and his fellows their prosperity was of course the trade which the Bristol of their time was well placed to attract by its very geography. Nationally the city was the natural manufacturing and market-centre for the entire south-western quarter of England, with wool, hides and cloth being brought to it from the west, Wales and Monmouth, timber, iron and coal from the Forest of Dean, and tin and fish from Cornwall.

Internationally likewise it was well placed to command an impressive arc of trade-routes ranging far to the west, north and south. There was nothing accidental in its sporting of a shrine to St Brendan. The south and west of Ireland was a long-established run for Bristol's ships, with fish and hides being the most popular commodities brought back in exchange for the English cloth. According to a common saying:

> Herring of Sligo and salmon of Bann
> Has made in Bristowe [Bristol] many a rich man

As already noted, Iceland was another popular Bristol run, also for fish. Others were to Brittany for salt, to Bordeaux for wine and woad, and to the Basque region of France for iron. By a peace treaty signed between Richard II and King John I of Portugal there was a particularly flourishing trade with that country, its wine being exchanged for English cloth, and Bristolian carriers progressively outnumbering their Portuguese counterparts. The Andalusian region of southern Spain was another regular port of call for more wine, together with honey, almonds, figs, liquorice, wax and more iron.

And although the fifteenth century was marked for England politically by the loss of France, by the Wars of the Roses, and by serious weakening of central government's grip on the country, the tunnages of Bristol's merchant ships tell their own story of a burgeoning commerce more than keeping pace with its counterparts on the European mainland.

Thus while early in the century very few of Bristol's vessels had a carrying capacity of more than 100 tuns, even by the middle of the century this average had doubled, with some vessels carrying as much as 250. Such was the further progress that by around 1475 William Canynges's fleet was reliably listed as comprising four ships under 200 tuns, three between 200 and 250, a *Mary Canynges* at 400 tuns, a *Mary Redcliffe* at 500 tuns (the size of the nation's largest battleships), and a *Mary and John* of, for the period, a quite colossal 900 tuns, rivalling the great Mediterranean carracks of Spain and Italy. Wherever possible these ships were built in Bristol's own quayside ship-yards.

Equally impressive was the relative routine solidity and safety of the business the Bristol merchants built up. Of course there were the occasional losses, some of which could even happen very close to or actually at home, as in 1484 when a fierce storm grounded two ships waiting at Kingroad, sank some other smaller vessels, and flooded some of Bristol's cellars, ruining the merchandise stored there.

But on the whole these were as exceptional as the ferry disasters that can happen to this day. Thus merchants of Waterford, Ireland so trusted a Bristolian merchant with whom they did business that they put in his care the royal letters patent by which they enjoyed certain special liberties. The Bristol to Spain run was considered so safe that before the end of the century it became the preferred route for the sending of state correspondence to and from Spain, sometimes without even the precaution of putting it into cipher.

But despite or perhaps because of the very solidity of the more routine trade routes, one intriguing characteristic of certainly the more entrepreneurial among the Bristol merchants was the urge to reach out to new destinations, to test to the very limits the sturdiness of their ships, the navigational powers of their seamen, and the extent to which they could break into markets either untapped, or jealously guarded by others.

One somewhat ill-fated example of this, back in the 1440s, had been that of Bristol merchant Robert Sturmy, who tried to challenge the Genoese and Venetians' monopoly of the Mediterranean. The

Sturmy plan was first to take wool, tin and cloth to Pisa, the port for Florence, then to continue with a party of pilgrims to the Holy Land. It was arranged for the pilgrims to make their return by road, while Sturmy's crew stuffed the ship's hold with spices, pepper, ginger and other Eastern commodities intended to make them a handsome profit back in England. All went according to plan until the return journey, when Sturmy's vessel went down with its entire 37-man crew during a storm off Greece.

Even so, Sturmy was sufficiently undeterred as to try again in 1457, personally accompanying this second attempt. But this time, despite having arranged for two caravels as escorts, he was ambushed by the Genoese near Malta, and although by way of reprisal the London community of Genoese back in England were seized and £6,000 compensation obtained, Sturmy himself seems to have died at the hands of his ambushers.

Of prime interest, however, were Bristol's battles with the equally aggressive and monopolistically-minded Hanseatic League, centring on Iceland's staple export product, dried cod.

In the twentieth century cod might not seem the sort of commodity to cause major upheavals, even though there actually have been cod wars in our own time. We might also think of it as a product of very marginal practicality for fifteenth-century ships to venture as far as Iceland to fetch. Yet we would be wrong on both counts.

First, it has to be remembered that as at 1475 all Europe was still staunchly Roman Catholic, Martin Luther being not yet a gleam in his mother's eye. On Friday every European housewife had therefore to be able to provide meatless dishes for her family. She also had to find the same on the church's many prescribed days of abstinence. Far worse, she was burdened with the culinary nightmare of no fewer than 40 days' prescribed meatlessness every Lent. From the very earliest centuries the Church, mindful perhaps that its very first pope had been a humble fisherman, considerately allowed the consumption of fish as a meat substitute on the days of abstinence. But no one particularly considered how fish could be made available on Fridays and other prescribed days all year round, including in inland districts. There was also the not insignificant problem of how its supply could be maintained day after day over nearly six weeks for an entire population.

In fact, so mesmerised are we of the twentieth century by living in the age of refrigeration that we tend to forget that people in earlier times were not short of some perfectly satisfactory alternative methods of food preservation. While fresh fish was a luxury mostly enjoyed only by the rich, ordinary folk did not go without. Their fish was chiefly of the dried, salted or smoked variety, preservation by such means, both for meats as well as fish, having been well developed from at least as far back as Ancient Egyptian times.

Such long experience had also shown that certain preservation methods were more suitable for some products than for others. The herring, for instance, is an oily fish, and when these moved to the North Sea the Dutch, who fished them from their large three-masted 'busses', developed a highly acclaimed method of first de-gutting them, then curing them on-board by heavy sprinkling with coarse salt, then packing them head to tail in wooden barrels, being careful to top up the barrels after settlement to make them airtight. By this means herring could be kept for up to a year.

But the North Atlantic cod, besides being less seasonal in its movements than the migratory herring, was also much simpler and cheaper to preserve, given certain optimum climatic conditions. As the Norse discovered in their own homeland, if cod were simply de-gutted, lightly salted and laid out in the open, the dry, windy weather typical of a Norwegian spring, combined with cool sunshine and a bacterial action akin to that of cheesemaking, would desiccate them to a mummified form that could keep equally as long as the Dutch herring. Nor did they need expensive barrels.

When the Norse arrived in Iceland they found they were able to use exactly the same preservation methods there, with the added bonus of much more plentiful quantities of the fish around them. Furthermore, the simple product they were able to prepare, a triangular slab of hard, dry, pale amber-coloured fish, with minimal bones and a not unappetising smell, was one ideal for sale to visiting merchant ships. It could be fitted by the tens of thousand into a ship's hold, and back in Europe stored for up to a year to be brought out for all times of high demand, most particularly the peak season of Lent. Known variously as 'stockfish' or as 'Poor Jack' or 'Poor John', for the European housewife it provided an inexpensive meat substitute that she could rehydrate and, if resourceful, prepare to dozens of different recipes.

When, as described earlier, Bristolians began venturing 'by needle and stone' to Iceland sometime before 1436, this dried cod was the product they particularly sought to take back with them. Furthermore the Bristolians were just the sort of traders the Icelandic peoples welcomed, for as currency they brought from England products the Icelanders could not make for themselves; quality cloth, meal, beer, wine, longswords, silver buttons, knives, glasses, combs, etc.

But again as earlier noted, in seeking such trade the Bristolians ran the gauntlet of every bit as much hostility from the Hanseatic League as Sturmy had encountered from the Genoese. With regard to North Atlantic fish the League's prescribed staple was Bergen in Norway, anyone wanting to purchase Icelandic fish being theoretically therefore supposed to deal only there, and to pay whatever dues or delivery charges the Hanseatics imposed. Trading direct with Iceland was only permissible by a special licence that could on some occasions be obtained from the King of England, rationed to a special quota prescribed by the Hanseatics, and on others only from the King of Norway/Denmark, whom the Hanse even more directly controlled.

For the Bristolians, dealing with Bergen was a non-starter, not least because of its geographical inconvenience. The city's merchants' success in obtaining the special licences, whether from the King of England or Norway, fluctuated greatly according to the prevailing political circumstances. In 1449, for instance, the English government needed the Scandinavians as allies against France and so accepted a ban on any trading with Iceland except by licence issued only by Norway/Denmark's King Christian I. Although William Canynges obtained such a licence, he was a very rare exception. In 1461, when a licence from the King of England was regarded as sufficient authorisation, Edward IV issued 16 after winning the battle of Towton, which was the most granted at any time during the operation of the licence system. But since Edward owed his victory as much to the Hanseatics as to English merchants, he was soon obliged by the League to be much less free with any later favours.

Historically much of our knowledge of this derives from fifteenth-century licences, law-suits, and customs records that can be inspected to this day on time-darkened rolls of parchment preserved in London's Public Record Office. Although they contain much useful data on the ships, their cargoes and destinations, many are incomplete and provide in any case only a partial picture of what was going on.

Thus there can be little doubt that there were many otherwise perfectly honest and upright Bristol merchants who during the times of licensing difficulties kept up unlicensed trading with the Icelanders, their consciences as well as their pockets reassured by the knowledge that their goods were as welcome to the Icelanders as the Icelanders' were to them. Even the official records seem to indicate that by the second half of the fifteenth century the Bristolians trading with Iceland had gained a substantial ascendancy over their east coast counterparts, their voyages via Ireland being far more straightforward than those of the latter, who were in any case both geographically disadvantaged and far more beholden to the Hanseatics.

One quite independent indication of the extent to which the Bristolians familiarised themselves with Iceland and its people derives from a Catalan chart of the second half of the fifteenth century, preserved in the Biblioteca Ambrosiana, Milan, which shows an unusually accurate delineation of Iceland, referred to as 'Fixlanda' [see fig. 9]. According to one authority:

> ... the contours ... leave no doubt that this ... owes its origin to some person or persons who were fairly well acquainted with Iceland from personal experience, and we doubtless owe it to some traders or fishermen ...

Since the 25 place-names indicated around Iceland's coast have a distinctively English ring, several scholars have suggested that such detailed knowledge was most likely acquired from Bristolian traders. Another indication of the close relations developed with Iceland is the fact that Englishmen were often chosen as bishops of Icelandic benefices.

Accordingly up until 1467 Bristolians both licensed and unlicensed seem quietly to have built up better and better trading relations with Iceland, those lacking official licences still being well received on Iceland itself, because it was to the Icelanders' benefit. But about this time the Hanseatic problem, never far beneath the surface, began to boil over in earnest. It began with the seizure of four English ships, followed by an English retaliation with the arrest of all Hanseatic merchants in London. Although these latter were relatively quickly released, formal war with the Hanseatics broke out soon after, papered over with a truce in 1471, the fragility of which was all too evident from the way it subsequently had to be renewed every two or three years.

What made matters worse for the Bristolians was the fact that a faction of the Hanseatics who did not belong to the Bergen monopoly now decided that they wanted to follow the Bristolian example and sail direct to Iceland. Hamburgers and Danzigers began pursuing this trade with such Teutonic pushiness that they were soon jostling even

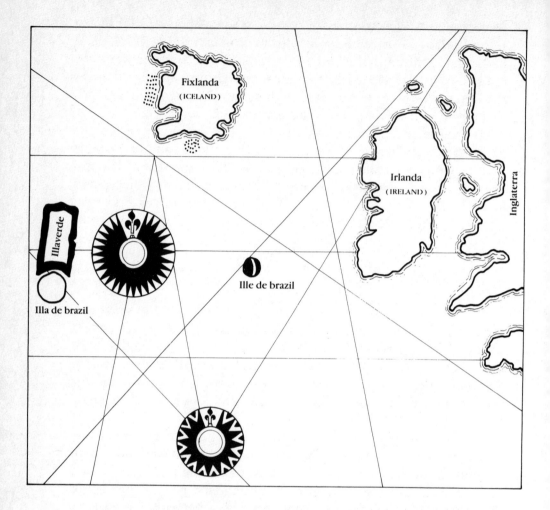

Fig. 9: Iceland, or 'Fixlanda', detail after Catalan chart of the second half of the fifteenth century, (Biblioteca Ambrosiana, Milan). The topographical information (with many place-names in the original), is thought to have been gained from Bristolian voyages to Iceland. Note also the two 'islands of Brasil', the second indicated far to the west, south of the square-shaped '*Isla Verde*', or Greenland. These latter were of course delineated unconvincingly, because of the lack of authoritative information available to the cartographers.

to carry fish from Iceland to England. Then their success so infuriated the Wendish, or Bergen-oriented, Hanseatics that these decided to follow suit. Soon, from having been a long-neglected outpost, Iceland became the battle-ground for a full-scale trade war, with repeated armed clashes on the high seas and in harbours between English ships and those of either faction of the Hanseatics.

Nor was the conflict only around Iceland. The Hanseatics, taking every advantage of the legal stranglehold they enjoyed because of the licence system, had no scruples about bringing before the English court complaints of acts of violence which they alleged against some of the most thoroughly upright Bristol merchants. It speaks volumes for the high regard of the Icelanders for the Bristolians that the island's high dignitaries actually wrote letters to the English monarchy in the Bristolians' defence.

But the Bristolian merchants were nothing if not realists. Although they had built up a large and highly profitable market for the fish they brought from Iceland – so large, indeed, that they onward exported also to Portugal – they had to recognise that their legal rights to trade with Iceland had never been more than tenuous. And now that the Hanseatics were taking up the fight in such earnest, even backing it up with the gun, clearly their days were numbered. Somehow they had to seek what they had been obtaining in Iceland from elsewhere.

Here all too frustratingly the customs accounts and licences that are our prime sources, by their very nature begin to fail us regarding what might have inspired the Bristolians, alone of any Europeans, to seek their fortune further westwards. From the evidence of the St Brendan shrine at their portals, the Bristolians had quite clearly long known of the fabled, far-westward fog-enshrouded isle that the saint was said to have visited. From their close relations with the Icelanders they are also likely to have learned at least something of the Icelandic sagas' stories of far-westward voyages beyond Greenland to Vinland and Markland. Independently, some may perhaps have come across Hugh of Ireland/Nicholas of Lynn's *Inventio Fortunatae* with its mention of 'brazil-wood' in the land beyond Greenland. They may have associated this with the mysterious island of 'Brasil' marked on some maps as to the far west of Ireland and south of Greenland, as on the earlier-mentioned Catalan chart with its highly accurate delineation of Iceland. And alongside their interest in finding a new supply of cod, they may well have fancied the 'brazil-wood' as a possible new source of dye for the red cloth for which Bristol was famous.

It can scarcely have been coincidence that it was in 1480, the very time when the strife with the Hanseatics reached its height, and four years before Columbus first put forward his ideas of finding the Orient by sailing westwards, that the Bristolians very quietly sent a lone ship on a little-known westward voyage of discovery. And what we most certainly do know is that the ship's intended destination was none other than the mysterious far-westward isle of Brasil.

CHAPTER 5

Bristol's Fishy Secret?

. . . a very ancient and fish-like smell,
a kind of not the newest Poor-John

Shakespeare, *The Tempest*, Act II, Scene 2

Although we have all too little pictorial support for most of Bristol's involvement in transoceanic voyages, one happy exception is to be found in St Mary Redcliffe, the Bristol church so lovingly restored by William Canynges. Walk the length of its nave and at the south side of the chancel, beneath a piece of protective carpet, can be seen a well-preserved funeral brass of a clean-shaven man in late-fifteenth-century-style tunic, a purse and rosary hanging from his belt, and his hands brought together in prayer. Beside him stands the slighter figure of his wife, her hands likewise joined in prayer, and her hair encased in a contemporary-style cloth head-dress. The Latin inscription, though incomplete, identifies the couple as:

> . . . John Jay, formerly Sheriff of this town, and Joan, his wife, which John died on . . . day of the month . . . 148 . . . On whose souls may God have mercy . . .

As evidenced by a line of much smaller figures depicted below the inscription, the Jays produced a large family, comprising six sons and eight daughters. Also evident is the fact that John earned his living as a merchant, for two of four shields show his merchant's mark, the distinctive monogram which mediaeval merchants used to identify their respective goods, and which each cherished with as much pride as a nobleman his coat of arms. The two other shields display a 'fuller's bat', an instrument used in the cloth trade.

On the face of it, this John Jay might appear to be just another of the many English merchants whose memorials have survived but whose

Fig. 10: Memorial brass of the Bristol merchant John Jay and his wife
Joan, from the chancel of the church of St Mary Redcliffe, Bristol.

lives were too ordinary to make any significant mark in the pages of
history. Among Bristol's fifteenth-century customs records the name
John Jay does, in fact, recur quite often, both in licences and customs
accounts, but not without a certain element of confusion for some
of these entries relate to John Jay's father, another John, who died
in 1468, others to our St Mary Redcliffe John Jay's son, who also
had the same name, all three of these John Jays earning their living
as merchants engaged in the same family business.

Thankfully, however, we know a little more about the St Mary

Redcliffe John Jay (whom we may best call John Jay the second), due to a curious fifteenth-century notebook preserved in the Library of Corpus Christi College, Cambridge. Consisting of 332 pages of jottings, mostly in Latin, the notebook's author was antiquary William Worcestre, none other than the brother of Joan Jay, wife of John Jay the second, whose features we have already observed on the St Mary Redcliffe memorial brass. Apparently one-eyed and swarthy-looking, Worcestre lived mainly in Norfolk, where he had his own large family. But having been born in Bristol, he appears to have revisited his native city quite often, making copious notes of its buildings. He also clearly visited his sister, jotting down of her husband John:

> John Jay the second, husband of my sister Joan, died on 15 May in the year of Christ . . .

Frustratingly, and in a curious coincidence with the St Mary Redcliffe brass, Worcestre omitted the exact year of his brother-in-law's death, though this seems merely to have been typical of Worcestre's tendency to leave blanks to indicate information he did not possess or could not remember. Since Worcestre himself died no later than 1485, John Jay must inevitably have died early in the 1480s.

But for us the most fascinating information occurs in the very next jotting in Worcestre's notebook:

> 1480. On the 15 day of July the ship belonging to. . . . and John Jay junior, of 80 tons burthen, began a voyage from the port of Bristol at King Road to the Island of Brasil to the west of Ireland, ploughing the seas for . . . and. . . . Lloyd was master of the ship, the [most] competent seaman of the whole of England; and news came to Bristol on Monday 18 September that the said ship had sailed the seas for about 9 months [mistake for 9 weeks], but had found no island and had been forced back by storms at sea to the port of . . . in Ireland to rest the ship and the seamen

Now this might seem only a simple paragraph, and with some frustrating gaps. But what we have here, from a date securely 12 years before Columbus's First Voyage, is a quite unequivocal record of a Bristol ship, owned by at least one merchant of that city, setting off on a westward-bound transatlantic voyage of discovery, its intended goal clearly stated as the island of 'Brasil', which as we have seen earlier may or may not have been St Brendan's isle, alias Newfoundland. And although Worcestre does not name the ship involved in this voyage, we do at least know that the first John Jay, who died in 1468, had bequeathed to his son his eighth share of the vessel *Trinity*.

Also evident from further jottings in Worcestre's notebook is that John Jay the second, who traded with Portugal, had taken quite an interest in the islands believed to lie westward in the Ocean Sea. Worcestre specifically recorded having seen in the Jay household a 'new chart' of the latest discoveries of Atlantic islands 'painted to show these islands'. This apparently showed Madeira, Tenerife, the various islands of the Azores, the Cape Verde islands, etc, together with the sailing distances between each. Since these islands were mostly discoveries made earlier in the century by the Portuguese it is reasonable to infer that Jay had obtained the chart during his dealings with Portuguese merchants.

Additionally, in his listing of the various islands of the Azores, Worcestre noted:

> Three small islands lying in a triangle, perhaps inhabited
> St Brendan's Isle, a large island due east of Jesus Christo island [the Azores island of Terceira], a long way further east

As commented by Worcestre's present-day editor, John Harvey, by 'east' in this context, Worcestre almost certainly meant 'towards the east', i.e. to the west, the consistent location for St Brendan's isle both in literature and on maps. Furthermore, while it is impossible to be sure of the exact chart that John Jay had acquired, Worcestre's reference to the 'three small islands' suggests it may have been closest to one made circa 1475 by Cristofal Soligo, preserved today in the British Museum as Egerton manuscript 73. Harvey conjectured that the '*ya, del Brazil*' marked on Soligo's chart could well have been what Worcestre jotted down as St Brendan's Isle, a point itself indicative of the interchangeability between these two names.

Now by itself Worcestre's reference would of course mean very little, particularly since he stated that the voyage had been unsuccessful. But the plot thickens when we learn that the Lloyd/Jay voyage seems to have been authorised by a surviving licence issued by England's King Edward IV on 18 June, 1480, i.e. under a month prior to its known date of departure as recorded by Worcestre. This licence permitted two or three Bristol ships of 60 tons or under 'to trade for three years to any parts with any except staple goods'. Although Jay is not named in the licence, which may indicate that he was a relatively junior partner in the enterprise, four other Bristol worthies are: Thomas Croft, William Spencer, Robert Strange and William de la Fount.

In themselves these names give us some indication that the 'Brasil' expedition was no idle, one-off whim, but a venture with a great deal of clout behind it, indicative perhaps of the urgent desire to find another Iceland for the supply of dried cod.

Thomas Croft, for instance, was none other than King Edward IV's Collector of Customs for Bristol, he and his brother Richard, of the well-to-do Croft family of Croft Castle, Herefordshire, having both been child companions to Edward when he was a young prince. Croft's very appointment as Collector seems to have been the King's reward for this childhood friendship, and three years before he had also served as Member of Parliament for his family's local town of Leominster.

William Spencer, like Jay, was a Bristol merchant, but one more on a par with the late William Canynges. Sixty years old in 1480 (yet unusually for the times with another 15 years to live), he had been bailiff and sheriff of Bristol in his earlier years, once the city's Member of Parliament, and three times its mayor, the last occasion only the year before. In an old mayoral book preserved in the Bristol Record Office an exquisitely coloured drawing [pl. 2] shows him officiating at the mayor-making ceremony of September 29, 1479, holding the Bible for the swearing-in of his successor, Edmund Westcott.

Robert Strange, although fifteen years younger than Spencer, was a similarly well-established merchant, vintner and shipowner who had likewise been bailiff, sheriff and mayor, and would go on to serve two further terms as mayor, also twice as the city's MP. In 1465, with William Spencer and others, he had founded a Guild of the Holy Cross at Bristol's St John the Baptist church. He also had something of the previously mentioned Robert Sturmy's adventurousness in the Mediterranean, having, like Sturmy, suffered a spice ship being spoiled in the Mediterranean.

William de la Fount, though perhaps less civic-minded than the others, seems to have been no less prosperous, frequently named as a merchant in customs accounts, and having built a ship of his own, of 201 tuns, only five years before. Indeed, among these other four, John Jay, although obviously the best known to Worcestre, would seem to have been a junior partner.

That these were rich, powerful men, often metaphorically sailing very close to the wind in their commercial dealings, is evident from the fact that only the previous year Strange had spent seven weeks imprisoned in the Tower of London accused of coining money, a charge of which he was eventually cleared. His accuser was hanged.

Perhaps the most fascinating feature, however, is that it was from a not dissimilar corruption accusation made against Customs Collector Thomas Croft that there comes the next vital clue that the reportedly unsuccessful voyage of 1480 was not the last and had by no means diminished these Bristol men's resolve to find their 'Brasil' somewhere out to the west.

For in the autumn of 1481 there arrived in Bristol a royal commission to inquire into all matters relating to Bristol's shipping activities, and the collection of royal revenues therefrom. A jury of 44 persons was empanelled to hear the cases brought before the commission, one of which was a charge that:

> Thomas Croft of Bristol . . . Customer of the said lord the king in the port of his town of Bristol aforesaid on the sixth day of July in the aforesaid year [1481] . . . was owner of an eighth part of a ship or balinger called the *Trinity*, and of an eighth part of a certain ship or balinger called the *George*, and in each of the said ships or balingers . . . laded, shipped and placed forty bushels of salt . . . with the intention of trading.

Immediately noteworthy here is that the first of the ships referred to, the *Trinity*, bears the same name as that of which John Jay the second had inherited a share from his father. The proportions of ownership, i.e. in eighths, are also the same. It may well therefore have been the very same vessel as the unnamed one which Worcestre reported 'Lloyd' to have captained across the Atlantic the previous year.

However, also to be noted, in order properly to understand the charge against Croft, is that one of the most cardinal rules that Edward IV and other monarchs had set down for their customs collectors was that they should be prohibited from any personal trading. It was an understandable and straightforward enough rule, to prevent corruption. Yet even the very licence issued by Edward IV for the 1480 voyage, and still applicable, specified that its purpose was 'to trade for three years to any parts'. So how could Croft even have considered associating himself with such a venture – and also have been allowed to do it in the first place?

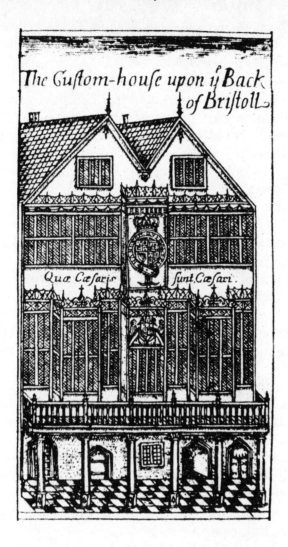

The Custom-house upon y^e Back of Bristoll

Quæ Cæsaris sunt Cæsari.

Fig. 11: The Bristol Customs House, headquarters of Bristol's customs collectors, from a seventeenth-century engraving by James Millerd.

Here is where some extraordinary interest pertains to Croft's defence before the charges brought against him. He did not deny association with the *Trinity* and *George* venture. Nor did he deny responsibility for the loading of salt on to the two vessels. But what he did argue was that this latter was for the ships' 'repair, equipment and maintenance'. He also insisted that the purpose of their voyage was 'not with the intention of trading', but of 'examining and finding a certain island called the Isle of Brasil' (*causa scrutandi et inveniendi quandam insulam vocatum le Ile of Brasile*).

The jury which listened to this case had something of the powers of a modern magistrates' court, and had Croft been found guilty he would then have been sent for more formal trial before the High Court of Exchequer who could then have stripped him of his office. But Croft was cleared on both charges, an official pardon to this effect being still preserved in London's Public Record Office in one of the Memoranda Rolls for Edward IV's reign.

Nonetheless the Croft case leaves for us a whole series of unanswered questions. Although it provides us with the highly important information that the Bristolians sent out a second expedition, with two vessels, in search of Brasil only a year after the apparent failure of the first, it gives no accompanying information on whether these may or may not have been successful. There is, for instance, a frustrating ambiguity to the Latin words '*scrutandi et inveniendi*', which could conceivably be construed to mean the examination and exploration of a land already found.

There is also confusion concerning the vessel involved, the *Trinity*. The customs records show that the *Trinity* of Bristol as part-owned by John Jay was a major cargo-carrying vessel of some 300 tuns, regularly making voyages to Spain and Portugal with large consignments of cloth, returning with equally large consignments of wine, oil, fruit, etc. She was at least three times larger than Columbus's *Santa Maria* and five times larger than *Pinta* and *Niña*. Unless there was another Bristol ship of the same name, she was rather too valuable a vessel to be risked on any mere exploratory voyage. Her size was also in contravention of Edward IV's licence.

And here it is important to emphasise that for us not to be told of the 1481 voyage's success by no means necessarily implies its failure. Had the Bristolians found Brasil, and found it to be just the new location for the cod that they needed, their unhappy treatment over Iceland would have given them every motive for keeping very quiet about this news so that it should not be learned by the Hanseatics. And since the Hanseatics still had many ears in London the Bristolians would have felt equal chariness about releasing any news in that direction also.

Indeed, home events gave the Bristol merchants all the more reason and excuse to keep very quiet about any such discovery, had it indeed occurred. When Edward IV died in April 1483 leaving the kingdom to his twelve-year-old son Edward V, England swiftly became embroiled in the final phase of the Wars of the Roses, involving Edward V's usurpation and secret murder by Richard III, followed by Richard's own bloody defeat by Henry Tudor on Bosworth field in 1485. With central government in disarray, it was a time for keeping one's head down and waiting to see who might emerge victorious before beginning to impart confidences. Thomas Croft was actually shrewd enough to change his allegiance to Henry Tudor shortly before Bosworth, but the new king bestowed no special favours on him, and in any case Croft died no later than 1488.

But why should we be disposed even to begin to believe that the 1481 voyage might have been successful? Here of prime interest in the accusations against Croft is the fact that the *Trinity* and the *George* were said to have been 'laded' or loaded with salt. Salt was not a normal English export item, certainly not on its own, for during the fifteenth century England's supply was predominantly imported, most coming from Bourgneuf Bay, Brittany, with further quantities brought by Bristol ships from Lisbon, Oporto, and occasionally Andalusia. Furthermore Croft successfully defended himself against the charges that he had any intention of trading in this commodity.

But if not for trading, what was the salt's purpose? Croft, as we have noted, claimed it was for the ships' 'repair, equipment and maintenance', yet this has a less than convincing ring about it. Fifteenth-century wooden sailing ships needed to carry a variety of materials for their repair and maintenance, including timber and caulking. Salt may have been among these for the odd shipboard purpose, such as when a vessel was thoroughly cleaned from time to time. But the quantity of salt and its singling out for special mention scarcely makes much sense.

Where it would, however, make a great deal of sense is if a new but uninhabited equivalent of Iceland had been discovered, somewhere with plentiful cod, but where, unlike in Iceland itself, the actual catching and shore-curing of the fish had to be done by the Bristolians themselves.

Had this been the case, certainly the one commodity they would have needed to bring with them for this operation would have been salt. So could it be rather more than coincidence that salt was the very commodity which the *Trinity* and *George* were specifically reported to have carried in significant amounts in 1481? Indeed, might we not suspect that this new Iceland had been found even before their departure on 6 July of that year, hence the fact that the two ships were travelling out ready equipped?

Now if we at least allow the possibility that this was indeed the case, and that the *Trinity* and *George* just *might* have been en route to some such new Iceland, exactly where was this new location? We already know the ships' stated destination to have been the 'Isle of Brasil'. Similarly, we have already seen the case for identifying Brasil as Newfoundland. And in fact, given the Bristolians' overriding need in the early 1480s for an alternative source of cod, Newfoundland makes sense from many other points of view.

For first, of course, and quite overridingly, Newfoundland had the cod, and in even greater abundance than Iceland. While *Gadus morhua*, the North Atlantic cod, can be found right across the Atlantic, including off English shores, the very same mixing of the cold Labrador current with the warm Gulf Stream that creates Newfoundland's fogs also creates paradisical breeding conditions for plankton, bringing higher forms of marine life that in turn attract cod by the million.

Perhaps the most spectacular demonstration of this occurs every July in eastern Newfoundland when literally billions of capelin, or smelt, arrive to spawn on its beaches, hotly pursued by whales and squid, but most of all by millions of cod. As Captain John Mason, an early settler who wrote a tract on Newfoundland around 1618, described this phenomenon:

> cods so thick by the shore that we nearly have been able to row a boat through them, I have killed of them with a pike.

But even aside from the extremes of this season, cod are found throughout the year in such abundance in Newfoundland's waters that during a personal visit in September 1990, I watched a boat-party of tourists pull them from the sea at the rate of one every few seconds, using mere hooked hand-lines. The fish hardly even struggle. On Newfoundland anyone, even the most inexperienced, can be an instant cod fisherman.

Another argument for Newfoundland having been the fifteenth-century Bristolians' 'Brasil' is that it was one of the few locations they would have found virtually devoid of any competitive human inhabitants, its 'Red Indian' population of the now extinct Beothuk tribe being peaceable and very thinly distributed. The Bristolians would therefore have been able to set up their own seasonal shore

stations for the drying of the cod in Newfoundland's hundreds
of quiet inlets, an added bonus being the island's plentiful
supply of timber for the making of the necessary wharves, or
'stages' and 'flakes' or drying platforms, on which this had to
be done.

And not least of the reasons for identifying Newfoundland as the
Bristolians' 'Brasil' is the fact that with absolute certainty from at
least as early as the first decade of the sixteenth century, Bristolians

Fig. 12: Traditional method for the splitting and drying of cod, as
practised on Newfoundland. From inset to H. Moll's map of North
America, London, 1720.

and other West Country entrepreneurs very definitely did set up a seasonal fishing industry on Newfoundland, involving the catching of cod and the drying of this in the open air, just as they had observed in Iceland. As the procedures were described in the previously mentioned Journal of the seventeenth-century Plymouth surgeon James Yonge:

> As soon as we resolve to fish here, the ship is all unrigged, and in the snow and cold all the men go into the woods to cut timber, fir, spruce and birch being here plentiful. With this they build stages [and] flakes. . . .

About five men would go out in a ship's boat, and in a few hours might catch up to 1,200 cod, whereupon:

> They bring the fish at the stage head . . . and throw them up. Then a boy takes them and lays them on a table in the stage, on one side of which stands a header, who opens the belly, takes out the liver, and twines off the head and guts (which fall through the stage into the sea) with notable dexterity and suddenness . . . When the header has done his work, he thrusts the fish to the other side of the table, where sits a spoilter, or splitter, who with a strong knife splits it abroad, and with a back stroke cuts off the bone, which falls through a hole into the sea. There are some that will split incredibly swift, 24 score in half an hour.

Next it was the turn of the salter, economically using a supply of salt arguably just such as that with which Thomas Croft loaded the *Trinity* and *George*. According to Yonge:

> The salter comes with salt on a wooden shovel and with a little brush strews the salt on it. When a pile is about 3 foot high they begin with another. A salter is a skilful officer, for too much salt burns the fish and makes it break, and wet, too little makes it redshanks, that is, look red when dried, and so is not merchantable. The fish being salted, lies 3 or 4 days, sometimes (if bad weather) 8 or 10 days, and is then washed by the boys in salt or fresh water and laid in a pile skin upward on a platt of beach stones, which they call a horse. After a day or thereabout, it's laid abroad on flakes . . . that is boughs thinly laid upon a frame, like that of a table, and here the fish dries . . . When well dried, it's made up into prest pile, where it sweats; that is, the salt sweats out, and corning, makes the fish look white. After it's so done, it's dried one day on the ground and then put up in dry pile,

as they call it, that is a pile bigger than the prest by 3 times. There it lies till shipt off, when it's dried part of a day, then weighed, carried on board, laid, and prest snug with great stones.'

So like a production-line was the Newfoundland cod-fishing and curing business that according to the previously mentioned early-seventeenth-century settler Captain Mason 'three men [going] to sea in a boat with some on shore to dress and dry them' could make ready for shipment 'commonly between 25,000 and 30,000' fish in as little as 30 days. In Mason's time as many as 250 West Country vessels were engaged in the Newfoundland trade. It was also certainly well established as early as 1589 because we know there was a serious dried fish shortage in that year, an alarmed Lord Burghley reporting 'the whole country cannot supply above one hundred thousand Newfoundland fish for the fleet', against normal stocks exceeding two million. This was apparently due to so many normally Newfoundland-bound vessels having stayed back in England the previous year to defend it against the Spanish Armada.

Even earlier, in 1541, the 'Newland' fishing trade was apparently already sufficiently flourishing to be mentioned in an Act of Henry VIII 'Concerning Buying of Fish upon the Sea' of that year. In fact, as early as 1504 can be traced the first absolutely definite cargo of Newfoundland cod brought back to Bristol.

The problem for us, however, is that virtually our entire knowledge of the whole development of the Newfoundland dried cod fishery derives only from when things went wrong, as when it became interrupted in 1589, and (arguably) when some common informer made a charge against Thomas Croft in 1481. Back in the 1970s Henry Forbes Taylor, a Bristol engineer who became fascinated by the problem, made the most exhaustive study of Bristol's customs accounts in an endeavour to argue that the Bristolians had been falsely declaring Newfoundland voyages as to 'Ireland' in order to keep their activities secret from the Hanseatics and from officialdom in general.

In reality, no such complex argument is needed. Historically there are no records of the Newfoundland fishery's beginnings, and thereby of the success or otherwise of the 'Brasil' voyages of the 1480s, because there did not need to be. As the maritime historian Professor Quinn has pointed out, if the Bristolians were making fishing voyages to Newfoundland in which they caught the cod and shore-dried it themselves before bringing this back to England, then they would not have been trading with another sovereign nation, as they had been in Iceland, but in effect only fishing. And ordinary fishing catches were not liable to customs duty.

Therefore so long as the royal customs officers were aware that this was how the fish had been obtained (and as we have seen, Thomas Croft was a partner in the enterprise, and had quite possibly been invited to be so for this very reason), there would have been no requirement for the catches to be entered on any customs records. Similarly, it was in these very circumstances that a customs officer such as Croft could have put money into the enterprise yet in all justice plead complete innocence of any charges of trading, because trading meant an exchange of goods and/or money, and on Newfoundland no such exchange occurred.

The difficulty for us, however, particularly given that the Bristolians had every motive for wanting to keep their new source of cod secret from anyone who might leak the knowledge to the Hanseatics, is that we are thereby deprived of the very evidence we would most like to have that Bristolians began fishing off Newfoundland as early as the 1480s.

For instance, if lacking documentary records we might be minded to look for archaeological evidence of the Bristolians' earliest cod-drying stations on Newfoundland, this, frustratingly, has to be worse than finding a needle in a haystack. Bristolians, along with fishermen of several other nationalities, set up shore stations by the hundred in Newfoundland's myriad of inlets throughout the days of sail, invariably using wooden materials that simply ended up either burnt for firewood or cannibalised and replaced by the next generation. For centuries nothing permanent was set up because the fishermen almost invariably returned to their home base at the end of each season. Given such a paucity of archaeological remains (and those there are have hardly begun to be investigated), there is hardly a chance of finding anything that could be specifically attributed to the years 1481 to 1492.

Nor are some of the alternative clues particularly promising. One is a possible indication that the Bristolians might have received some initial instruction and help from sympathetic Icelanders in the setting up of the Newfoundland cod-drying methods. By chance there has survived in the Public Record Office a register of taxable foreign servants employed in Bristol for the year 1484. Although Bristol's trade with Iceland was theoretically virtually dead by this time, this register, the only one of its kind to survive for Bristol, most curiously and intriguingly shows no fewer than 48 Icelandic men and boys employed in Bristol households. One of the employers was the William Spencer whose association with the 'Brasil' voyages we have already noted. Another was a merchant whose name will recur later, Richard Ameryk. At least one of the Icelanders, William (one of only two to be listed by name), went on to become a naturalised Englishman and Bristol merchant in his own right, listed as such in the customs accounts for 1492. So could these Icelanders have been recruited to help teach the Bristolians the best methods of cod-drying on Newfoundland?

A similar and equally non-specific clue is that while we might expect the Bristol merchants, having lost their trade with Iceland, to have suffered a marked decline in their fortunes, there are signs that they remained rather more prosperous than they cared to make out. Part of Bristol's folklore relates that when King Henry VII visited the city in 1486, shortly after his Bosworth victory, the merchants who welcomed him told him that trade was bad, specifically because of the fall-off of the Iceland market. Henry was, however, too astute not to notice that the merchants' wives were all looking rather suspiciously well dressed. He was even more suspicious when he returned in 1490 to find the wives all looking even more richly apparelled and bejewelled than before. Without further ado he therefore insisted upon a £500 'benevolence' for the royal coffers, together with £1 from every man who was worth £200 'because men's wives went so sumptuously apparelled.'

A modern painting by Tom Mostyn, displayed in an upstairs court room of Bristol's Old Council House, immortalises this particular Bristol historical anecdote. And while we have no way of being sure whether success in the Newfoundland fishery was responsible for this clandestine prosperity, we do know that in the very same year of 1490, following a final, final treaty which the English crown negotiated with the Hanseatics, the Bristolians were given the opportunity to renew their old trade with Iceland, yet for unexplained reasons chose not to do so.

Clearly, however, something rather more positive than these indications is needed for there to be any measure of certainty that Bristolians had indeed reached their 'Brasil', alias Newfoundland, before Columbus reached the West Indies. It is important to realise that even had they done so, there is no reason to suppose that they, any more than the Norse before them, believed themselves to have

found a hitherto unknown new continent. Just as the Norse had seen
Newfoundland as a heavensent new pasture-land, so the Bristolians
arguably would have regarded it simply as the answer to their prayers
for a non-Hanseatic-dominated source of supply for dried cod.

But there is one person who if he had heard even a whisper of
the Bristolians' activities, might have viewed them in an altogether
different light: Christopher Columbus. When the Portuguese made
their first voyage to Greenland as late as the early 1500s they mapped
even this as a 'peninsula of Asia'. Had Columbus heard anything of the
Bristolians' 'Brasil' voyages he might well have leapt to the conclusion
that they had found a new short route to 'Asia'. As we will learn, from
unimpeachable evidence to emerge later, Columbus unquestionably
did learn of the Bristolians' 'Brasil' voyages, his knowledge of these
in the event representing the strongest evidence of their success. But
our first concern has to be to establish exactly *how* Columbus could
have come by information of this kind.

CHAPTER 6

Columbus:
The Bristol Connection?

At the very beginning of this book we noted Columbus's reticence and tendency to untruthfulness concerning his early life. But there is one passage in the biography written by his son Fernando potentially highly relevant to any consideration of how he came by his idea of voyaging westwards in search of Asia. It consists of a note or memorial by Columbus which Fernando seems to have found among his father's papers, and which he quoted verbatim:

> In the month of February 1477, I sailed one hundred leagues beyond the island of Tile [Thule], whose southern part is in latitude 73 degrees N. and not 63 degrees as some affirm; nor does it lie upon the meridian where Ptolemy says the West begins, but much farther west. And to this island, which is as big as England, the English come with their wares, especially from Bristol. When I was there, the sea was not frozen, but the tides were so great that in some places they rose fifty feet, and fell as much in depth.

Scholars are essentially agreed that by 'Thule' Columbus would have meant what we now know as Iceland. And of course if Columbus had personally visited Iceland in 1477, then he could readily have heard about the 'Vinland' voyages of the sagas direct from the Icelanders. Given that he would thereby have supposed that the Norse had reached the northern parts of Asia, it would have been all too easy for him to deduce that if he sailed westwards at a more southerly latitude, he would come to the much richer parts of Asia, such as the lands of the Great Khan, that were reliably believed to lie at those latitudes. Indeed, accepting at face value this single passage quoted by Fernando, some Scandinavian writers have postulated that Columbus's whole discovery of America was based on such 'secret knowledge' of the Icelanders' 'Vinland' voyages.

If true this would of course seriously undermine any hypothesis that knowledge of Bristol's 'Brasil' voyages might have had some influence upon Columbus's thinking. But the validity of the Fernando passage has in fact been very percipiently challenged by British maritime historian Dr Alwyn Ruddock, retired reader in history at London University's Birkbeck College. As she pointed out, not only is the passsage in Fernando's biography the only one in all the Columbus source material to suggest that he visited Iceland, it is also full of mistakes.

For instance, the calculation of latitude is in error by at least ten degrees. And while in itself this is nothing unusual for Columbus (who as we have earlier established, made quite a practice of falsifying such information), much more seriously wrong is the reference to unusually high tides. Iceland has some remarkable features, such as its volcanoes, but the height of its tides is not one of these, the absolute maximum being 10–12 feet. There seems therefore to have been some muddle with Bristol, which is also mentioned in the same passage, and where, as we have already learnt, the tides genuinely can reach 50 feet. Since no one who had actually visited Iceland and/or Bristol was likely to have become confused in this way, Dr Ruddock has strongly argued that Columbus never did visit Iceland, Fernando simply having garbled something in his father's notes.

And a further indication that Columbus, for all his boasting and untruthfulness, never claimed to have visited Iceland is the entry in his Journal for 21 December, 1492 in which, directly describing his seafaring experience, he stated that he had sailed the Mediterranean east to west, and had travelled southwards as far as Guinea and northwards as far as England. Here would have been his natural opportunity for stating he had visited Iceland, had he indeed done so. It can only therefore be supposed that he did not.

All this gives rise to two questions. First, if not a visit to Iceland, what was it that gave Columbus the whole idea for mounting his voyages to the west? And second, how did such a strangely garbled note concerning Iceland and Bristol happen to be among Columbus's papers?

Given the many hundreds of books written on Columbus, the first of these questions might seem the easiest to answer. Yet in fact, curiously, there is no historical consensus concerning how Columbus developed the idea that gave him his place in history. Even his most authoritative biographer, Admiral Samuel Morison, has felt bound to acknowledge:

> Whilst no valid ground exists to question the traditional concept
> that Columbus's purpose was to reach Asia by sailing west, there is
> plenty of room for argument as to where he got the idea, and when
> . . . Columbus apparently never told anybody, and perhaps himself
> did not remember . . .

For Morison, and several others, the prominent Florentine banker,
doctor of medicine and grand old man of astronomy Paolo Toscanelli,
who died in 1482, has been most frequently tipped as the likeliest
major source of influence on Columbus. This is because in Fernando
Columbus's biography of his father, as well as copied into the back of
one of the books that Columbus personally owned, is to be found a copy
of a letter purportedly sent in 1474 by Toscanelli to Fernão Martinez,
an advisor and confessor to the Portuguese King Alfonso V.

In this letter, which had apparently been accompanied by a map,
'Toscanelli' relayed with great enthusiasm Marco Polo's reports of
the riches of the East, explaining how:

> spices grow in lands to the west, even though we usually say the
> east; for he who sails west will always find these lands in the west,
> and he who travels east by land will always find the same lands in
> the east.

In the same vein 'Toscanelli' described the 'sea route from here to
India, the land of spices' as 'shorter than that by way of Guinea'.
And besides this letter to Martinez, Fernando's biography reproduced
another, one purportedly sent directly from 'Toscanelli' to Columbus,
explaining how he had sent the copy of the Martinez letter in order to
convey to Columbus how much he endorsed his ideas.

Scholarly opinion has been deeply divided on the authenticity of this
Toscanelli correspondence. Early this century it was very forcefully
debunked by one researcher, Henry Vignaud, on the grounds that the
views expressed in the Martinez letter mimicked suspiciously closely
those of Columbus, and that there was no independent indication,
either in Portugal or in Italy, of the real Toscanelli ever having
held any such ideas. The historical existence of Martinez has also
been doubted. Although the authoritative Admiral Morison, for
his part, was inclined to believe the correspondence was genuine,
recently opinion has again begun to harden against this, the finger

of suspicion being pointed sometimes at Fernando, sometimes at Columbus's brother Bartholomew, as having devised the letters as fake 'testimonials' for Columbus's ideas. Among the latest remarks on the subject are those of Dr Robert Fuson, professor of geography at the University of South Florida:

> The best evidence that the Toscanelli correspondence was a fake rests with the fact that the information in the letters is ridiculously out-of-date. No informed scholar in Florence would have written such a letter in 1474; only someone in Spain who was not current with the sophisticated learning of the Florentines could have been responsible.

If therefore the Toscanelli correspondence is rejected, and similarly any likelihood of Columbus having visited Iceland, this begins to reduce substantially whatever factors might have influenced Columbus to seek Asia via the west. Chapter Ten of Fernando Columbus's biography of his father enumerates some minor anecdotes which must certainly have helped Columbus with his ideas. One of these was the story of a Portuguese pilot who had apparently told Columbus that:

> on one occasion 450 leagues to the west of Cape St Vincent, he saw and took into his ship from the sea a piece of wood artificially worked, and as he judged, not by means of an iron tool, from which circumstance, and because there had been west winds for many days, he imagined that this timber came from some island or islands lying to the westward.

Another was how Columbus had been told:

> . . . that in the isle of Flores, which is one of the Azores, the sea had brought up the bodies of two dead men who seemed very broad in the face and of an appearance different from that of Christians. Another time . . . they saw hollowed trunks or canoes with a movable covering, which by chance . . . the force of the winds and the sea brought thither.

However something more than mere anecdotes such as these has to have been responsible for persuading Columbus to pursue his ideas over several years, sometimes in circumstances of considerable penury. There also has to have been something that particularly caused him to believe that Asia was near enough to be within reasonable sailing distance, not least because it was on this very point that Columbus met with the strongest opposition to his ideas from scholars both in Spain and Portugal. According to the best-informed thought of the late-fifteenth century, based on Arab geography and mathematics, the circumference of the earth was calculated to be relatively close to the currently accepted figure of 25,000 miles. This meant that Asia's distance westward across the Ocean Sea had to be some 11,000 miles, way beyond the capabilities of the vessels of the time. But Columbus, by contrast, calculated the distance from the Canaries to Cipango, or Japan, as 2,400 miles, and to Cathay, or China, as 3,500. It was these calculations which both Portuguese and later Spanish experts very justifiably rejected in the strongest terms, dismissing them as pure fantasy.

Unquestionably Columbus gained at least some of these ideas from geographical treatise, the *Imago Mundi*, written back in 1410 by the French cardinal and armchair geographer, Pierre d'Ailly. The published edition of this was printed at Louvain during the early 1480s, and Columbus's personal copy survives in the Biblioteca Colombina in Seville, complete with heavy annotations in his own handwriting. Evidence enough of his particular interest in the Europe to Asia distance problem is quite apparent from the heaviness of his annotations to those passages referring to the comparative narrowness of the ocean between western Europe/Africa and easternmost Asia, as for example:

> Between the end of Spain and the beginning of India is no great width
> India is near Spain
> The beginnings of the Orient and of the Occident are close
> Aristotle says that the sea is small between the western extremity of Spain and the eastern part of India . . . Moreover Seneca in the fifth book of the things of nature says that this sea is navigable in a few days if the wind be favourable.

However, most of Pierre d'Ailly's ideas were already seriously out of date by the early 1480s, as no doubt scholars of the time would repeatedly have reminded Columbus. So arguably there has to have been something else which lay behind his dedication to his scheme, something which in a much more down-to-earth way convinced him that Asia lay only one-third of the distance westwards generally supposed, and which in particular sustained him in this belief during the bitter years of rejection.

Here is where some considerable interest pertains to the origin of the curious and muddled note, preserved in Fernando's biography, concerning Iceland and mentioning also Bristol. During the years 1476 to 1484 Columbus seems mostly to have been employed as a map-maker in Lisbon, which had a substantial Genoese community. And since we have already established that Bristolian ships were regular visitors to Lisbon's harbour, it would obviously have been easy enough for Columbus to have picked up some information concerning Iceland – and, by the same token, concerning the voyages to 'Brasil' – in casual conversation with some Spanish or Portuguese-speaking Bristol seaman or trader on Lisbon's waterfront.

However one scholar who has taken a particularly close interest in this issue is the previously mentioned Dr Alwyn Ruddock. And she has argued strongly against Columbus having obtained his information by any such direct means. As she has pointed out, it is rather unlikely that a Bristolian would have imparted privileged information directly to any Genoese, these being hardly the best loved of people in Bristol, bearing in mind Robert Sturmy's fate. There is also the curious mix-up between Iceland and Bristol's 50-foot tides. This is something a Bristolian is hardly likely to have been responsible for, even allowing for language difficulties. And when referring to Iceland, a Bristolian is also rather more likely to have used the mariners' name 'Islonde', rather than the 'Thule' of the professional cosmographers.

For these and similar reasons Dr Ruddock has therefore argued for an indirect point of connection between Columbus and men of Bristol. And her attention has focused on a particular geographical region for this point of connection, a somewhat uninspiring area of Andalusia in southern Spain that was particularly significant to Columbus: the marshy Rio Saltés estuary, with its then sleepy seaports of Palos and Huelva, the latter today the site of oil refineries and other unattractive looking industrial works. Not only was it from Palos that Columbus would set out on his historic First Voyage in 1492, but at next-door Huelva there lived Columbus's wife's sister, together with her husband Miguel Molyart. And certainly it was to this same region that no later than the end of 1484 (if he had not already visited before) the recently widowed Columbus came to lodge his five-year-old son Diego with the local Franciscan friary of Santa Maria de la Rábida [pl. 5]. This would seem to have been just after the first rejection of his ideas by Portugal.

Now, sadly, all too little is known of Columbus's actual dealings with

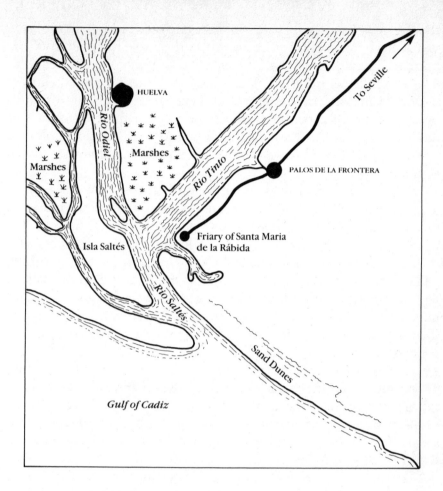

Fig. 13: The Rio Saltés estuary of Andalusia, southern Spain, late-fifteenth century, showing the locations of Palos, Huelva and the La Rábida friary. After a map of 1755.

the La Rábida friars on this occasion, beyond the fact that he lodged little Diego, who was his first-born, and legitimate, with them. What is, however, certain is that the head friar at this time was the Franciscans' regional head, Antonio de Marchena, a man specifically noted for his cosmographical interests. Also quite definite is that later in his life (and arguably as a result of this single known meeting at La Rábida), Columbus gave Antonio de Marchena unusual and specific credit as being one of the few Spaniards who believed he was right and furthered his enterprise. Given their common interests, a conversation of some considerable importance between these two men must therefore quite clearly have taken place at La Rábida at this time. But what could de Marchena have known that so supported Columbus in his ideas that Asia was much closer than most scholars of the time would allow?

Documents of crucial importance here are a set of late-fifteenth-century shipping accounts which came to light quite by chance at the Mercers' Hall in London during the 1960s, the elucidation of which is again directly owed to the patient scholarship of Dr Alwyn Ruddock.

For as Dr Ruddock was quick to spot, these accounts were of a ship with a name highly relevant to us, the *Trinity* of Bristol, the very same name at least as the vessel part-owned by John Jay which Thomas Croft was accused of loading with salt along with its companion vessel the *George* for the voyage to 'Brasil' of 6 July, 1481. Conscientiously prepared by the ship's purser, John Balsall, the accounts show that some of the very same 'big league' of Bristol merchants, John Jay, William Spencer and Robert Strange, loaded their goods on *Trinity* for the particular voyage involved, and that a Harry Jay, arguably one of the family of John Jay, was among the crew. They also show the departure date of the voyage as 18 October, 1480, and its return in the spring of 1481. It must therefore have taken place just after the unsuccessful John Jay/Lloyd 'Brasil' venture of 1480 (the ship of which went unnamed), and just before what seems very likely to have been this same *Trinity*'s departure loaded with Croft's salt on the (possibly) successful 'Brasil' voyage of 1480.

Nonetheless even though the *Trinity*'s destination was not 'Brasil', at least some of the places we find she did call on turn out to be of almost equal interest. Thus it emerges that after leaving Bristol with a company of 34 (including soldiers and gunners), and a cargo consisting mainly of cloth, *Trinity* made a brief stop first at Kinsale in southern Ireland, from where after taking on more crew she headed due south, her first main port of call none other than Huelva in the very Rio Saltés estuary of Andalusia with strong Columbus associations. Here her crew spent a leisurely four or five weeks during which purser Balsall sold a substantial amount of the cloth cargo, and purchased various armaments, including some gunpowder.

Balsall's accounts go on to show that the *Trinity* then moved on to nearby Puerto de Santa Maria, from there to Gibraltar, where a pilot was taken on board, and then eastwards to Oran in present-day Algeria, at that time a Moorish stronghold greatly feared by the Venetians and

Genoese. This latter has to have been a particularly hazardous part of the voyage (almost certainly the reason for the arms purchases), and offers perhaps another hint of the Iceland-expelled Bristolians trying to open yet another new market for themselves. Whatever, the *Trinity* then returned to the Saltés estuary for a refit, and after a few final cloth deals (this time taking on Andalusian wine and oranges in exchange), began her return to Bristol late April.

It is absolutely clear from the Balsall accounts that this *Trinity* was one and the same vessel as that which Croft loaded with salt for 'Brasil' within just a few weeks of its return from the Huelva/Oran expedition. Not the least part of the evidence for this is the fact that when Balsall purchased gunpowder at Huelva, some of this was apportioned to a companion ship called the *George*, the very same name as that of the *Trinity*'s companion for the 'Brasil' voyage.

Second, it is equally clear that Bristolians of the very ships associated with the 'Brasil' voyages made virtually a second home of the Rio Saltés estuary of Spain which, as we have noted, had such strong Columbus associations. There is every reason to believe that they had called regularly before, and would do so again.

But third and most important of all, the Balsall accounts show quite explicitly that the men of the *Trinity* and *George* struck up some very friendly relations with the friary of Santa Maria de la Rábida, whose head friar, as we have already seen, had such a supportive influence upon Columbus. The vital clue to this is the fact that clearly itemised among the voyage's expenses is a donation: 'to the friars of Our Lady of Rábida to pray for us' [pl.6].

Here we have then the scenario of a friary under the charge of an individual, Antonio de Marchena, known to have been keenly interested in cosmography, the fifteenth-century science of learning all that was yet to be known of the unknown parts of the world. As the accounts make clear, Bristolians of the very ships associated with the voyages to 'Brasil' enjoyed friendly relations with this friary, if not with this very friar. And quite independently we know that Columbus visited the same friary and regarded Antonio de Marchena as a most valuable source of support. All this in the early 1480s, the very time when by what may be rather less than coincidence the Bristolians ventured on their 'Brasil' voyages and Columbus first developed his ideas of finding 'Asia' by a western route.

In Dr Ruddock's view the 'Iceland' note found among Columbus's papers most likely had its origins in the 'Columbus connection' at La

Rábida. It would, after all, have been quite natural for the Bristolians, in friendly conversation with de Marchena, to have imparted information both concerning Iceland and the 50-foot nature of their own tides, this information very understandably then becoming garbled in the course of a later onward transmission from de Marchena to Columbus, hence the confusion.

And equally likely is that in very similar circumstances, with one or more Bristolians feeling relaxed by Andalusian wine and very far removed from any threatening Hanseatics, there may have been imparted to Marchena a few careless words on the finding of 'Brasil'. Although it might only have been a passing reference, it could well have been enough to trigger the cosmographically interested Franciscan into reckoning that these unwitting Englishmen had most likely found a northern part of Asia, and that here lay a wonderful opportunity for someone like his friend Columbus to try to win the route to the lands of the Great Khan for Spain. De Marchena may even have sworn Columbus to secrecy concerning his source, hence the cryptic manner in which he acknowledged the friar's help.

All this essentially represents the case for how Columbus could, with considerable ease, have learned the key information concerning the Bristolians' voyages to Brasil via the La Rábida connection, information which would have given him the confidence he so clearly exhibited in maintaining that Asia lay within sailing distance across the Ocean Sea.

Also worth mentioning, however, is one further document which, although fraught with uncertainties, at least suggests that Columbus's information may have been more elaborate still. This is a near four-foot-wide double map preserved in the Bibliothèque Nationale, Paris, consisting primarily of a portolan sea chart of Europe and Africa, but with the unusual feature of a circular *mappemonde* or map of the world set to the left. The place-names, and the extensive knowledge of the African coast exhibited, suggest it was made in Portugal sometime after Bartholomew Diaz's rounding of the Cape of Good Hope in 1488, most likely c.1490. Among its several interesting features [fig.14a] is its accurate delineation of Iceland, indicative, as in the case of the Catalan chart in Milan [see fig.9], of at least some element of English, and arguably, specifically Bristolian, influence. The same map also shows the island of Brasil as a mere tiny mid-Atlantic blob, consistent with the usual map-makers' renditions of anywhere still semi-mythical and unmapped.

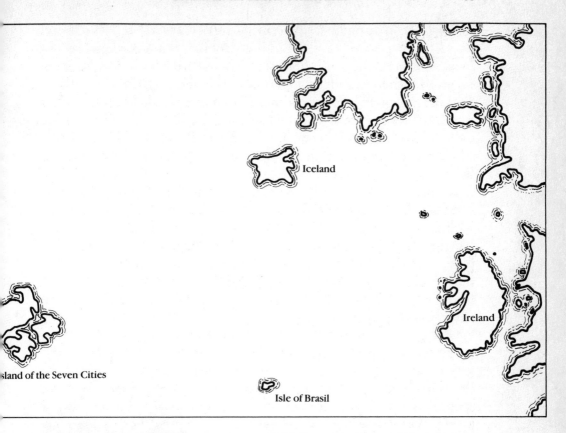

Iceland

Ireland

Island of the Seven Cities

Isle of Brasil

(b)

(c)

Fig. 14: (a) 'Island of the Seven Cities', detail after portolan sea chart of c.1490 AD, Bibliothèque Nationale, Paris, with (b) Newfoundland as shown on Mercator map of 1569; and (c) the true outlines of Newfoundland.

Particularly intriguing, however, is that to the west of 'Brasil', and as convincingly drawn as the 'English' delineation of Iceland, appears a jagged-outlined cluster of three islands labelled the 'Island of the Seven Cities'. This name itself is not particularly important, being simply the Portuguese equivalent of, and often interchangeable with, the other semi-mythical westward islands such as 'Brasil', 'St Brendan's isle', and 'Antillia', relating to a vague and thin Portuguese legend of an island founded in the eighth century by Portuguese Christians who had fled from the Moors.

Far more interesting is that the island cluster is not only drawn at roughly the correct latitude for Newfoundland, it has convincing-looking outlines that are if anything slightly more accurate for Newfoundland than some of the *definite* maps of this drawn even up to nearly a century later. These latter, as in the case of Mercator's of 1569 [fig.14b], show Newfoundland similarly fragmented into three islands, seemingly because of its actual geography of three extremely jagged peninsulas.

Given this feature (and it is by far the most convincing-looking rendition of any 'semi-mythical' island on any pre-1492 map), yet more intriguing are some of the ideas advanced concerning the Paris map's authorship. There is general agreement among specialists that it was drawn by a Genoese map-maker employed by the Portuguese, among whose number figured both Columbus and his brother Bartholomew.

And indeed in 1924 one French expert, Charles de la Roncière, went even further and argued outright for the map having been made by none other than Columbus himself. De la Roncière showed parallels with the Columbus/Fernando note on Iceland, parallels with Columbus's understanding of the Island of the Seven Cities, and above all parallels between Columbus's annotations in his copy of Pierre d'Ailly's *Imago Mundi*, and extracts from the same work that flank the *mappemonde* on the Paris map, even down to an identical misunderstanding of a phrase concerning the length of the passage down the Red Sea. De la Roncière's daughter Monique has more recently supplemented her father's research by finding among Columbus's notes a reference to his 'four charts on paper, all of which also contain a sphere', a strikingly accurate description of the Paris map's unusual two-maps-in-one format.

So is the map visual evidence of Columbus's knowledge of Newfoundland/'Brasil'/'the Island of the Seven Cities' as learned via the La Rábida connection from the Bristolians? Considerable caution is needed in reaching any such conclusion, not least because the de la Roncière attribution of the map to Columbus, although respected among scholars, has by no means won consensus of acceptance. One problem is that Columbus might have been expected to include 'Cipango' or Japan on the *mappemonde*, yet this does not appear. Another is that it is thought unlikely that either Columbus or his brother, who was also a map-maker, would have been capable of achieving the map's high degree of professional finish. A third is that the inclusion of a Spanish flag on the city of Granada suggests the map might date from after 1492, when the previously Moorish-held Granada fell to Ferdinand and Isabella. None of these problems is insuperable, one possible solution being that the map was made by a slightly later cartographer using data earlier gathered by the Columbus brothers. In itself, however, undated as it is, the map can still only count for very little.

Altogether different, however, is the evidence we will be considering shortly, positive documentary evidence not merely as to how Columbus *could* have known about the Bristolian voyages to 'Brasil' and/or the 'Island of the Seven Cities', but that he actually *did* know. But first patience is necessary, for this evidence will come to light not only after Columbus had made his First Voyage of 1492, but also after Columbus's fellow-Genoese, John Cabot, had made his near equally historic voyage – from Bristol – to North America in 1497.

CHAPTER 7

Columbus and Cabot – The Race for 'Asia'

It is now part of the stuff of history that Columbus set off on his famous voyage on August 3, 1492, leaving from the very same Rio Saltés estuary that we have now established was a regular haunt of the Bristolians.

Intriguingly the La Rábida friary, which Columbus's *Santa Maria* had to pass on its port bow as it made its way down river, played a second major part in bringing the whole venture into being. Just a year earlier Columbus, seemingly defeated in his attempts to win backing from Ferdinand and Isabella, had returned to La Rábida to collect his first-born son Diego (now an eleven year old), intending to leave Spain forever and to try his fortune in England or France. By this time Antonio de Marchena was no longer head of the friary, his successor being Fray Juan Pérez, a former confessor to Queen Isabella. And while we have no inkling whether Pérez knew anything of the Bristolian ventures, unquestionably it was he who for undisclosed reasons persuaded Columbus not to leave Spain but to make one last appeal to Ferdinand and Isabella. Pérez even went to the trouble of writing a personal letter to Isabella on Columbus's behalf, following this up with a visit to the royal court. This led to Columbus receiving the vital royal summons that ultimately resulted in his venture getting the go-ahead.

In fact, given the almost absurdly high price Columbus had all along been demanding for his backing – an immediate cash advance, three ships and their crews, and in the event of success, the title of Grand Admiral and a tenth of the profits from all trade opened up – the surprise has to be that he *ever* received royal sanction. However, there has to have been something that Pérez was able to tell Isabella that persuaded her to back the venture. And so, after getting his vessels, leaving Palos in these, and stopping over briefly in the Canaries,

Columbus duly made his historic arrival at the island that he called San Salvador on October 12,1492.

Now of course it is also the stuff of history that while we know that Columbus had reached an island off the shore of the American continent (according to the latest thinking, most likely the Bahaman island of Grand Turk, rather than the present-day San Salvador), he himself was utterly convinced, and would remain so, that he had reached the portals of Asia. The world maps with which he would have been familiar in the 1480s and early 1490s show the western Asian coastline as running relatively straightforwardly north to south [fig.15], so he may well have reasoned that it should take him little further to reach the Great Khan's wealthy seaports of Quinsay and Zaitun to the south than it had for the Bristolians to reach their 'Brasil' to the north.

Some maps known to have had the greatest influence on Columbus, most notably the famous Martin Behaim globe of 1492, also showed Quinsay and Zaitun on roughly the same latitude as the Canaries, with in between the fabled island of Cipango or Japan, which Marco Polo had described as 'very large' and with 'immense quantities of gold'. The natural course for Columbus to take, therefore, was one due west of the Canaries by which first Cipango then Cathay should be reached, and hopefully both [fig.15].

Accordingly, when Columbus arrived at San Salvador and found it to be simply a tiny island with a few stark naked inhabitants and no quantities of gold, it had to be obvious even to him that it was neither Cipango nor Cathay. But from his point of view he still had no cause to believe he was in anything else but the right region, and on the right track. After all, Marco Polo had specifically written of the sea around Cipango that it: '. . . contains no fewer than seven thousand four hundred and forty islands, mostly inhabited.' And the maps of Columbus's time that reflected Marco Polo, including Behaim's, similarly featured the China Sea dotted with islands.

Accordingly Columbus refused to be discouraged, even as day after day, wandering from one West Indian island to another, and continually meeting mere variants of the same naked Arawak peoples, he failed to find anything of the great commercial centres and gold-encrusted buildings that Marco Polo's descriptions of Asia had led him to expect. Repeatedly his Journal shows him anticipating a breakthrough, as on approaching the genuinely large island of Cuba, which he thought must be Cipango; also on being told by natives

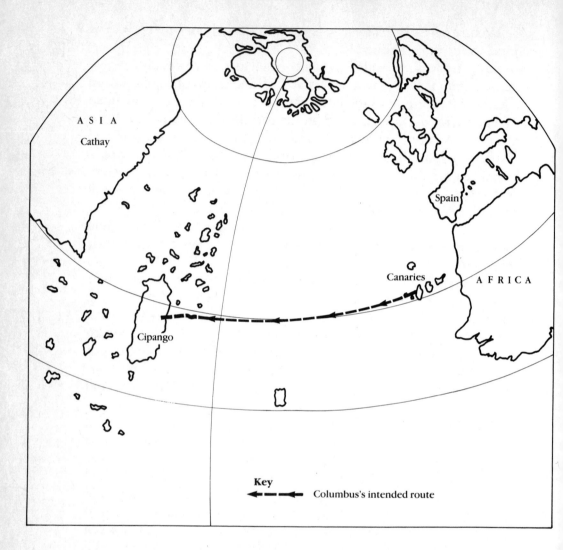

Fig. 15: Columbus's intended route to 'Cipango', as superimposed on the Martin Behaim globe of 1492.

that there was gold in 'Cubanacan', or central Cuba, only for him to suppose that the Great Khan must be in the island's interior.

Even so, when on March 15, 1493 he arrived back at the Rio Saltés estuary minus the *Santa Maria* (grounded on a Hispaniola reef), and relatively empty-handed, he was far from despondent. As proof that he had achieved his promised goal of finding a new westward route to Asia he had brought back with him a troupe of six 'Indians', 'Indian' golden ornaments, cages containing colourful parrots and large 'Indian' rats, small dogs that would not bark, barrels of strange salted fish, chests of cotton and other similar exotica. And he was totally confident that given a second, larger expedition (and he had to go back anyway to collect men left on Hispaniola), he would easily find the plentiful gold and flourishing oriental commercial centres that had eluded him in the First.

Even one of the greatest homecomings in history can have its down-side, and for Columbus this was that on landing at Palos he learned that Ferdinand and Isabella, to whom he needed to report, had made one of their habitual moves of the royal court, on this occasion to Barcelona in the furthest north-eastern corner of Spain, some 800 miles from Palos. Nonetheless it probably suited Columbus's vanity to use the journey as an opportunity to show off to all Spain what he had found, for instead of taking an arguably easier sea voyage, he set off overland, triumphantly processing with his men, the troupe of 'Indians' and accompanying trophies through every big city along the way.

Now it so happens that one of the cities through which Columbus had to pass in this manner was the major Mediterranean port of Valencia, where according to the local records, one John Cabot Montecalunya had been working on plans for an improved harbour during the time Columbus had been at sea. This John Cabot had had two interviews with King Ferdinand, and his plans had actually been approved by the king at the end of February, only to be shelved a month later when Valencia's local aldermen cancelled the project through lack of funds.

Of considerable interest therefore is that in the opinion of most historians this John Cabot Montecalunya was one and the same as the John Cabot who four years later would sail from Bristol on the first 'official' voyage to North America. And if correct it is not too difficult to gauge something of Cabot's frame of mind when, still smarting from the crash of his harbour scheme, a few days later he stood with all the rest of Valencia as his fellow Genoese Christopher Columbus proudly paraded his 'Indians' and other 'Asian' trophies through the streets, claiming to have reached 'the Indies' by sailing westwards.

For as it happens, despite the comparatively scanty surviving information concerning the Bristol-associated John Cabot, it is certain that he knew rather more about the genuine Asia than most other Europeans of his time, including Columbus. As would be reported of him only four years later by the Milanese Ambassador in England:

> He [Cabot] says that on previous occasions he has been to Mecca,
> whither spices are borne from distant countries. When he asked
> those who brought them what was the place of origin of these
> spices, they answered that they did not know, but that other
> caravans came with this merchandise from distant countries, and
> those again said that the goods had been brought to them from
> other remote regions.

Arguably, therefore, Cabot may well have been virtually alone among
the crowds applauding Columbus as he passed through Valencia able to
recognize that his clearly primitive 'Indians', along with the goods they
carried, were a significantly far cry from the true Indian caravaneers
and other oriental merchants whom he had almost inevitably met in
Mecca.

This is not to suggest that he did not share Columbus's idea that the
East could be reached by sailing west, for the same ambassador's letter
makes clear that in this the two Genoese thought alike. But it is perhaps
not stretching history too much to surmise that Cabot, baulked of his
harbour plans, and recognizing that Columbus had not yet reached
the true Asia of the Great Khan, saw at this very moment in 1493
the idea for his next great project: to copy Columbus in seeking Asia
westwards, but to sail more to the north of where Columbus had
been, and thereby to succeed where he had so far failed.

As might be expected, the next few years were ones of frantic
activity for everyone interested in voyages of discovery. Columbus
very quickly went off again, this time with 17 ships, to find those
he had left on Hispaniola all dead, and predictably again to fail to
find either the Great Khan or his riches. The monarchies of Spain
and Portugal, anxious to reach some amicable agreement whereby
they would not clash with each other over new-discovered lands,
sought the doubtful arbitration services of the Spanish Borgia, Pope
Alexander VI.

By the Treaty of Tordesillas, which they signed on 7 June, 1494
a longitudinal line was drawn 370 leagues west of the Cape Verde
Islands. This gave the Portuguese entitlement to all non-Christian
lands east of this, and thereby recognition of their rights to Africa and
beyond, while the Spanish, for their part, became entitled to all that
lay to the west, the lands that so far as all at that time were concerned,
were those of the Great Khan's easternmost Asia. Cabot, meanwhile,
appears to have made approaches to both the Spanish and Portuguese
to gain approval for a more northerly route than Columbus had taken,

only to have been rebuffed by both. Although nothing is known of the exact reasons given, Spain would have rejected him because of the exclusivity of its contract with Columbus, from whom success was still expected; Portugal because they would have been in breach of the Treaty of Tordesillas.

So it is that when Cabot eventually re-emerges in historical records we find him in London, at the court of King Henry VII, sometime around the end of December 1495/beginning of January 1496. Here his presence is signalled by correspondence between Ferdinand and Isabella and London's Spanish Ambassador Gonzalez de Puebla, surviving in the form of a letter of 28 March in which Ferdinand and Isabella remarked in response to an earlier, lost letter sent by Puebla:

> In regard to what you say of the arrival there of one like Columbus [i.e. Cabot] for the purpose of inducing the King of England to enter upon another undertaking like that of the Indies, without prejudice to Spain or to Portugal, if he aids him as he has us, the Indies will be well rid of the man ... Take care that you prevent the King of England being deceived in this or in anything else of the kind ...

In fact, despite Ferdinand and Isabella's warning, Henry VII had already come to a deal with Cabot, the terms of this being drawn up in an official Licence, signed by Henry on March 5, 1496 and still preserved in the London Public Record Office. This grants:

> to our well-beloved John Cabot, citizen of Venice, and to Lewis, Sebastian and Sancio, sons of the said John, and to the heirs and deputies of them ... full and free authority ... to sail to all parts, regions and coasts of the eastern, western and northern seas under our banners, flags and ensigns, with five ships or vessels of whatsoever burden and quality they may be ... to find, discover and investigate whatsoever islands, countries, regions or provinces of heathens, in whatsoever part of the world placed, which before this time were unknown to all Christians.

Ponderous as the wording might sound, the careful stipulation that Cabot was entitled to sail the 'eastern, western and northern seas' effectively meant that the one route he was not authorised to take was a southern one. By this Henry VII, although not a signatory of the Treaty of Tordesillas, was clearly carefully trying to avoid unnecessarily offending Spain, Ferdinand and Isabella being useful allies against the common enemy, France.

Even so, the licence entitled Cabot, on arriving at any new non-Christian land *in whatsoever part of the world placed* to 'conquer, occupy and possess' all that he found. And for this reason alone Cabot's and Columbus's ventures were unavoidably in direct competition with each other, the main point of distinction being that Cabot's approach was a more northerly one. Another difference, and one indicative of Henry VII's notorious parsimony, was that the Cabot venture was to be 'at their own proper costs and charges', that is, at Cabot and his supporters' own expense. Also noteworthy was that Cabot was 'bounden and holden only to arrive' from 'our port of Bristol'.

Now Bristol would certainly have been a logical port for Cabot to choose as his base, both because it faced the direction he wanted to go, and (quite aside from any considerations of the 'Brasil' voyages) because its mariners had well-recognised long experience of sailing in northern waters. Most historians have assumed that Cabot must have set up base in Bristol before approaching Henry VII, although there is no direct evidence of this.

But what is known is where Cabot and his family lived for at least part of their time in Bristol. Preserved in the Gloucester Record Office is a Bristol rent book of the year 1498–9 in which among the rents paid to two Bristol property-owners, Philip Green (Bristol's sheriff in 1499–1500), and John Kemys is listed 40 shillings (£2) from one 'John Cabotta' for a house in Bristol's St Nicholas Street.

From this we are able to locate in present-day Bristol the very street in which Cabot lived, for the name survives today in the same location. Sadly, due to redevelopment and the ravages of war, only the parish church, St Nicholas's (the patron saint of mariners), remains from the mediaeval buildings that Cabot would have known.

But the amount he paid as rent gives us a clue to his status at the time. A rent of 40 shillings was significantly higher than that of most other tenants listed in the same rent book, though not as high as that of John Jay (almost certainly the son of the 'Brasil' voyage John Jay), who is listed as paying five pounds for a house in nearby Broad Street. Elsewhere Cabot was described as a 'poor man', a relative term, but certainly indicative that he was not conspicuous for his wealth.

Careful consideration is needed concerning the exact degree of support that Cabot might or might not have received from Bristol's

Fig. 16: St Nicholas Street, Bristol, detail from a seventeenth-century print by James Millerd. This and neighbouring street names still exist in the same locations to this day.

coterie of merchants. Remembering the fate of Sturmy, any Genoese is likely to have been unwelcomed, by them. But even more so one proposing to venture on to the very route that (if our earlier deductions are valid) they had been quietly keeping to themselves for their Newfoundland/ 'Brasil' cod-fishing runs.

As we saw earlier in the licence granted to Thomas Croft, Robert Strange, and the Williams Spencer and de la Fount for the 'Brasil' voyages, it was common Bristolian practice for several merchants to band together for entrepreneurial ventures, thus sharing both the risks and the potential profits. It is arguably more than a little significant, therefore, that absolutely no accompanying 'mafia' of Bristol merchants is listed in Henry VII's licence of 1496, nor is there any similar document in which a Bristol merchant is listed as associating with Cabot.

Another indication that the Bristolians may well have been less than enthusiastic in their reception of this Genoese newcomer is that although Henry VII's licence allowed for a five-ship expedition, the vessel in which Cabot actually set out was, in the words of the Milan Ambassador, merely a single 'little ship, with eighteen persons'.

Frustratingly, as with the vessels which sailed on Columbus's voyages, all too little information is known about this 'little ship' of Cabot's. Although a mid-sixteenth-century Bristol chronicle called it the *Matthew*, the only customs records to have survived for Bristol around the period of the Cabot voyage derive from 1492–3, and the *Matthew* does not appear in these. All we know is that in the next records to survive, those for 1503–4, there is a 'bark' called the *Matthew* listed as plying busily between Ireland, Bristol and Bordeaux. On the meagre basis of the *Matthew*'s absence from the 1492–3 records the vessel may possibly have been newly built for Cabot's voyage, perhaps specially commissioned by him from a Bristol ship-builder. Indeed it has even been suggested that Cabot's wife Mattea might have been the inspiration for the vessel's name, for as remarked by maritime historian the late Dr James Williamson:

> The name indeed may have been *Mattea*, anglicised by the Bristolians, who had no English feminine form of the word. It is pleasant to think of John Cabot's compliment to his wife, perhaps the only wife of a great explorer to see her name borne by her husband's ship.

As for the voyage itself, its dates and those who took part in it, the fact that there has survived no direct eyewitness account inevitably demands our reliance on secondhand sources, predominantly the sharp-eared ambassadors and other foreign notables hanging around the court of Henry VII. Nonetheless these were men who tried to get the facts right for those they wrote to back in their own countries, and some of the details they supply are clearly authoritative.

For instance, the first to send back a despatch that has been preserved was the Venetian merchant Lorenzo Pasqualigo, who on 23 August, 1497 wrote to his family back in Venice:

That Venetian of ours [Cabot, it is to be remembered, had acquired Venetian citizenship] who went with a small ship from Bristol to find new islands has come back and says he has discovered mainland 700 leagues away, which is the country of the Great Khan, and that he coasted it for 300 leagues and landed but did not see any person; but he has brought back here to the king certain snares which were spread to take game and a needle for making nets, and he found certain notched [or felled] trees, so that by this he judges that there are inhabitants. Being in doubt he returned to his ship; and he has been three months on the voyage, and this is certain. And on the way back, he saw two islands, but was unwilling to land, in order not to lose time, as he was in want of provisions.

The very day after this was sent, someone from the Milanese Ambassador's office (Ambassador Soncino being still en route back to London) sent to Milan a briefer, but otherwise similar, note to the same effect, to be followed, on 18 December by a much fuller account from Soncino, which we have already had occasion to quote from. According to the main elements of this:

There is in this Kingdom [i.e. England] a man of the people, master John Cabot [Zoan Caboto] by name, of kindly wit and a most expert mariner . . . After obtaining patents that the effective ownership of what he might find should be his, though reserving the rights of the Crown, he committed himself to fortune in a little ship, with eighteen persons. He started from Bristol, a port on the west of this kingdom, passed Ireland, which is still further west, and then bore towards the north, in order to sail to the east, leaving the north on his right hand after some days. And having wandered for some time he at length arrived at the mainland, where he hoisted the royal standard, and took possession for the king here; and after taking certain tokens he returned.

This master John, as a foreigner and a poor man, would not have obtained credence, had it not been that his companions, who are practically all English and from Bristol, testified that he spoke the truth . . . They say that the land is excellent and temperate, and they believe that brazil-wood and silk are native there. They assert that the sea is swarming with fish, which can be taken not only with the net, but in baskets let down with a stone, so that it sinks in the water. I have heard this master John state so much. These same English, his companions, say they could bring so many fish that this kingdom would have no further need of Iceland, from which place there comes a great quantity of fish called stockfish.

This is clearly an important document, one of the key sources for information on Cabot's voyage, because Soncino makes clear that on getting back to England he personally heard everything at first hand from Cabot himself, seemingly in a sort of illustrated lecture which Cabot gave at the court in London:

> This master John has the description of the world in a map, and also in a solid sphere, which he has made, and shows where he has been ... He tells all this in such a way, and makes everything so plain, that I also feel compelled to believe him.

Also quite apparent from Soncino is the fundamental difference between Cabot and his personal entourage, and the 'English ... from Bristol' who comprised the bulk of his crew.

Thus for the Bristolians, besides a significant belief that the land would be found to be a source of brazil-wood, clearly of very major interest were the fish, the quantities of which make it quite apparent that Cabot had reached somewhere along the cod-rich Grand Banks of the North American seaboard. In this regard the Bristolians' apparent surprise at the fish, and their remark that they were 'so many ... that this kingdom would have no further need of Iceland' might seem to contradict the hypothesis that anyone from Bristol could already have found the Newfoundland fishing grounds during the 1480s.

But this is by no means necessarily so. Since we have already argued that the Bristolians hid the news of Newfoundland from London for fear of the Hanseatics, they would have been bound to have feigned surprise. Also, since both Pasqualigo and Soncino spoke of Cabot having found mainland, the crew may possibly have deliberately taken Cabot some way south of Newfoundland, where they may genuinely not have expected to find cod still so abundant.

A further point, though one to be treated cautiously, relates to Pasqualigo's mention of the Cabot party finding 'a needle for making nets.' As has been remarked by the Newfoundland author-historian Harold Horwood:

> For centuries this was assumed by all historians to have been an Indian artefact. But no Indian ever made or used anything that a

European would call a net needle. It could only have been a relic of an earlier fishing voyage.

Whatever the truth, our prime interest at this point concerns the insights Milanese Ambassador Soncino's letter sheds on the fundamental difference between the Bristolians' interests and the far grander ambitions of Cabot. For immediately after mentioning the abundant fish Soncino goes on:

> But master John has his mind set upon even greater things, because he proposes to keep along the coast from the places at which he has touched, more and more towards the east [Soncino seems to mean here 'towards the Orient'], until he reaches an island which he calls Cipango, situated in the equinoctial region, where he believes that all the spices of the world have their origin, as well as the jewels.

Clearly revealed here is that even as at the end of 1497, four years after he had watched Columbus's triumphal procession through Valencia, Cabot saw himself as still very much in direct competition with Columbus, battling to be first to achieve the same goal of reaching Cipango and the lands of the Great Khan. Soncino goes on to describe Cabot grandly promising islands to the non-English among his companions, the first 'a Burgundian . . . who corroborates everything'; the second his Genoese barber, both these men apparently 'consider[ing] themselves counts, while my lord the Admiral esteems himself at least a prince.' There is no mention of such favours to any Bristolian.

Accordingly, while the paucity of our documentation has to be stressed, the prevailing impression is that Cabot was essentially using the Bristolians' port, and commissioning such of its men and resources as he could afford, for a venture that was really a London-sanctioned quest to reach 'Asia', the real 'Great Khan's' Asia, before Columbus. In effect, Cabot's venture was a straight piece of rivalry to Columbus's, the one backed by the Spanish crown, the other at least sanctioned by the English crown, and both suffering from the same delusion as to Asia's nearness. Any Bristolian cod-fishing enterprise, established or otherwise, and known or unknown to Cabot, would certainly have been of absolutely no interest to him.

Specifically because of this rivalry with Columbus, centring as it did on the reaching of Cipango and Asia, some considerable interest pertains to the exact date of Cabot's voyage, also to exactly where he may have arrived on North America's coast, bearing in mind he told both Soncino and Pasqualigo that he had found a mainland that he and most others of the time assumed to be Asia.

The date can in fact be established with reasonable ease. Extant in Bristol until destroyed in a fire in the last century was a sixteenth-century chronicle which listed Cabot's departure from Bristol as occurring 2 May, 1497 (actually given as 1496 because of the Bristol civic year reckoning), his single landfall as on 24 June, and his return to Bristol as on 6 August of the same year. Although a non-directly contemporary and no longer extant document such as this chronicle has to be treated with caution, nonetheless these dates are in fact broadly corroborated from other sources. The Pasqualigo letter, for instance, makes clear that Cabot had managed both to return to Bristol and to make the then three-day overland journey to London sometime before 23 August, 1497. That Cabot reached somewhere in America in the June, and had returned by the August, is to all intents and purposes fully accepted by all serious historians.

But given that Cabot claimed to have found mainland during this time, mainland that of course he regarded as 'Asia', exactly where had he reached? Highly relevant in this regard is the fact that Columbus, although in August 1497 he had been back from his Second Voyage for more than a year, had so far come across only more and more of Marco Polo's 7,440 islands, yet still nothing that seemed to resemble his descriptions of the Great Khan's Asian mainland.

Indeed, just how sensitive he was on this point may be gauged from the fact that during his Second Voyage, a voyage to which he had attracted many with the promise that he was leading them to mainland Asia, he resorted to one of his typical perversions of the truth. While on Cuba he had been told by the natives that it was an island, and in fact circumnavigated it to within 50 miles of the point at which it should have been obvious to both him and his crews that it was an island. Yet at this point, dogged by leaking ships and low food supplies, and in a move that can only be interpreted as to save face for the return to Spain, he despatched a notary to every one of his ships demanding that each and every officer and crew-member sign a sworn statement that Cuba was the Asian mainland:

> If they had any doubt or knowledge of it, then he besought them to declare it, in order that at once he might remove the doubt and make

them see that this is certainly mainland. And if any should contradict him at any time, there should be imposed upon him on behalf of the Admiral a fine of one thousand maravedis for each occasion, and that his tongue should be slit; and if he were the ship's boy or a person of such degree, he should be prepared for this penalty by receiving a hundred lashes.

To reinforce this, on June 12, 1494 he signed a declaration that again could only be for the benefit of those back in Spain:

> that he had never heard of or seen an island having an extent of three hundred and thirty-five leagues of coast from east to west, without having got yet to the end of it, and that he now perceived that the mainland turned toward the south-west and south-south-west; that he had no doubts about its being a mainland, but on the contrary, believed and would maintain that it was a mainland and not an island, and that before one had gone many leagues, sailing along the said coast, he would find land inhabited by civilized people instructed, and with a knowledge of the ways of the world.

In the event Columbus would not reach the true American mainland until his Third Voyage when he briefly touched the Paria peninsula of what is now Venezuela on 4 August, 1498. And ironically, as we will learn later, it was at a time he was so ill he did not recognise it as such.

But the question for us is that if Columbus, as at August 1497, had not actually reached what he believed to be the Asian mainland (and which of course we know as the true American mainland), had Cabot? Here the problem is to know whether what Cabot described as 'mainland' was the island of Newfoundland (which, of course we suspect the Bristolians already to have reached more than a decade before), or whether his crew, as earlier suggested, had taken him further south, to avoid their fishing grounds, and therefore to American mainland territory that was genuinely new to them.

In this regard it is important to recognize that the name Newfoundland, which in the wake of Columbus's voyage the English quickly gave to their 'new found land', was in the sixteenth century by no means confined to the large island of that name that we know today. At that time it was applied to all new land of the new continent. It is therefore important not to be too beguiled by the 'official' tradition that it was on the present-day island of Newfoundland that John Cabot made his landfall on June 24, St John the Baptist's Day, 1497.

Thus particularly associated with Cabot on present-day New-foundland is Cape Bonavista, a very rugged and weather-beaten part of Newfoundland's north-eastern coast where there stands an imposing statue officially marking it as the spot at which he first set eyes on North America.

Thirty-three miles to the south of Cape Bonavista is a cove claimed to have been the site of Cabot's first and only landfall of this voyage, Grate's Cove, where purportedly there was once visible an inscription carved by Cabot to commemorate the event.

But seriously casting doubt on whether Cabot arrived at the Newfoundland we know today is the fact that nowhere do the Pasqualigo and Soncino accounts mention either fog or icebergs, even though both would be expected to be encountered by almost any vessel arriving in Newfoundland around June. Similarly, if Cabot had 'coasted' Newfoundland for the 300 leagues (approximately 900 miles) reported by Pasqualigo he could scarcely other than have crossed the Strait that bears his name. Yet neither Pasqualigo's nor Soncino's reports give any indication of this.

So could Cabot's voyage of discovery have taken him further south, perhaps to the genuine North American mainland somewhere along the coasts of Nova Scotia and Maine? As it happens, comparatively recently discovered is a document so far little known outside academic circles that throws important new light on this. And as we are about to discover, it also at last gives us that long awaited positive evidence that the Bristolians really had reached their 'Brasil' during the 1480s.

CHAPTER 8

Columbus and the
English Double-Agent . . .

The most important piece of evidence to come to light in the
twentieth century touching the discovery of America . . .

Dr Alwyn Ruddock

The discovery was made at Simancas, a Roman-founded town in a
particularly hot, barren and treeless region of central Spain, eight
miles from Valladolid. Here a moated and slate-roofed castle has
been a repository for Spanish national archives ever since 1545,
and it was while working in these archives in the spring of 1955
that a Dr Hayward Keniston, professor of romance languages at
the University of Michigan, happened to come across a seemingly
misplaced document relating to English voyages to America. Almost
by chance Keniston mentioned this document to fellow American
researcher Dr Louis André Vigneras, and unknowingly thereby set
in motion a detective trail with the profoundest consequences for any
understanding of the discovery of America.

Vigneras had already long been researching material on early
voyages to America, and was initially frustrated when on a first search
at the location described by Keniston he failed to find the document in
question. Nonetheless he persevered, and on a second attempt three
weeks later it came to light as folio 6 in a file named '*legajo 2 of
Estado de Castilla*' [pl.7]. The reason why he had initially failed to
find it, and also why it had hitherto been consistently overlooked,
was because its cover described it as concerning an English voyage to
Brazil, creating confusion with the Brazil of South America. In reality
it was concerning the 'Brasil' that we have already come across as the
goal of the Bristolian 1480s voyages.

Although the document was in Spanish, this posed no difficulty to Vigneras. Also it was well preserved, and the handwriting, in a style characteristic of the late-fifteenth century, clearly legible. But nothing had quite prepared Vigneras for the extraordinary nature of its contents, even though it began innocuously enough.

> Johan Day to the Most Magnificent and Most Worthy Lord, the Lord Grand Admiral:
> Your Lordship's servant brought me your letter. I have seen its contents and I would be most desirous and most happy to serve you. I do not find the book *Inventio Fortunatae*, and I thought that I [or he] was bringing it with my things, and I am very sorry not [to] find it because I wanted very much to serve you. I am sending the other book of Marco Polo and a copy of the land which has been found.

Ostensibly this might not seem much to raise eyebrows. Yet even from the outset it seemed curious to Vigneras that an Englishman (for the surname 'Day' is difficult to ascribe to any other nationality) should have been writing to an apparently Spanish 'Grand Admiral'. Nor did this seem to be the first time these had been in correspondence, for the 'Admiral' had clearly sent the Englishman an earlier, non-extant letter which had prompted this reply.

Also the two were apparently already on book-loaning terms, and with regard to some unusually specialist works pertaining to world travel. The ownership of a copy of Marco Polo was still comparatively rare for anyone of the fifteenth century, but for an Englishman particularly so, since Polo was not published in England until the next century, and hardly anyone would have heard of him there.

It was equally unusual for this 'Day' to have possessed a copy of the *Inventio Fortunatae*, the already mentioned lost treatise by the fourteenth-century Oxford friar describing his voyage to Greenland and mentioning 'brazil-wood' in what seemed to be Labrador. Since this book was never printed, Day could only have possessed a Latin manuscript copy, rare even for his own time.

But what did Day mean about 'the land that has been found'? The first clues to this were soon to become evident from the letter's next paragraphs:

> I do not send the map because I am not satisfied with it, for my many occupations forced me to make it in a hurry at the time of my departure; but from the said copy your Lordship will learn what

you wish to know, for in it are named the capes of the mainland and the islands, and thus you will see where land was first sighted, since most of the land was discovered after turning back.

Thus your Lordship will know that the cape nearest to Ireland is 1800 miles west of Dursey Head which is in Ireland, and the southernmost part of the Island of Seven Cities is west of Bordeaux River, and your Lordship will know that he landed at only one spot of the mainland, near the place where land was first sighted, and they disembarked there with a crucifix and raised banners with the arms of the Holy Father and those of the King of England, my master

'... the King of England, my master'. So 'Johan Day' (or John as we can now call him), was quite definitely English. And the 'departure' he mentioned was clearly from England to Spain, for the letter showed that it had been written from Puerto de Santa Maria, one of the Andalusian ports that had been (and may well have continued to be) a regular port of call for Bristolians of the *Trinity* and its like. But what then was Day doing sending such a clearly detailed 'copy' of the apparently newly discovered land to this Spanish 'Grand Admiral', together with some rather exact-sounding sailing directions, including, not least, very authoritatively mentioning the 'Island of the Seven Cities'? And who was the 'he' referred to as setting up the crucifix and banners? If this was not already evident to Vigneras at this point, it had to be from what immediately followed:

... and they found tall trees of the kind masts are made, and other smaller trees and the country is very rich in grass.

In that particular spot, as I told your Lordship, they found a trail that went inland, they saw a site where a fire had been made, they saw manure of animals which they thought to be farm animals, and they saw a stick half a yard long pierced at both ends, carved and painted with brazil, and by such signs they believe the land to be inhabited. Since he was with just a few people he did not dare advance inland beyond the shooting distance of a cross-bow, and after taking in fresh water he returned to his ship. All along the coast they found many fish like those which in Iceland are dried in the open and sold in England and other countries, and these fish are called in England 'stockfish'; and thus following the shore they saw two forms running on land after the other, but they could not tell if they were human beings or animals; and it seemed to them that there were fields where they thought might also be villages, and they saw a forest whose foliage looked beautiful.

Quite unmistakably this Englishman John Day was describing the Cabot voyage, evident not least from the stick that seems to have been one and the same as the controversial net needle mentioned by the Venetian Pasqualigo. (The additional information that the stick was 'painted with brazil' incidentally reinforces our earlier inference that the north-east American 'Red Indians'' use of red paint was readily confused with brazil-wood red dye.) Equally indicative was that the sea was described as teeming with cod, or 'stockfish'.

But most importantly here were some interesting extra details which were either omitted from the Pasqualigo and Soncino letters or, rather more likely, which the foreign ambassadors had never been allowed to hear, because it would have been considered prejudicial to English national interests. For just how much detail Day was able and willing to disclose, detail of very considerable value to anyone interested in transatlantic navigation, was quite clear from the next paragraph:

> They left England toward the end of May, and must have been on the way 35 days before sighting land; the wind was east north-east and the sea was calm going and coming back, except for one day when he ran into a storm two or three days before finding land; and going so far out his compass needle failed to point north and marked two rhumbs below. They spent about one month discovering the coast and from the above mentioned cape of the mainland which is nearest to Ireland, they returned to the coast of Europe in fifteen days. They had the wind behind them, and he reached Brittany because the sailors confused him, saying that he was heading too far north.

For anyone considering venturing in a sailing-boat westwards on Atlantic waters, here was a recommended time to sail, indication of available winds, likely lengths of outward and return voyages, and some compass problems that might be encountered; in other words, a brief but most invaluable navigational and meteorological service. Also dispelling any further doubt that the 'he' being referred to was Cabot was the very next paragraph:

From there he came to Bristol, and he went to see the King to report
to him all the above mentioned; and the King granted him an annual
pension of twenty pounds sterling to sustain himself until the time
comes when more will be known of this business, since with God's
help it is hoped to push through plans for exploring the said land
more thoroughly next year with ten or twelve vessels – because
in his voyage he had only one ship of fifty 'toneles' and twenty
men and food for seven or eight months – and they want to carry
out this new project.

From all these details, the arrival back in Bristol, the approximate
size of the ship and the number of its men, the plans for a further
much larger voyage, there could be no reasonable doubt that Day was
referring to the Cabot voyage. Indeed, there is complete consensus to
this effect among all interested historians.

Furthermore, to the gratitude of these same historians Day also
provided some hitherto unsuspected information concerning an
unsuccessful earlier voyage that Cabot had made:

Since your lordship wants information relating to the first voyage,
here is what happened: he went with one ship, his crew confused
him, he was short of supplies and ran into bad weather, and he
decided to turn back.

This can only have been a voyage made by Cabot in 1496, not long
after Henry had granted the letters patent. It is also notable for being
the second mention of Cabot's crew 'confusing' him, the other being
on the return from the successful voyage, when the crew led him too
far south.

But it was the next paragraph immediately following the mention
of Cabot's 'new project' that astonished Vigneras, and has delivered a
bombshell topic of controversy for all those professionally interested
in the discovery of America. As Day went on:

It is considered certain that the cape of the said land was found and
discovered in the past by the men from Bristol who found 'Brasil' as
your Lordship well knows. It was called the Island of Brasil, and it is
assumed and believed to be the mainland that the men from Bristol
found.

Here we have an unequivocal and seemingly authoritative statement,
from none other than the Spanish archives, that men of Bristol had

indeed quietly found their 'Brasil' sometime before Cabot, and arguably before Columbus, just as we have already suspected. Not only had this been earlier hinted at from Day's confident reference to the Island of the Seven Cities, but Vigneras also found a majority of Spanish historians and archivists confident that the phrase *'en otros tiempos'*, which he translated as 'in times past', suggested a substantial time gap of around a generation, thus easily encompassing the likeliest period of the Bristolian 'Brasil' voyages. Near equally explosive was the cool assertion, from Day's words 'as your Lordship well knows', that this Spanish 'Grand Admiral', whoever he was, was already well aware of the Bristolian priority. So can this document, and more precisely this particular passage, be regarded as the sought-for proof positive that the Bristolian 'Brasil' voyages of the 1480s really had reached America before Columbus?

Vigneras was a very cautious historian, not given to rushing into any conclusions of this kind, and he rightly recognised that among the first priorities were to establish approximately when the letter, which carried no date, was written; also the exact identities of the two clearly high-placed individuals between whom it was exchanged: the Spanish 'Grand Admiral' who was its recipient, and who had clearly asked for the information given, and its actual sender, the mysterious Englishman of 'many occupations', John Day.

With regard to the date, this presented no serious difficulty. As already noted, Day mentioned that the king had granted Cabot a pension of £20, and since the official document for this, still preserved in the Public Record Office, is dated December 13, 1497, Day is not likely to have written his letter before then. Time also has to be allowed for Day to have travelled from England to Puerto de Santa Maria (from which he sent the letter), and for the 'Admiral' to get in touch with him. As for the latest when the letter could have been written, a crucial clue is Day's mention of Cabot's plans for sending a new expedition 'next year', an expedition which we know set out in the May of 1498. Since the mediaeval English New Year began on March 25, Day has therefore to have written it sometime between the late January and early March of 1498.

Scarcely more problematic was the task of establishing the identity of the 'Muy Magnifico Y Virtuoso Señor el Señor Almirante Mayor' (the most magnificent and most worthy lord, the Lord Grand Admiral) to whom Day's letter was addressed, for as relatively quickly recognized by Vigneras, in late 1497/early 1498, as indeed for some years either side of that time, there were only two possible candidates to this title.

The first was Fadrique Enriquez, hereditary Grand Admiral of Castile from 1490 to 1537. And as Vigneras was well aware, Enriquez was a courtier rather than a sailor, whose greatest responsibility seems to have been that of commanding the wedding flotilla of the Spanish princess Juana on her marriage in Flanders. He is not known to have had any serious interest in transatlantic exploration, and is actually thought to have been out of Spain at the time the letter was written.

Absolutely fascinating, therefore, is the fact that the second and only alternative to Enriquez is none other than Columbus himself. As will be recalled, part of the very hard bargain that Columbus had driven with Ferdinand and Isabella was to be granted the title of 'Grand Admiral' in the event of success, a bargain which the Spanish monarchs immediately honoured. No fewer than ten directly contemporary documents identify Columbus by this title, in addition to which his son Fernando and others used it repeatedly. Furthermore, Columbus was definitely in Spain, mostly at the monastery of Las Cuevas, Seville, only just up the road from Day's base of Puerto de Santa Maria, at the very period that Day's letter has to have been sent.

Not only has this identification been generally accepted by historians, but the fact that Day specifically used the phrase 'as your Lordship well knows' when referring to the Spanish admiral's awareness of the earlier Bristolian 'Brasil' voyages dovetails with, and corroborates, all our earlier suspicions of precisely this knowledge on Columbus's part. Hitherto we have been largely dependent on establishing how Columbus *could* have known about the 'Brasil' voyages, i.e. by the La Rábida connection. Now we have the positive evidence that he indeed *did* know.

Rather more of a grade one detective mystery, however, lies in the task of determining the exact identity of the letter's sender, the mysterious Englishman John Day. This is not least because of the unmistakable air of cloak and dagger which pervades the letter's contents. This has already been indicated to us by the almost certainly deliberate way the main subject, John Cabot, went throughout unmentioned by name. But it is also apparent from the sycophantic concluding sentences:

... Rest assured, Magnificent Lord, of my desire and natural intention to serve you, and when I find myself in other circumstances and more at leisure, I will take pains to do so; and when I get news from England about the matters referred to above – for I am sure that everything has to come to my knowledge – I will inform your Lordship of all that would not be prejudicial to the King my master.

In payment for some services which I hope to render you, I beg your Lordship to kindly write me about such matters, because the favour you will thus do me will greatly stimulate my memory to serve you in all things that may come to my knowledge . . . I kiss your Lordship's hands.

Clearly, while covering himself a little by the insistence that he could not give information prejudicial to Henry VII, Day was effectively saying that any equivalent information that Columbus could pass his way would greatly lubricate his disposition to furnish further information of the same kind.

Indeed, that something of a cat-and-mouse game was in progress is also evident from Day's earlier mention that he had a map of Cabot's discoveries, but had not sent it 'because I am not satisfied with it, for my many occupations forced me to make it in a hurry.' Had Day been a mere common spy we might have expected his reward from Columbus to have been hard cash. But the currency passing between these two was clearly not cash but information, at the very edges of the 'cosmography' of the period and of as key political sensitivity as space technology in our own time. The lines are carefully blurred as to the extent to which Day may even have been in league with the English government by giving out a controlled amount of information to the Spanish, with whom England was still on reasonably cordial terms, in return for valuable data on what they were up to. Certainly we seem to be glimpsing, perhaps more than in almost any other document of this time, the shadowy world of the late-fifteenth-century double agent.

So who, then, was 'John Day'? The remark in his letter 'I am sure that everything has to come to my knowledge', strongly hints that he was in the right circles to gather information. He also spoke of 'many occupations', and after mentioning Cabot's first, unsuccessful voyage, told Columbus:

... as to other things pertaining to the case, I would like to serve your Lordship if I were not prevented in doing so by occupations of

great importance relating to shipments and deeds for England which
must be attended to at once.

From this we can glean that at least one of Day's occupations was
something to do with shipping. And in this regard Vigneras found
at Simancas one document clearly corroborative of Day's mercantile
dealings. Dated 20 December, 1500 this concerned a cargo of lead
to be handed over to '*Roberto Espexforte yngles*' in the name of
'*Juan Day yngles*', to replace a similar quantity of lead belonging
to Day which had been requisitioned at Malaga.

Another clue came from study of Bristol's customs account for
1492–3, showing the name John Day as that of a shipper importing
wine in a Portuguese vessel from Lisbon in November 1492; also,
again from Lisbon, wine and oil in an English ship, *Nicholas of the
Tower*, the following April of 1493. Since Columbus, returning from
his First Voyage, had reluctantly harboured in Lisbon between March
4 and March 13 1493, it is even possible that he and Day may first
have met on this occasion.

So was John Day just another Bristol merchant? If so, and if
he was as high-powered as he made out, it was curious that he
should have had such a meagre showing in shipping and customs
records, incomplete though these are. In the event one crucial Bristol
archival mention, in the records of the city's historic Tolzey Court,
provided a most important further lead. This showed one John
Day, 'merchant of London', having been admitted to the Bristol
Staple on 10 May, 1494, on payment of the not inconsiderable fee
of £6.13s.4d.

This led historian Dr Alwyn Ruddock, who has worked to continue
Vigneras's researches, to make a characteristically meticulous search
for John Day among the records of the merchants of London. Once
again initial enquiries drew a blank. Although Dr Ruddock found
no fewer than three John Days among the city's merchants during
the late-fifteenth century, a variety of factors eliminated each in turn
from having been one and the same as the writer of the letter to
Columbus.

Then she tried the records of London's Chancery Court, which at
that time incorporated lawsuits pertaining to contracts and disputes
that had originated outside England. Among these she found the
name of a John Day associated with two lawsuits conducted during
the years 1502–3, lawsuits in which, although documents regarding

Fig. 17: Bristol's historic Tolzey Court, which preserved a record of John Day as a 'merchant of London'. Detail from a seventeenth-century engraving by James Millerd.

their actual outcome have not survived, this Day appears as a none too savoury plaintiff.

The background circumstances were that a trader-merchant John Rokes of Bristol had fallen ill and died before he was able to honour two mercantile transactions with Day, the first relating to payment for some Spanish wine, the second to the export of some woollen cloths which had to be received in Andalusia by a specified date.

With regard to the first of these Day successfully sued Rokes before the latter's death, to the extent of gaining a half-share in Rokes's ship. Then, once Rokes had died, Day claimed that he had still not been fully compensated, and went on to sue a Bristol bowmaker who had stood surety for Rokes, prompting the bowmaker to appeal for justice to the Lord Chancellor.

The second lawsuit, the one involving the cloths, also involved a man who had stood surety for Rokes, a Bristol merchant called John Jonys. On being sued by Day, Jonys counter-claimed that because Day was part-owner of the ship that was supposed to carry Rokes's cloths to Andalusia, Day had deliberately held up its sailing so that it would be unable to deliver the merchandise on the contracted date. In neither suit do we know the final outcome.

The fascinating feature, however, was that in each of these lawsuits Day was described as 'John Day, *now calling himself Hugh Say*'. Furthermore, strong corroboration that this John Day also known as Hugh Say was one and the same as Columbus's correspondent derived from a third lawsuit, also at the Court of Chancery. In this 'Hugh Say', now plaintiff in an action against his Spanish business manager, described himself both as 'citizen and mercer of London' and as one by occupation 'continually to make his adventure with his goods and merchandise out of this realm into the parts of Castile (of which Andalusia was part) and Portugal'.

Accordingly, as swiftly recognized by Dr Ruddock, not only was it apparent that our most intriguing double-agent had even resorted to the ruse of an alias, there was also now a new and potentially more rewarding name, that of Hugh Say, to search for among the archives.

And indeed, in Alwyn Ruddock's own words, 'Hugh Say proved a much easier person to track down than the elusive John Day.' The most unequivocal references to Say occur towards the end of his life, when he seems to have given up the rôle of merchant and become a retainer to Lord Mountjoy, a friend of Erasmus. In March 1514 he was recorded as Mountjoy's servant when the latter officiated at an assay of English and Flemish coin at the Goldsmiths' Hall, London. In 1515 he kept for Mountjoy a muster-book of the labourers fortifying the defences of Tournai, in what is now Belgium. In 1516 he came close to being promoted to the position of Tournai's joint controller, but Henry VIII refused to ratify the appointment, and soon he was sent back to London. Shortly after, he fell ill, making out his will in December 1517, a valuable still extant document that provides insights on a few key earlier elements in his life.

As Dr Ruddock has succinctly summarised these, the will reveals Say 'as a man who had travelled widely, lost most of his patrimony, committed deeds for which he despaired of making restitution, and at the end had very little left to bequeath to his son and daughters'. Although he indeed left little money, he was clearly from a family once rich enough to have owned a fine London house with its own private chapel, for he instructed that the furniture and fittings from this should be sold and put towards the building of the new St Peter's in Rome.

Further clues from the will indicate that the house to which this chapel belonged had been lost by Say in a legal dispute around 1505, after being inherited by him from his great-grandfather Robert Colbrook, a prominent London trader. Although the lineage cannot be traced exactly Colbrook left a sole daughter who married probably a brother of Sir John Say, a prominent Hertfordshire landowner who held various high offices during Edward IV's reign.

Closely associated with this Sir John Say was Sir Hugh Wyche, who married Colbrook's widow Joanna, thereby becoming step-father to the Colbrook daughter who had married into the Say family. One of the most prominent men in the City of London, Sir Hugh Wyche similarly held a variety of high offices in Edward IV's reign, even being knighted on the same day as Say in 1465. It is also known that in 1452 he took on an apprentice called Robert Say who became a full member of London's Mercers' Company, this Robert Say being most probably Hugh Say/Day's father. Hugh Wyche may also have had Bristol connections for there was a John Wyche of unknown relation who was a wily Customs Collector who foiled inquiries into his Icelandic fishing deals back in 1440.

Tangled though it all is, somewhere in this background, involving two important mercantile families particularly prominent in London but possibly linked also to Bristol, would seem to have been the circumstances in which our shadowy double agent Hugh Say/John Day received the education and wheeler-dealing knowhow implicit in the Columbus letter; how he also inherited the big London house that he lost in 1505, and learned so much about the Cabot voyage and the earlier ventures from Bristol.

Many questions remain unresolved. Day's letter is, for instance, in impressively fluent and accurate Spanish. Since he clearly lived and worked in Spain for extended periods, it is conceivable that he personally acquired this command of the language. But it is also quite possible that the letter was simply set into Spanish for him by a Spanish associate, perhaps even the business manager whom he later sued in the Court of Chancery.

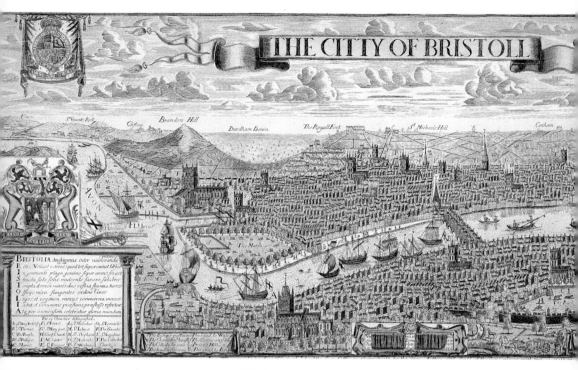

1   The city of Bristol, detail from a seventeenth-century view showing how all ocean-bound ships had to pass Brandon Hill (dedicated to St. Brendan) on their journey to and from the city. The original shrine to St. Brendan that topped the hill was destroyed during the Reformation.

2   Bristol merchant William Spencer (just left of centre), one of the backers of the 'Brasil' voyages, depicted swearing in his successor as Bristol's Lord Mayor, during the mayor-making ceremony of 29 September, 1479. From a contemporary illumination in the *Kalendar* of Bristol Town Clerk Robert Ricart, preserved in the Bristol Record Office.

3   Hibbs Cove, Conception Bay, a typical Newfoundland fishing harbour, showing the wooden 'stages' traditional from the very beginnings of the Newfoundland cod industry.

4   Cod laid out on the traditional 'flakes', as used in the traditional drying process.

5   The friary of Santa Maria de la Rábida, near Palos, Spain, where Columbus received the vital encouragement to pursue his westward voyage project with the Spanish monarchy.

6   Detail of page from the accounts of the *Trinity of Bristol*'s 1480-81 voyage to southern Spain; the seventh line shows clear evidence of the Bristol crew having visited the La Rábida friary.

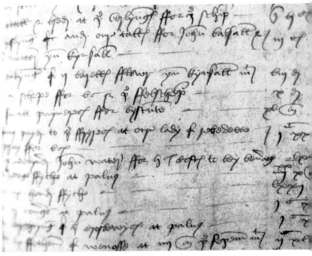

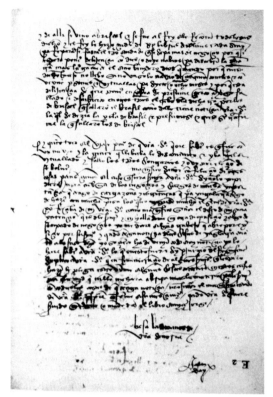

The crucial letter written by English double agent John Day/Hugh Say to Columbus, as preserved in the Spanish national archives at Simancas, northern Spain. This shows unequivocally Columbus's knowledge of the earlier 'Brasil' voyages.

Bristol customs roll of 1498, as found in the Westminster Abbey archives. The eighth line shows the payment of John Cabot's pension. The top line shows that one of his two paymasters was the Bristol Customs Collector, Richard Ameryk.

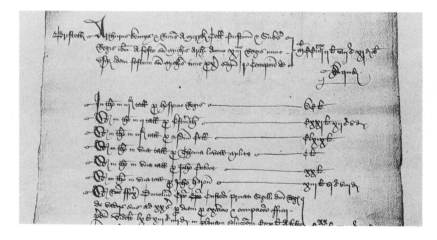

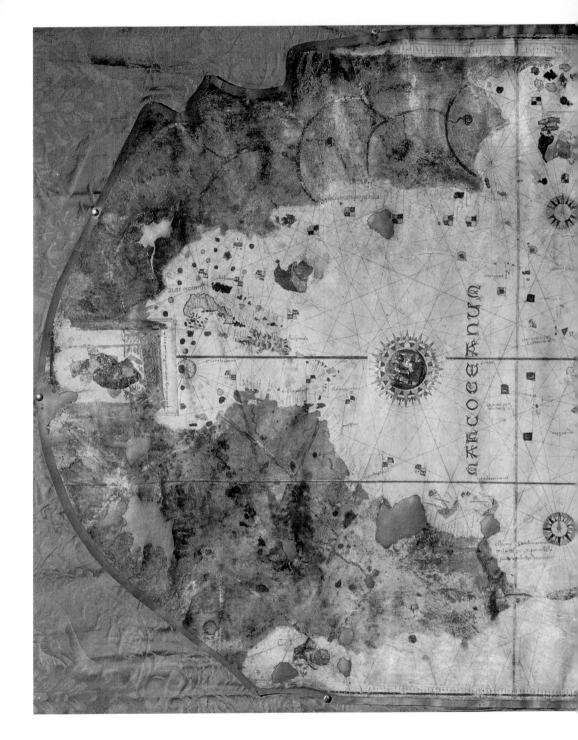

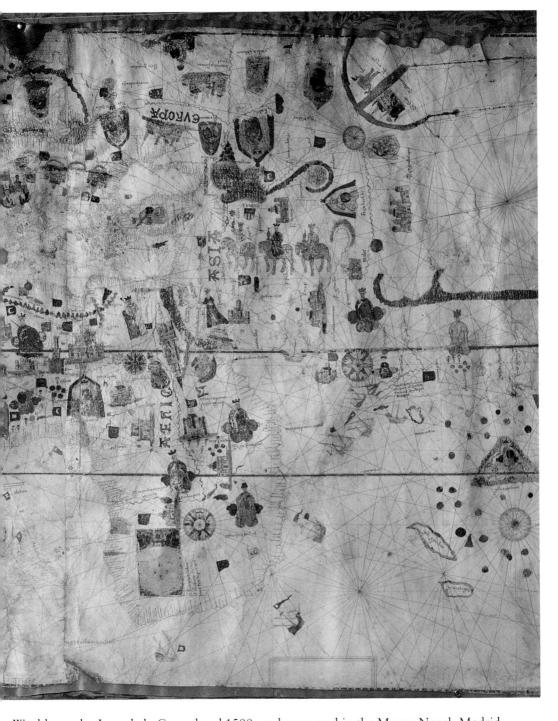

World map by Juan de la Cosa, dated 1500, and preserved in the Museo Naval, Madrid. This is the first known map indisputably to show America, its particularly curious features being the five English flags shown along the northern coastline; also the remarkable near entire rendition of the Caribbean coastline, when theoretically most of this had not yet been reached by any European.

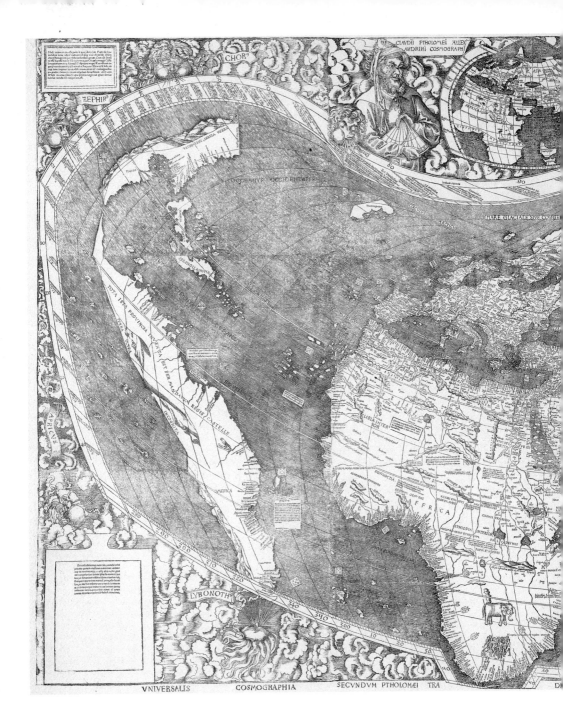

UNIVERSALIS   COSMOGRAPHIA   SECUNDUM PTHOLOMÆI TRA

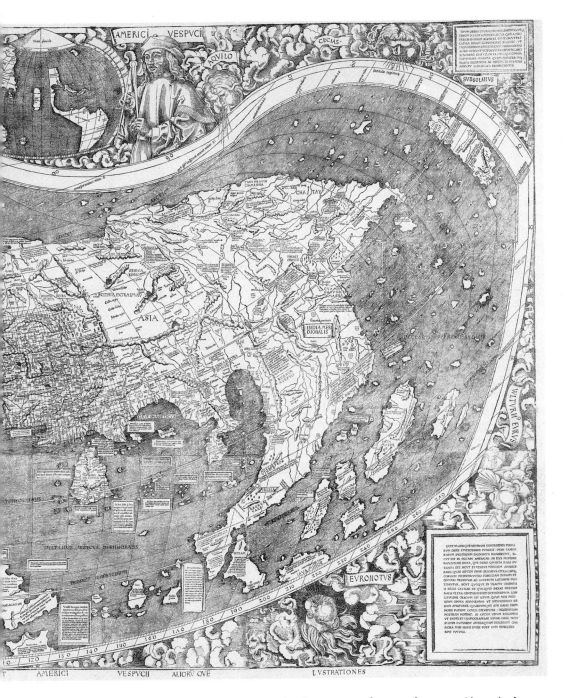

10　World map by Martin Waldseemüller, 1507, the first-ever to feature the name 'America' as preserved in the Schloss Wolfegg, Württemberg, Germany. At the top Amerigo Vespucci can be seen (at right) accorded equal ranking to the great classical geographer Ptolemy (seen left). The strikingly accurate rendition of Central and South America (with apparent knowledge of the Pacific) seems to derive from Amerigo Vespucci, yet Vespucci's source for this information is undetermined.

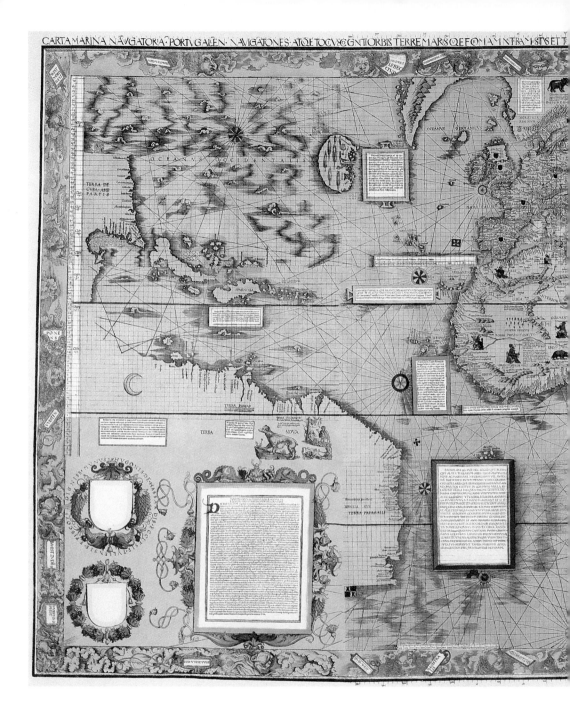

11 World map by Martin Waldseemüller, 1516 (detail). By the time of the creation of this map, Amerigo Vespucci seems to have suffered some serious demotion in Waldseemüller's eyes. Not only Vespucci's image, but also the use of his name for the continent, and the geographical information seemingly deriving from him, has been studiously deleted. This latter seems to be the only explanation for this map's altogether inferior understanding of Central and South America, compared to that of the map of 1507 reproduced as plate 10.

Interest also relates to the 'book of Marco Polo' which he apparently supplied to Columbus. Columbus's actual copy of Marco Polo is still preserved, along with other items from his book collection, in the Biblioteca Columbina, Seville. It is an abridged Latin version made by Francesco de Pepuriis of Bologna, and probably printed in Antwerp in 1485. It contains 366 marginal notes in different handwritings, critics being agreed that considerably less than half of these are by Columbus. So who wrote the rest? Could this book be the very copy supplied by Day, with earlier annotations by him? It is a possibility perhaps deserving of future research.

But what can be said with absolute certainty is that the Day letter was written by an individual who, although we might not find his business morality particularly appealing, was unquestionably very well acquainted with mercantile circles both in Bristol and London, had clearly learned more from Cabot than had been overheard by Soncino and Pasqualigo, and could therefore give with considerable authority and accuracy the information he imparted to Columbus. With every justification the letter has been described by Dr Alwyn Ruddock as 'the most important piece of evidence to come to light in the twentieth century touching the discovery of America.' Its authenticity is unimpeachable, and it effectively provides the strongest grounds for believing that the Bristolians genuinely had reached 'Brasil' alias Newfoundland some years before Columbus reached the West Indies.

Having established this we are now able to focus attention on the question which we first sought to answer via the Day letter: the extent to which it may also help determine exactly where John Cabot reached during the 1497 voyage. Was this just the island of Newfoundland, or had Cabot gone one further than either Columbus or the Bristolians (or indeed the Norse, as at the present state of our knowledge), and reached the American mainland proper? If we can establish the latter, then Cabot would certainly have pre-empted Columbus by more than a year, since as earlier remarked Columbus quite definitely did not touch the South American mainland until August 1498.

Now if only the 'copy of the land which has been found' which Day mentioned as accompanying his letter had also come to light in the Simancas archives, it might be easier to determine the exact path of Cabot's 1497 voyage with much greater assurance. But since it has not, we are therefore obliged to deduce what we can from Day's verbal descriptions. And although these are precise and detailed, they still suffer from ambiguities similar to those preventing the identification of the exact Bahaman island of Columbus's first landfall.

Thus, since Day spoke of 'capes of the mainland and the islands' (a notable echo of the wording of Columbus's licence), there seems to have been a definite distinction between what Cabot perceived as mainland, whether or not this actually was mainland, and what he thought to be islands. Day also seems to make it clear that the 'only one spot of the mainland' where Cabot landed, planted his flags and took on fresh water (very necessary after 35 days at sea), was indeed what Cabot believed to be mainland.

But complicating the whole issue are two other most enigmatic pieces of information from Day. The first of these is his remark that 'most of the land was discovered after turning back', from which we may not unreasonably infer that Cabot's 'about one month's coasting' (independently reported by Pasqualigo as of some 900 miles) was in an easterly direction; i.e. in a general direction away from the westerly course they had assumed on their outward voyage. In this same context it is to be noted that Day's words 'all along the coast', and 'following the shore' suggest a relatively continuous west-east running coastline.

Yet as Day also reported, with seemingly great precision: 'the cape nearest Ireland is 1800 miles west of Dursey Head, which is in Ireland, and the southernmost part of the Island of the Seven Cities is west of the Bordeaux river'. And here is where the problems begin.

For Dursey Head on western Ireland's beautiful coast of County Cork, effectively the Irish equivalent of England's Land's End, is at latitude 51 34 N. So if we were to accept this latitude at face value, we would assume Cabot's 'cape nearest Ireland' on the American continent to be at the northernmost tip of Newfoundland, e.g. Cape Bauld, just a few miles from the Norse settlement at L'Anse aux Meadows.

Similarly the mouth of France's Gironde river, leading to the port of Bordeaux, with which any Bristol wine trader would have been familiar, is at latitude 45 35 N. So again accepting Day's information at face value, the southernmost part of the Island of the Seven Cities would be located roughly at Cape Canso on the eastern coast of Nova Scotia, only a few miles south of the southernmost part of Cape Breton Island.

Unfortunately, too great a reliance cannot be placed on either of these latitude readings. First, as noted earlier, late-fifteenth-century astrolabe and quadrant readings, even when not actually lied about (as in the case of Columbus), tended to be notoriously inaccurate. The instruments were best used on land, and since Cabot made only one landfall, at least one of his must have been taken on the unsteady deck of his ship.

Second, while it is possible that Cabot might from Newfoundland's Cape Bauld have coasted very roughly south south-easterly down the island's extremely jagged eastern coastline, or that from Nova Scotia's Cape Canso he might have coasted east north-easterly along what is mainly regular mainland American coastline towards Cape Breton, it is most unlikely that he would have done both. This would have demanded a very marked change of direction and the crossing of a substantial body of uncharted water (the present-day Cabot Strait), neither of which is indicated either in Day's account or in the other two surviving descriptions.

Accordingly, given the stark alternatives of Cabot either having coasted eastern Nova Scotia or eastern Newfoundland, the majority of historians, including Vigneras, have opted for the Day letter indicating that Cabot did not touch Newfoundland at all – just as we had earlier suspected. Indeed this neatly explains the lack of any mention of either fog or icebergs, an omission which Day notably repeats despite the otherwise greater amount of information he provides.

In this light Cabot's first land-sighting might possibly even have been as far south as Maine, in which case Maine would have been his 'mainland', and Nova Scotia his Isle of the Seven Cities. But the more favoured view is that he arrived somewhere between Nova Scotia's Capes Sable (its most southerly point) and Canso, and then worked his way east north-eastwards along Nova Scotia. Here he would still have seen tall trees and cod a-plenty, and his departure point, Day's 'above-mentioned cape of the mainland which is nearest to Ireland', would then have been Cape Breton. Sailing from this he might well have mistaken spurs of Newfoundland for the two mysterious islands as 'with the wind behind them' he and his crew sped for home.

And that his departure point was a relatively southerly one is further indicated by Day's curious mention that 'his sailors confused him, saying that he was heading too far north', thus causing him to arrive off Brittany, rather than at the approaches to the Bristol Channel. As earlier remarked, this was the second instance of Cabot's crew confusing him, suggesting either that they were novices, or perhaps

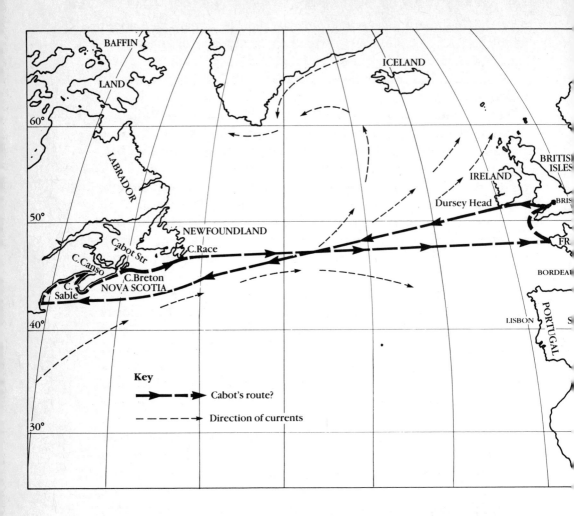

Fig. 18: John Cabot's most likely outward and return routes for the voyage of 1497, as reconstructed from information in the John Day letter. Note the apparent deliberate avoidance of Newfoundland.

rather more plausibly that they deliberately kept him to the south of Newfoundland so that he might not come across their fellow Bristolians' ready established cod-fishing stations.

Whatever the truth of this matter, it is now quite clear that Bristolians not only preceded Columbus in reaching an offshore island of the American continent, rediscovering Newfoundland some eleven years before Columbus reached what he called San Salvador, but they and Cabot were also very likely the first fifteenth-century

Europeans to reach what all parties of the time, of course, could only suppose to be the Asian mainland. It is equally evident, not least from the very fact of the Day letter, that Columbus knew of Cabot and the Bristolians' achievement, knowledge which to him must have been all the more bitter in view of his guilty awareness that he had lied to the Spanish sovereigns that he had found the Asian mainland, when in reality the closest he had come to this was the island of Cuba.

Quite clearly, then, the Columbus and Cabot ambitions were on a highly dangerous collision course. And as we are about to learn, although for Columbus there would lie ahead years of troubles, for Cabot and for those Englishmen who were to accompany him on his next transatlantic voyage, a swifter and far murkier fate lay in store.

CHAPTER 9

Cabot's Mysterious Disappearance

Reposing like the Day letter among the archives in Simancas, but known for much longer by historians, is a letter sent from London by Pedro de Ayala, Spanish envoy to England. Unlike the Day letter, it carries a date, 25 July, 1498. So it was written some five to six months after Day's. Also unlike the Day letter, it clearly identifies its recipients. They were Columbus's patrons, the Spanish monarchs Ferdinand and Isabella.

The sender of the letter, Pedro de Ayala, was a shrewd and observant envoy to whom the king and queen had entrusted some important missions. Through his eyes, for instance, they had obtained a particularly percipient assessment of the young and personable James IV, King of Scots. Currently Ayala was carefully preparing the ground for a delicate treaty of alliance between England and Spain, to be marked by the marriage of Ferdinand and Isabella's daughter Catherine to Henry VII's eldest son and heir the Prince Arthur, brother to the future Henry VIII. For the utmost confidentiality, therefore, Ayala transposed his letter into cipher, so that it might not be intercepted and read in transit to Spain. Accordingly it carries some considerable authority, as well as relevant interest, its mention of Cabot beginning:

> I think Your Highnesses have already heard how the king of England has equipped a fleet to explore certain islands or mainland which he has been assured certain persons who set out last year from Bristol in search of the same have discovered. I have seen the map made by the discoverer, who is another Genoese like Columbus, who has been in Seville and at Lisbon seeking to obtain persons to aid him in this discovery.

This is interesting from several points of view in relation to our previous sources. For instance, Ayala seems better informed than most others that Cabot was of Genoese birth. Also, solely from

Ayala do we learn that Cabot had been in both Seville and Lisbon trying to gain support for his voyage before approaching Henry VII. As already remarked, it was quite possibly in one or other of these cities that Cabot and Day first met. Again we find reference to the map which Cabot made of his discoveries, and which he seems to have been quite freely showing to all interested persons in the English court. Again we have reference to 'islands or mainland'.

Quite clear also from what follows is Ayala's recognition already that Cabot and Columbus were on a collision course, so much so that having only a limited understanding of the geographical arguments, Ayala told Ferdinand and Isabella that he thought that the 'islands' that Cabot had come across and was claiming for England were the very same as those that Columbus had already discovered for Spain. As he remarked later in the letter:

> I told him [Cabot] that I believed the islands were those found by your Your Highnesses, and although I gave him the main reason, he would not have it. Since I believe Your Highnesses will already have notice of all this, and also of the chart or *mappemonde* which this man has made, I do not send it for now, although it is here, and so far as I can see, exceedingly false, in order to make believe that these are not part of the said islands . . .

Now a fascinating feature here, particularly from the line 'Since I believe Your Highnesses will already have notice of this, and also of the chart . . .', is that it would appear that Columbus had forwarded all the information he had received from Day straight on to Ferdinand and Isabella. Indeed the chart as mentioned may well have been the very 'copy of the land which has been found' which Day spoke of as being appended to his letter. Alternatively it may have been the map which Day did not send 'because I am not satisfied with it', but which he may have forwarded later.

Equally intriguing is the line of Ayala's letter immediately following his reference to Cabot having sought support in Seville and Lisbon. He went on:

> For the last seven years the people of Bristol have equipped two, three [and] four caravels to go in search of the island

of Brasil and the Seven Cities according to the fancy of this Genoese.

Here yet again, it would seem, we have an explicit reference to Bristolians purportedly 'searching' for the island of Brasil. While on the one hand we have to be impressed that by now even the Spanish envoy had heard that something of this kind had been going on for a period as long as seven years, it would be straining credulity altogether too far to suppose that the Bristolians could have sent so many substantial ships for so long without actually finding anything. For while from all we have seen, Bristolian merchants were a hard-headed, entrepreneurial lot, not averse to taking the odd risk or two in the hope of turning a fair profit, it beggars belief that they should have continued to venture so many vessels over so many years to no avail. The true value of Ayala's statement is that it offers yet another important piece of evidence that the Bristolians had indeed been making voyages to 'Brasil and the Seven Cities' for some long while, just as we have already deduced.

But while this is yet another helpful pointer, the true purpose of Ayala's letter was to inform Ferdinand and Isabella of a highly sensitive development: that even at that moment Cabot was on the high seas with a new and much more impressive expedition, potentially poised to make proper diplomatic contact with, and commercially exploit, the very same 'Asian' mainland that had so far eluded their man Columbus. Ironically, as previously mentioned, Columbus would actually touch the South American mainland for the first time within three weeks of the very despatch of Ayala's letter, reaching most likely the modern Punta Bombeador in the great delta of the Orinoco river (though he would not realise this when he did so).

But Ferdinand and Isabella could know nothing of this as they read and re-read the transcription from code of Ayala's carefully measured words:

> The fleet he [Henry VII] prepared, which consisted of five vessels, was provisioned for a year. News has come that one of these, in which sailed another Friar Buil, has made land in Ireland in a great storm with the ship badly damaged. The Genoese [i.e. Cabot] kept on his way. Having seen the course they are steering and the length of the voyage, I find that what they have discovered or are in search of is possessed by Your Highnesses because it is at the cape which fell

to Your Highnesses by the convention with Portugal. It is hoped they
will be back by September. I let [? will let] Your Highnesses know
about it. The king has spoken to me several times on the subject.
He hopes the affair will turn out profitable. I believe the distance
is not 400 leagues . . .

Lacking as we do any proper biography or journal of Cabot's life and
voyages, what this tells us, in economical but precise detail, is that with
Henry VII's full backing Cabot set out in 1498 now with five ships,
just one of which apparently was forced to turn back because of a
severe storm. That this returned vessel was not Cabot's is apparent
from Ayala's remark 'the Genoese kept on his way'.

Independent reference to this same voyage, clearly the one which
Ambassador Soncino had reported to be planned back in the
December of 1497, derives from *The Great Chronicle of London*
for the year September 1497 to September 1498. According to this,
as rendered into modern English:

> This year also the king by means of a Venetian which made himself
> very expert and cunning in knowledge of the circuit of the world
> and islands of the same, as by a chart and other demonstrations
> reasonable he showed, caused the king to man and victual a ship
> at Bristol to seek for an island which he said he knew well was
> rich and replenished with rich commodities. Which ship thus
> manned and victualled at the king's cost divers merchants of
> London ventured in [her] small stocks, [there] being in her as
> chief patron the said Venetian. And in the company of the said
> ship sailed also out of Bristol three or four small ships stocked with
> small and large merchandise such as coarse cloth caps, laces, points,
> and other trifles. And so departed from Bristol in the beginning of
> May . . .

So we know that Cabot's new expedition sailed from Bristol very
early in May 1498. We also know that one of the vessels that took
part was a 'king's ship', i.e. one specially sponsored by Henry VII.
Of the other vessels, it is generally assumed that some at least were
Bristol-based and manned, but there is no certainty of this, the only
definite information being that they sailed from Bristol and that
at least a proportion of the merchandise with which they were
freighted was provided by London merchants. The very character
of this merchandise indicates that it was intended for trade with the
'Asians' with whom this time Cabot anticipated proper contact, and

that spices, not fish, were the commodity with which they hoped to return. That London not Bristol was the city to which Cabot hoped to bring the lion's share of the profit is evident from the earlier quoted letter of Soncino:

> By this means they hope to make London a more important mart for spices than Alexandria.

It is also noteworthy that Cabot's letters patent for the 1498 voyage, which have survived in the London Record Office, no longer insist on Bristol as the required port of departure or return. These allowed Cabot to 'take at his pleasure six English ships in any port or ports or other place within this realm of England', increasing the suspicion that the project may well have raised considerably more enthusiasm in London than in Bristol. Overall, there are several indications that perhaps not many Bristolians shared Cabot and the Londoner's anticipations of trading with the lands of the Great Khan.

Unfortunately, as with the first voyage, we know all too little about the people who sailed with Cabot on this 1498 expedition. Nonetheless a clue to just a few of these derives from entries in Henry VII's Household Books for Spring 1498, in which we find Henry bestowing some varying cash gifts on certain Londoners taking part in, or sponsoring, the expedition. Thus for the period March 17–22 there occurs the entry: 'Item, to Lancelot Thirkill of London, upon a prest [advance payment] for his ship going towards the new Island, £20'. For March 25–31: 'Item delivered to Lancelot Thirkill going towards the new Isle in prest, £20'. For April 1–3: 'Item, to Thomas Bradley and Lancelot Thirkill going to the new Isle, £30'. For April 4-6: 'Item delivered to Thomas Bradley and Lance Thirkill in full payment of £108 8 shillings, £43.8 shillings'. Then, for April 8–11: 'Item to John Cair going to the new Isle, in reward, 40 shillings'.

Among the several indications to Spanish envoy Ayala that the expedition was a scant-disguised rival to Columbus's was the undoubted fact that it included priests. Back in the previous December Milanese Ambassador Soncino had hinted at this with the heavily sarcastic remark 'I . . . believe some poor Italian friars will go on this voyage, who have the promise of archbishoprics'.

But that this intention had been actually implemented is quite evident from Ayala's notification to Ferdinand and Isabella that the Cabot venture included 'another Friar Buil'. As Ferdinand and

Isabella would have been well aware, Friar Buil was a Benedictine whom they had appointed to accompany Columbus's Second Voyage, with special responsibility for conversions. It was he who at Epiphany 1494 celebrated on Hispaniola the first Catholic Mass known ever to have been held anywhere in the New World.

In this regard it is actually possible with reasonable certainty to pinpoint the exact identity of the 'another Friar Buil' who accompanied the Cabot 1498 expedition. On 30 June, 1498 Agostino de Spinula, another of the Duke of Milan's eyes and ears at the London court, wrote to his master of:

> ... three other [recently arrived] letters, one for Messer Piero Carmeliano, one for Messer Piero Penech, and one for Messer Giovanni Antonio de Carbonariis. I will keep the last until his return. He left recently with five ships, which his Majesty sent to discover new islands.

This gives us the name Giovanni de Carbonariis as that of one individual whom we can say positively accompanied Cabot on the 1498 expedition. From earlier documents we know him to have been a cleric of some importance. Nine years before, for instance, he had been deputed to act as messenger between Henry VII and the Duke of Milan. In 1497 Ambassador Soncino spoke of Carbonariis as the 'reverend master' to whom he would look for advice on arriving in England. Only shortly prior to his departure on the Cabot expedition, the Duke of Milan had written him a personal letter, as a trusted confidante.

Otherwise we know only that five ships set out in the early May of 1498, and that by a little before 25 July (the date of Ayala's letter), news had reached London that one of these had been beaten back by 'a great storm' to seek refuge and repairs in Ireland. Of the four others, *The Great Chronicle of London* in its entry for the year ending September 29, 1498 sombrely reported: 'Of whom in this mayor's time returned no tidings'.

Lancelot Thirkill, the Londoner, seems to have survived the voyage, for he appears in a record of 1501. This may have been because he did not actually sail with the expedition but acted as a form of procurement manager for Henry VII, possibly buying up consignments of merchandise with which the thrifty-minded king hoped to reap a handsome personal profit from the voyage.

Alternatively Thirkill may have been on the ship beaten back to Ireland. Of Carbonariis nothing more is ever heard.

Nor are there any other documentary references to sightings or news of Cabot and the rest of his men. The fact that his £20 pension from Henry VII is recorded as being paid from Bristol customs receipts for the year September 29, 1497–September 19, 1498, and again for the same period 1498–9, was once regarded as evidence that he did manage to return. Today, however, the prevailing historical opinion is against this. Not only would it have been perfectly legitimate for Cabot's wife Mattea or another senior member of the family to claim the money on his behalf while they believed him still alive somewhere overseas, a reference to him in a manuscript copy of the *Anglica Historia* written by Italian chronicler Polydore Vergil in 1512–13 strongly indicates that he never did return. In this Vergil wrote of Cabot (whose name had apparently been almost forgotten, because Vergil left a space for it which had to be filled in later):

> . . . he is believed to have found the new lands nowhere but on the very bottom of the ocean, to which he is thought to have descended together with his boat, the victim himself of that self-same ocean; since after that voyage he was never seen again anywhere.

But could all four unaccounted-for vessels, and Cabot along with them, simply have sunk without trace somewhere in mid-ocean as a result of the 'great storm' referred to by Ayala? In the opinion of the already-mentioned naval historian Dr James Williamson this is most improbable:

> In the history of Atlantic exploration for the ensuing century, beginning with the Corte Reals of Portugal in 1500 and going forward to Gilbert and Frobisher and Davis and the Virginian pioneers of Ralegh's time, there is no instance of a multi-ship expedition having been entirely wiped out by an unknown disaster; and we are entitled to say that the odds were heavily against it in 1498.

As Williamson readily conceded, this is not to say that all four vessels necessarily survived the transatlantic journey and/or stayed together during it. Indeed, given both a storm and the perils of North Atlantic fog, they more than likely separated, and one or more of the company may indeed have disappeared in mid-ocean. But could at least one ship have reached and explored more of the American shore, only then to founder for some unknown reason before being able to return to England to tell the tale?

In fact, a little later in this book, for reasons that will become clear, we will be considering some intriguing indications of this. But assuming at least the possibility that something of this kind happened, it is obviously important for us to try to determine the direction that Cabot might have taken after making a successful landfall. As we learned earlier, the letters patent for his 1497 voyage allowed him to set the course for his outward voyage westwards but not southwards. And since those for his 1498 voyage, which also survive in the Public Record Office, simply required him to 'convey and lead [the expedition] to the land and isles of late found by the said John in our name', we may assume that he, or the masters of any ships that survived, would have followed the same general direction, insofar as they were allowed to by the effects of the 'great storm' they encountered.

But what cannot be emphasised enough, and what is confirmed by the very real concern behind Ayala's letter, is that as of the summer of 1498 Cabot's objective was exactly the same as that of Columbus, and one which the Spanish Admiral had still not achieved (indeed, never would), the reaching of 'Cipango'. The key indication comes in Soncino's previously quoted report to Ludovico Sforza, Duke of Milan, as penned 18 December, 1497:

> . . . he [Cabot] proposes to keep along the coast from the place at which he touched, more and more towards the east, until he reaches an island which he calls Cipango, situated in the equinoctial region, where he believes that all the spices of the world have their origin, as well as the jewels.

Soncino, it will be recalled, had directly listened to Cabot explaining his plans, and had apparently seen the map and globe by which he demonstrated these. His information that Cipango was Cabot's aim is further supported by the previously quoted passage in *The Great Chronicle of London* describing the 1498 expedition's goal as 'to seek for an island which he [Cabot] said he knew well was rich and replenished with rich commodities.' Also notable is Soncino's remarking, inevitably from what Cabot had told him, that Cipango was 'situated in the equinoctial region', i.e. within the tropics, exactly where Columbus, setting off from the latitude of the Canaries, had expected to find it during his First Voyage.

So the scenario we have is that if Cabot or other ships of his 1498 expedition had actually successfully reached the North American coastline somewhere in the region that they had found in the 1497 voyage (and they would naturally have aimed for this since, in another phrase of Soncino's, 'now they know where to go'), they would most definitely then have worked south, i.e. towards territory Columbus and the Spanish regarded as rightfully theirs under the Treaty of Tordesillas, between Spain and Portugal, of 1494.

Since we also know from Ayala that Cabot's ships were provisioned for a year, this, along with the many trading goods they carried, has to have been the strongest signal that the expedition was not only determined to reach Asia's great trading places, it was also confident of success. Small wonder, therefore, that the conscientious Ayala, while busy preparing the ground for the royal marriage-linked treaty of alliance between England and Spain, felt impelled to express under cover of cipher his most serious concerns to Ferdinand and Isabella:

> Having seen the course they are steering and the length of the voyage,
> I find that what they have discovered or are in search of is possessed
> by Your Highnesses by the convention with Portugal . . .

Independently Ferdinand and Isabella are likely to have received much the same message via Columbus's special English double-agent, our now familiar friend John Day/Hugh Say.

If Cabot or any of his party had survived the latest voyage (and Ayala gave no reason to doubt it: he reported 'It is hoped they will be back by September'), there lay a very powerful motive indeed on the part of those 'in the know' in Spain quietly to seek out and intercept the Cabot ships, and to make quite sure that they never managed to get back to Europe, either to breathe a word of their discoveries or to claim title to them.

Before any attention can be given to whether anything like this may actually have happened, it is important to turn to what actual evidence may have survived that a Cabot ship or ships actually did successfully cross the Atlantic in 1498. For this, short of the discovery off the American east coast of some wreck which could be linked with the Cabot 1498 expedition – and certainly nothing of this kind has yet come to light – we are obliged to turn to any information that might be forthcoming from other expeditions subsequent to Cabot's that successfully made the Atlantic crossing.

In this regard it is important to remember that there was another party who would have been keenly interested in what Cabot might or might not have been up to across the Atlantic: Portugal. Given that by the Treaty of Tordesillas Spain had been decreed as entitled to all undiscovered land more than 960 nautical miles west of the Azores, and Portugal to all undiscovered land east of this, Portugal had so far concentrated most of its activities on working its way slowly southwards down the African coast and then rounding this to reach India eastwards across the Indian Ocean. Indeed, within weeks of Cabot setting out on his 1497 expedition Vasco da Gama had left Lisbon with this very intention. Unknown to anyone in Europe he was actually succeeding at this time, returning to Lisbon on September 9, 1499.

But meanwhile Cabot's excited talk in 1497 that he had found 'mainland' relatively near across the Atlantic – as little as 400 leagues west of England according to both Soncino and Ayala, and therefore arguably less than 300 leagues west of the Cape Verde Islands – could only in Lisbon cause interested speculation that this was likely to be on their, i.e. the Portuguese, side of the meridian. While the friendship between England and Portugal was a much more mature and long-standing one than anything that England would ever enjoy with Spain, nonetheless Portugal's Dom Manuel, as a successor to Henry the Navigator, felt no constraint in issuing licences for his people to venture in the same direction that Cabot had taken.

The first to receive such a licence, a Terceiran called João Fernandes, was actually an individual well conversant with Bristol and the Bristolians, for he is shown in the city's customs records for 1492–3 to be a shipper of goods from Bristol to Lisbon at that time. Although he was granted his letters patent in October 1499 'to go in search of and discover certain Islands of our sphere of influence', the most he seems to have done in this direction was to 'rediscover' Greenland, his traveller's tales of finding only mountains of ice inevitably cutting very little of that commodity with the folks back home.

But in May 1500 Dom Manuel issued a second patent to a fifty-year-old *fidalgo*, or gentleman of the court, named Gaspar Corte Real. That same summer Corte Real set out and reportedly 'discovered' at about latitude 50°N (the parallel of northern France) 'a land that was very cool and with big trees'. Like Cabot, he seems to have taken a first, quick look, then returned with a major, three-ship expedition the following year. Of this expedition Pietro Pasqualigo, Venetian Ambassador to Portugal, and brother of the London-based Lorenzo Pasqualigo who gave us information of the 1497 Cabot voyage, sent home a particularly detailed report from Lisbon on 19 October, 1501:

> On the eighth of the present month arrived here one of the two caravels which this most august monarch sent out in the year past under Captain Gaspar Corterat [i.e. Corte Real] to discover land towards the north; and they report that they have found land two thousand miles from here, between the north and the west, which never before was known to anyone. They examined the coast of the same for perhaps six hundred or seven hundred miles and never found the end, which leads them to think it mainland. This continues to another land which was discovered last year in the north. The caravels were not able to arrive there on account of the sea being frozen and the great quantity of snow. They are led to the same opinion [i.e. that the land was mainland] from the considerable number of very large rivers which they found there, for certainly no island could ever have so many nor such large ones . . . They have brought back here seven natives, men and women and children, and in the other caravel, which is expected to be coming from hour to hour are coming fifty others. They resemble gypsies . . . are clothed in the skins of various animals, but chiefly otters . . . They speak, but are not understood by anyone, though I believe that they have been spoken to in every possible language. In their land there is no iron, but they make knives out of stones and in like manner the points of their arrows. And yet these men [i.e. the Corte Real expedition] have brought from there a piece of broken gilt sword, which certainly seems to have been made in Italy. One of the boys was wearing in his ears two silver rings which without doubt seem to have been made in Venice, which makes me think it to be mainland, because it is not likely that ships would have gone there without their having been heard of. They have great quantity of salmon, herring, cod and similar fish. They have also great store of wood and above all of pines for making masts and yards of ships . . .

Quite evident from this description is that the 'mainland' visited must be that of North America in the environs of Quebec and Nova Scotia. This not least from the reference to the 'very large rivers', the most impressive of which would inevitably have been the St Lawrence.

The poor 'natives' whom the Portuguese brought back with them would then probably have been of the Micmac tribe, one of the main inhabitants of those regions.

But the quite riveting item of information is the mention of the piece of broken sword, seemingly either proferred by the natives, or picked up by the Portuguese from the shore; also the silver ear-rings recognised as Venetian. The astonishment of the Portuguese at these obviously European finds is quite evident from the way they tried to explain them as evidence that this country must be mainland Asia, the items thereby having travelled overland eastwards from Europe 'because it is not likely that ships would have gone there without their being heard of.'

But since we know that the land was not mainland Asia (and any idea that the items might have travelled all the way across Asia, the Bering Strait and the entire breadth of North America, simply beggars belief), the only explanation can be that the items arrived by ships. And since the Portuguese clearly did not recognise them as theirs, the crucial question is: whose?

According to the great Columbus expert the late Admiral Samuel Morison, who believed that all four non-accounted-for vessels of Cabot's 1498 expedition simply sank without trace in mid-Atlantic, there could only be one answer: the Cabot expedition of 1497. The natives must have 'obtained' them from Cabot on that occasion.

But Morison wrote his account of the Portuguese voyages some years before the John Day letter had come to light. And it is quite obvious from the Day letter, though it was also evident enough from those by Pasqualigo and Soncino, that in 1497 Cabot had absolutely no contact with any native inhabitants. Nor would he or any of his companions have been likely to have left such items behind during the single flag-planting and water-gathering landing which they made at that time. A sailor might inadvertently have lost one ear-ring, but hardly two. And would Cabot, or anyone else on that particular occasion, have left behind either a whole or a broken sword?

There are therefore only two reasonable alternatives. The first, and less likely of the two, is that the items, of Italian manufacture and relatively easy for sailors to pick up in any port, came from the earlier Bristolian fishing visits. The second, and here the supposed Italian origin of the items assumes potentially greater significance, is that they came from Cabot's 1498 expedition.

If we opt for this, a possibility, albeit an extreme one, is that the Cabot expedition, arriving shipwrecked or exhausted, were simply murdered by the natives, the sword perhaps even being Cabot's own, broken during a last desperate skirmish. But why should the same natives appear to have shown no similar hostility towards the Portuguese?

The other possibility, based on one or more of the expedition ships arriving intact, is that the items were the very sort of 'trifles' with which the Londoners stocked Cabot's ships, specifically for trading with whosoever they came across. And on this hypothesis Cabot's men would have resourcefully exchanged them with the natives, perhaps for some valuable furs, and then moved on for the potentially more rewarding markets they expected to find further south.

Now on its own, without any more evidence to back it up, this second possibility might appear still very tenuous. But as we are about to see there is evidence, again from the still all too little plumbed Spanish archives, that at this very time a mysterious party of Englishmen did indeed move further south.

In doing so of course, they would have been failing to heed Envoy Ayala's warnings, moving right into the very latitudes visited by Columbus, latitudes which the Spanish, hyper-sensitive through not having yet found the expected rich cities of Asia, were most strenuously asserting to be their own. But that they might actually have done so, yet having got so far, failed to return, has to be one of the most intriguing elements in the whole story of America's rediscovery.

CHAPTER 10

'Certain Englishmen' in South America

As already remarked, it was within days of Ayala's intelligence to Ferdinand and Isabella of Cabot's 1498 expedition that Columbus, coasting the southern shore of Trinidad in the earliest weeks of his Third Voyage, unknowingly first sighted the South American mainland.

Seemingly badly affected by the heat at a latitude only 10 from the equator, he was by then suffering from such debilitating bouts of insomnia, blindness and gout that what survives of his diary from this time shows unmistakable signs of impaired mental judgment, a tendency to gross exaggeration, and even paranoia. Thus even the fact that the water around was very nearly fresh did not persuade him that he was at the outflow of one of the world's largest rivers (as we now know, the Orinoco), and that this had to signify the existence of a huge continental mass lying immediately to the south. Since Asia, according to his perception, was a land-mass to the north and west, any continent to the south simply could not, and therefore did not, exist.

Accordingly the landfall that took place on the lushly rainforested Paria peninsula of Venezuela on 5 August, 1498, a landing which with hindsight may be regarded as Columbus's one true 'first', as discoverer of mainland South America, was marked by no flag-planting of the kind that he had so proudly performed on San Salvador, and that Cabot had similarly enacted on mainland North America.

In fact, Columbus himself almost certainly did not even step ashore, for according to his diary:

> Some of the natives came out to the ship at once in their canoes and asked me, on behalf of their king, to go ashore. And when they saw that I was not inclined to do that, they came out in hordes to the

ship, and many of them wore pieces of gold on their breasts, and
some had pearls round their arms.

The further irony here is that at this moment when he had at last come
across gold and pearls in the sort of amounts that had prompted his
whole quest for Asia, he was too mentally and physically debilitated
to do more than make half-hearted enquiries concerning their origin.
Besides Columbus being far from well, in his ships' holds were
increasingly rotting supplies that he had brought from Spain to
re-provision the settlement that he had founded on Hispaniola
during his Second Voyage, and where his brother Bartholomew
was governor. It was imperative that these supplies be got out of
the equatorial heat and on to Hispaniola as soon as possible.

He therefore made the all too easy assumption that Paria must be yet
another of the many islands he had come across, and directed his ships
westwards along the peninsula's southern shore. He saw no reason to
suppose that he would not soon round it and thereby quickly be able
to head north for Hispaniola. On finding his way blocked by shallows
of yet more of the mysterious fresh water he had come across south of
Trinidad, he was eventually forced to double back. Yet still he refused
to believe the opinion of others that they were in the estuary of a huge
river.

In the event he managed to reach Hispaniola in about a fortnight,
and a few weeks later despatched a highly rambling report to
Ferdinand and Isabella explaining that he now believed the Earth
to be pear-shaped, and that the fresh waters he had found were
those of an 'Earthly Paradise' situated in the pointed part of the
pear. Intriguingly, the *mappamonde* on the Paris Map which Charles
de la Roncière attributed to Columbus actually shows an 'Earthly
Paradise', just to the south-east of Cathay, more or less precisely
where Columbus would have supposed himself to have been when
he was in Paria.

Indeed, although Columbus actually mused that the only alternative to this idea was 'a vast land to the south, of which
we know nothing', still he insisted he was 'quite convinced' of,
and much preferred, the Earthly Paradise notion, since this had
Biblical support. He assured the sovereigns that in due course he
would send his brother Bartholomew with three ships to explore
the 'Earthly Paradise' further. He also apparently still fully intended
to sail north-westwards to where he believed the land of the Great

Khan to be – and thus in the very direction from which any Cabot expedition survivors might have been coming in the course of their explorations southwards.

In fact, events were conspiring to baulk both Columbus and his brother Bartholomew of any such interception manoeuvres that they or Ferdinand and Isabella might have been considering. As Columbus was also obliged to admit to his royal patrons, on arriving in Hispaniola he had been confronted with some serious problems that had been frustrating his brother Bartholomew's attempts to govern the new settlement. Earlier friendly relations with the native population had been near totally ruined by the excesses of the incoming settlers. Among the Spanish there had been many deaths, not least due to the ravages of the mystery new disease syphilis. Yet worse, there had been in progress for some two years a bitter rebellion against Bartholomew led by the mayor of one of the settlements, Francisco Roldán. Although Columbus reasonably soon managed to reach some sort of working agreement with Roldán, nonetheless administrative problems so tied him to Hispaniola that he had no opportunity for further explorations. After two years he found himself shipped back to Spain in irons when the Spanish commander Francisco Bobadilla arrived to impose proper order where the Columbus brothers had so palpably failed.

But meanwhile Columbus's report to Ferdinand and Isabella, despatched by two ships which sailed from Hispaniola on October 18, 1498, had arrived back at the Spanish court, accompanied by what he described as a 'drawing of the land'. Although this has not survived, it has to have shown those places newly discovered during the early part of the voyage, notably Trinidad, Paria and the land of the Earthly Paradise, together with the location of the pearl fisheries.

At the royal court the official who would have received, scrutinised and held this report on Ferdinand and Isabella's behalf was Bishop Juan de Fonseca, a shrewd administrator who spent some thirty years in charge of Spanish overseas interests. Because of his rôle Fonseca would undoubtedly have been apprised of envoy Ayala's warning concerning Cabot and his Englishmen making their way southwards down the 'Asian' mainland. He may well also have shrewdly assessed that Columbus and his brother were beset by too many problems to be likely to be able to make an effective counter to any such competition.

But Fonseca was a resourceful individual and he had one secret weapon up his sleeve, in the person of Alonso de Hojeda, an Errol Flynn-like character who had once delighted Queen Isabella with a daring balancing feat on a 200-foot-high Seville tower. An intrepid gold-seeker, at only 22 Hojeda had captained one of the vessels on Columbus's Second Voyage, distinguishing himself by some exceptional cruelty when on Hispaniola. In one incident he personally cut off the ears of a native suspected of having stolen the clothes of three Spaniards, then sent the local chief and two relatives to Columbus for beheading (a sentence which Columbus, to his credit, mercifully annulled).

Intriguingly, therefore, while we have no explicit information concerning Fonseca's motives, we certainly know that he treated Hojeda as a favourite, and quite unethically gave him access to all the confidential information, charts, etc, which Columbus had sent back to Ferdinand and Isabella. Then, when Hojeda not surprisingly expressed more than a little interest in exploring the coast with the gold and pearls, Fonseca equally adroitly arranged a licence for him to do this, even though this was in breach of Columbus's agreement with Ferdinand and Isabella.

Now of course we cannot know whether, accompanying the licence, Fonseca gave Hojeda secret instructions to liquidate any party of English he might come across. But certainly Hojeda needed little more encouragement to set up a three-ship expedition, recruiting among his leading companions Juan de la Cosa, a seasoned mariner whom he already knew well as a fellow member of Columbus's Second Voyage, and Florentine merchant banker Amerigo Vespucci, for whom this was the first taste of transatlantic adventure.

Furthermore, even before setting out across the Atlantic, Hojeda began to behave as if he had some unwritten authority to behave as unspeakably as he pleased. Distrusting the seaworthiness of one of the vessels under his command, he blithely sailed her into Puerto de Santa Maria (the port from which Day had written his letter to Columbus), hijacked another vessel that happened to be berthed there, and left the old one in exchange. Moving south to catch the most favourable winds, he would feign distress to passing ships, then when these lowered sail to offer assistance, send over a boat of cut-throats to rob them like a common pirate. At Lanzarote in the Canaries he even plundered the town-house of the daughter of Columbus's lady-love, Doña Beatriz.

Probably due to Columbus's ever-inaccurate computations of latitude, Hojeda and his fellow pirates initially arrived too far south on the coastline of South America, most likely in the region of Guiana. They therefore had to work their way back north-westwards along the South American coastline, inevitably recognizing it as a huge area of mainland in a way that Columbus, only one year earlier, had not. Pressing on, they soon found Paria but acquired comparatively few of its pearls, once again, it would seem, because of Hojeda's ill-treatment of the natives. According to a contemporary description 'he went along killing and robbing and fighting, although these natives were peaceful and quiet'.

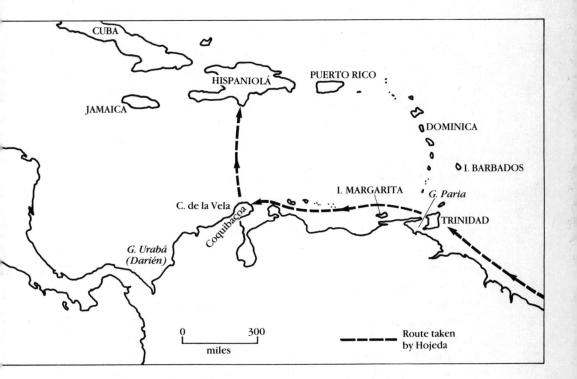

Fig. 19: Caribbean coast of South America, showing Coquibaçoa, and route taken by the Hojeda/La Cosa/Vespucci voyage of 1499.

Then, working further westwards than anyone had explored before, Hojeda and his companions came to the island of Curaçao, followed by a gulf which the local Arawak natives called Coquibaçoa, but which he renamed Venezuela, 'Little Venice', on account of a large, stilt-built native village which they came across at the waterside. Here, at the smallest pretext, Hojeda and his men shot some 15–20 natives, looted all their huts in search of gold, and carried off a pretty girl to be Hojeda's mistress and interpreter.

They then sailed around what is now the Guajira peninsula of eastern Colombia to reach Cabo de la Vela, the westernmost cape of a rather bleak stretch of coastline that came to be given the name Coquibaçoa on the earliest Spanish maps, after the Indian name for the adjoining gulf.

At this point they terminated their westward coasting, the reasons, so far as history is aware, being that their vessels were now badly in need of supplies and repairs. After loading logwood Hojeda is known to have sailed north for Hispaniola, reaching this on September 5, 1499. Here, to Columbus's chagrin, he immediately sided with the still troublesome rebel faction. But baulked, just as Columbus had been, of acquiring any significant quantities of gold or pearls, he contented himself with a raid on the Bahaman island, illegally capturing some 232 of the natives to sell back in Spain as slaves, a practice of which Queen Isabella strongly disapproved.

Since we know that Hojeda and his companions reached Hispaniola in early September 1499, it would have been in August or earlier that they were in the region known as Coquibaçoa, August 1499 being merely 15 months after Cabot and his men had set out from Bristol on the voyage from which they never returned. We can also be quite certain that there had been no further English voyage of transatlantic discovery, not least in view of no news having been received of Cabot. Although it had been hoped that his expedition might return to England by September 1498, it had been provisioned for a year, so there would have been no special surprise that it might take at least that long to return. Indeed, at this very time, September 1499, Vasco da Gama arrived back in Lisbon, having been away more than two years on his voyage to India.

It is therefore of extraordinary interest that in 1829 the highly authoritative Spanish historian Martín Fernández de Navarrete, the very man whose assiduous researches brought to light Las Casas's copy of Columbus's Journal, wrote in the third volume of his definitive history of the Spanish voyages of discovery:

> It is certain that Hojeda in his first voyage [that of 1499] encountered certain Englishmen in the vicinity of Coquibaçoa.

'Certain Englishmen' all that way south in 1499, when supposedly so far the only English feet on American soil had been those of Cabot's few companions in the environs of Nova Scotia in June 1497? The statement is one of the most tantalisingly enigmatic in the whole history of America's discovery, all the more so because of the insistent words 'it is certain', and because Navarrete, normally conscientious about quoting his sources, curiously omitted to do so in this instance.

So had Cabot and/or those who had survived from his 1498 voyage, diligently searching, like Columbus, for Marco Polo's 'Cipango . . . in the equinoctial region', been all this time making their way steadily southwards down the eastern American coastline, only to come face to face with Hojeda and his band of Spanish desperados in Coquibaçoa?

It is a tantalising thought that had they indeed done so they would have been virtually bound to have acquired more knowledge of America's geography than any other Europeans at this time, their peregrinations southwards inevitably convincing them that this had to be a whole new continent, just as Hojeda's men's coasting northwards had gained a corresponding understanding of America's southern half. Effectively they would have been the first to become aware of something approaching America's true vastness.

But it is also a much more sobering thought to realise that on meeting Hojeda any luck they might have had previously would very quickly have run out. Quite aside from the possibility of any secret orders that Fonseca may have given, Hojeda's well-practised ruthlessness towards natives and even fellow-Spaniards is indication enough that he and his men would have had little compunction about liquidating any such stray group of Englishmen, particularly since he could justify his actions on the grounds that they were trespassing on territory already allotted to Spain. Given that such an encounter ever took place, the English party may already have been enfeebled by the fevers and malaria endemic in this part of Colombia. But it is possible that they put up quite a resistance, since it was immediately after Coquibaçoa that Hojeda's ships needed substantial repairs (though this may simply have been because of the tropical climate's ravages upon wooden hulled vessels).

The root question is: can Navarrete's statement be trusted? It must be emphasised again that he was a sober and conscientious scholar, one who had personally made the most exhaustive researches in the Spanish archives at Simancas and elsewhere. So he is most unlikely to have made such a positive statement without some serious contemporary evidence to back it up. In the continued absence of this crucial document – perhaps a misfiled report or letter, just like the one Dr Louis Vigneras discovered of John Day/Hugh Say – the statement is too flimsy on its own to carry conviction.

Yet as it happens, it is by no means totally alone. Hojeda returned to Spain about the summer of 1500, but instead of being hung from the nearest yard-arm, as for his many acts of piracy he richly deserved, his 'achievements' (a 'slight profit' from his voyage was mentioned) earned him some exceptional favours. Not only was he granted a new licence, he was authorised this time to return to Coquibaçoa to set up a proper trading post, and given a respectable fleet for the purpose. He was also to have a grand title 'Governor of the Province of Coquibaçoa'.

Of particular fascination is the wording of this licence, issued 8 June, 1501, which has survived as yet another document from the Simancas archives. After being warned not to touch 'the land of the pearl-gathering' (the licence for this had been acquired by another adventurer, Cristóbal Guerra), also from Paria to the island of Margarita 'which you have no right to touch', Hojeda was told:

> Item: that you go and follow that coast which you have discovered, which runs east and west, as it appears, *because it goes towards the region where it has been learned that the English were making discoveries*; and that you go setting up marks with the arms of their Majesties, or with other signs that may be known, such as shall seem good to you, in order that it be known that you have discovered that land, *so that you may stop the exploration of the English in that direction* [Italics mine].

This alone has to be of enormous significance in support of Navarrete's statement that there had indeed been Englishmen at Coquibaçoa. The clear inference is that the English had been 'making discoveries' westwards of this, that Hojeda had stopped them, and was now to follow this up by pushing further westwards in the region where the English had been, setting up the Spanish standard instead.

Furthermore the licence goes on to indicate, somewhat mysteriously, that emeralds had come to light in this same region:

> Item: that you the said Alonso de Hojeda, for the service of their
> majesties, enter that island and the others that are around it which
> are called Coquibaçoa in the region of the mainland, *where the green
> stones are, of which you have brought a sample*, and that you obtain
> as many as you can, and in like manner see to the other things which
> you brought as specimens in that voyage.
> Item: that you the said Alonso Hojeda take steps to find out that
> which you have said you have learned of another gathering-place of
> pearls, provided that it be not within the limits above-mentioned, and
> that in the same way you look for the gold-mines of whose existence
> you say you have news.

No wonder that Hojeda, unfettered by Columbus's (and Cabot's)
compulsions to find fairy-tale Cipango and Cathay, was the Spanish
sovereigns' golden boy. Quite aside from any actual stopping of the
English (on which we can only speculate), he had brought back some
hard gems which we know can only have had their origins in the
emerald mines deep in Colombia's interior. He had also learned of,
but clearly not yet visited, another pearl-gathering place, which we
may identify as that along the coast about the Rio de la Hacha. He
had even gained report of gold-mines that according to the historian
Dr. Carl Sauer were most likely ones further towards the west, in the
mountains skirting Panama's Gulf of Darien.

How Hojeda had obtained all this information is unrecorded,
particularly regarding how it should have related to areas west of
where he had actually explored. Of course, it could have been from
the natives, via his interpreter mistress. But equally, it could well
have been extorted from the English, since the gold-mines certainly
lay in the very direction in which they had reportedly been 'making
discoveries'.

The documents have a suspiciously guarded air on these issues.
There seems also more than a touch of adroitness in the way the
Spanish sovereigns concluded the licence by rewarding Hojeda,
ostensibly not for what he had done, but for what he was to do.
After giving him the governorship of Coquibaçoa, they went on:

> Likewise their Majesties make you a gift in the island of Hispaniola
> of six leagues of land with its boundary, in the southern district which

is called Maquana . . . *for what you shall discover on the coast of the mainland for the stopping of the English* [italics mine], and the said six leagues of land shall be yours forever

Even so, the evidence so far that some members of the Cabot expedition really had survived to make their way all that distance south to Coquibaçoa, there to have their arguably fateful encounter with Hojeda, might still seem more than a little thin. But as it happens, there is yet another piece of the jig-saw yet to be considered — and it takes the form of one of the most enigmatic and historic maps of all time.

CHAPTER 11

An Enigmatic Map

In 1832 the wealthy aristocrat Baron Walckenaer was browsing in a Paris curio shop when he came upon an intriguing old *mappemonde* or world map drawn on oxhide. Measuring more than three feet by nearly six across, the map's early date was obvious from its primitive depiction of the continents, particularly America.

Then, as Walckenaer studied the map more carefully, he saw beneath a vignette of St Christopher the inscription:

> *Juan de la Cosa la fizo en el Puerto de S.Ma. en año de 1500*
> (Juan de la Cosa made this at Puerto de Santa Maria in the year 1500)

As Walckenaer immediately recognised, if this date could be believed, he was looking at the earliest extant map of America, and one drawn by a man known to have sailed with Columbus. He lost no time in purchasing the map, and after his death, in 1853 it was bought at auction by an agent of the Queen of Spain. Today it is displayed mounted on Russian leather inside a magnificent oak frame in the Spanish Naval Museum, Madrid [pl. 9].

Now one of the difficulties presented by a map of this kind turning up 'out of the blue', is that of determining where it might have been during the three centuries in which its existence went apparently unrecorded. Any deductions therefore need to be made with a reasonable degree of caution.

Nonetheless, for us not the least of the map's intriguing features is the name of its creator, that of Juan de la Cosa. To add to the confusion we have already experienced with the multiplicity of Bristolian John Jays, there are some scholarly uncertainties concerning whether there were one or two Juan de la Cosas associated with Columbus. Thus there was a Juan de la Cosa who captained the ill-fated *Santa Maria* on Columbus's First Voyage. There was also a Juan de la Cosa who was a seaman on *Niña* during Columbus's Second Voyage. According to some historians, most notably the late Admiral Samuel Morison, these were two quite separate individuals, though both of Basque origin. But according to others they were one and the same man, the main proponent of this latter view being the Spanish scholar Capitán de Corbeta Roberto Barreiro-Meiro of the Naval Museum, Madrid. To us the controversy is largely immaterial, there being no dispute that the second La Cosa was extremely highly regarded as a seaman. Queen Isabella herself provided a testimonial for him, apparently commenting, on granting a licence to another voyager: 'I would prefer that Juan de la Cosa make this voyage, for I believe that he would do it better than anyone else.'

Where the real interest of the map lies for us is in the fact that its authorship is not only very substantially attributed to this second la Cosa (if indeed there were two), but also that this same individual was one of the leading participants in the Hojeda voyage of 1499 which arguably encountered the Englishmen at Coquibaçoa. And this leads to the second of the map's major elements of interest, its understanding of world geography as at the year 1500.

For in its depiction of Europe, Asia and Africa it straightforwardly enough follows in the tradition of fourteenth- and fifteenth-century examples such as Abraham Cresques' Catalan Atlas of circa 1375 and Martin Behaim's globe of 1492. In common with these it features quaint and colourful mini-pictures of cities, monarchs, ships, national flags, etc, even of the three magi making their way to Jerusalem. Also in its depiction of the East African coastline and that of India it follows the old Ptolemaic tradition.

But where it differs from all that had gone before (at least, anything that has survived) is that its entire left-hand section depicts a huge continent, shaded green and stretching from the furthest north to the furthest south. This continent is nearly but not completely bi-sected by a bite-shaped area of sea in which can readily be recognized the characteristic shapes of Cuba, Hispaniola and other West Indian islands.

Now some allowance must be made for scholarly opinions that this side of the map has been drawn to a slightly different scale than that of the old world. Also it must be noted that La Cosa seems to have left deliberately vague whether this land-mass might or might not join up with, or actually be, Asia.

But the truly remarkable features are the hundreds of miles of named capes and bays, complete with national flags, that can be seen strung along two convincingly solid-looking northern and southern halves of the continent. Also clearly indicated is a continuous coastline all around what appears to us as the Gulf of Mexico punctuated only by a single area of uncertainty, the region of Nicaragua and Honduras, covered by the already-mentioned St Christopher vignette. Even more than a century and a half after it was first discovered by Walckenaer, the map remains essentially unrivalled as the first to show, albeit incompletely, something recognizably what we know today as the continent of America. The unresolved issue is how anyone in the year 1500 could have acquired sufficient information to put together a map that shows such a surprisingly advanced understanding of that continent's geography.

For most of the South American and West Indies landmarks the explanations are simple enough. The reasonably accurate drawing of South America's coastline from Guiana to eastern Colombia is nothing more than we would expect from La Cosa's known accompaniment of the Hojeda voyage of 1499. The accurate delineations of the West Indies also clearly derive from La Cosa's certain accompaniment of Columbus's Second Voyage; also from the fact that he would inevitably have seen Columbus's Third Voyage 'drawing of the land' that Hojeda had been shown by Bishop Fonseca, almost certainly at one and the same time being allowed to make a copy.

Of the West Indies, one so far insufficiently explained feature is La Cosa's quite emphatic and accurate delineation of Cuba as an island. As we noted earlier, Columbus did not fully circumnavigate Cuba on his Second Voyage, stopping just 50 miles short. Similarly, the reader may recall that all who took part in the Second Voyage, La Cosa included, had been obliged to sign a sworn affidavit that Cuba was part of the 'Asian' mainland. Since no one, on the Spanish side at least, was known to have visited Cuba since, a genuine mystery surrounds whether La Cosa simply guessed Cuba to be an island, or whether he had actually learned this from someone as yet unidentified. At the very least it reinforces how thin was belief in the truth of the affidavit that Columbus forced his crews to sign.

But by far the greater mystery (and one possibly carrying its own explanation of the Cuba delineation), is La Cosa's totally pioneering representation of the North American mainland. Quite indisputably this shows discoveries made by the English, not least because the sea off one area of the coast is specifically inscribed '*mar descubierto por*

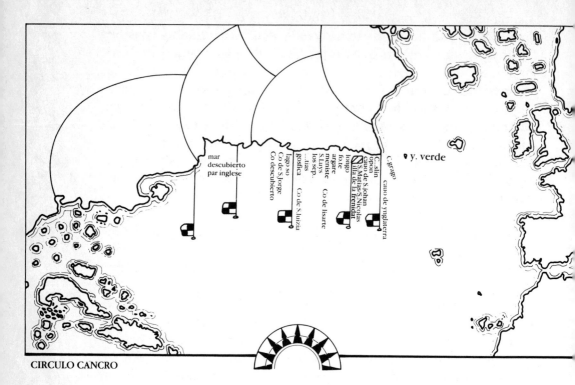

mar
descubierto
par inglese

Co descubierto
Co de S.Jorge
lago so

Co de S.luizia
gosfica
...tias
S.Luys
meniste
argare
longo
fo.te
cauo de S.johan
S.Matias/S.Nicolas
illa de la frenidat
C.slin
opoin
C.grago
cauo de ynglaterra

● y. verde

CIRCULO CANCRO

Fig. 20: Flagged area of coastline accredited to the English, detail
after Juan de la Cosa's map.

inglese' ('sea discovered by the English'), and this same area is also
decorated with no fewer than five English flags [fig.20]. Accordingly
there is full agreement among historians that La Cosa must have
received some detailed information of the discoveries made by
Cabot. The really thorny question is whether this derived merely
from Cabot's voyage of 1497, or whether we have in the map
unique data from the altogether more mysterious voyage of 1498.

Understandably, the safer money has been on the voyage of 1497.
We have already learned from the letters of Hugh Say/John Day and
from the envoy Ayala that a map of Cabot's 1497 voyage was all but
in Spanish hands by mid-1498, and would almost inevitably have been
so by the time of the Hojeda/La Cosa departure in May 1499. We have
also noted that La Cosa's inscription on the map showed he made it in
Puerto de Santa Maria, the very same port as that from which Hugh
Say/John Day wrote to Columbus. Furthermore the flagged area of

English coastline as marked on the map can be seen to be between the latitudes west of Ireland, to west of Bordeaux's river, precisely in accord with the description in the Say/Day letter. Again in accord with the Say/Day letter, the furthest-western named cape seems to be called 'Cavo Descubierto', or 'Cape Discovery', corresponding to Say/Day's remark to Columbus 'you will see [on the "copy of the land"] where land was first sighted, since most of the land was discovered after turning back'.

If La Cosa's map is indeed of the 1497 Cabot voyage, then it incidentally provides the strongest possible evidence that Cabot's landfall had indeed not been Newfoundland, but further to the south along the eastern American seaboard. For impossible as it is to identify La Cosa's coastline with any exactness, it is most certainly not that of a heavily indented island such as Newfoundland.

But the really curious feature of the La Cosa map, and one in which it is strangely both on its own and ahead of all other similar maps for some 30 years into the future, is its indisputably correct conception of continuous coastline from the flagged territory accredited to the English to all round the Caribbean, punctuated only by the single area of uncertainty denoted by the St Christopher vignette.

For it cannot be emphasised enough that no European is known to have touched the American coastline anywhere along the north of the Gulf of Mexico, until Ponce de Leon reached and explored some parts of Florida in 1513. Yet La Cosa, albeit without showing place-names, confidently delineated a continuous mainland north of the Caribbean islands and at approximately the correct distance from these. He equally confidently delineated the South American coastline stretching considerably further westwards than the Coquibaçoa region which was the furthest that he and Hojeda reached in 1499.

Furthermore, as particularly noted by the historian James A. Williamson, this section of the coastline happens also to be one of the most uncannily accurate of the whole map [see fig. 21], even though La Cosa makes quite clear that his expedition did not explore this section of coast. For although La Cosa shows a long line of new place-names stretching all the way from Guiana, the line abruptly stops at Coquibaçoa, which despite its aridity is accorded no fewer than seven place-name entries, terminated by an emphatic Spanish flag. So how could La Cosa have obtained his information about the coast west of Coquibaçoa, and could it have been from the same

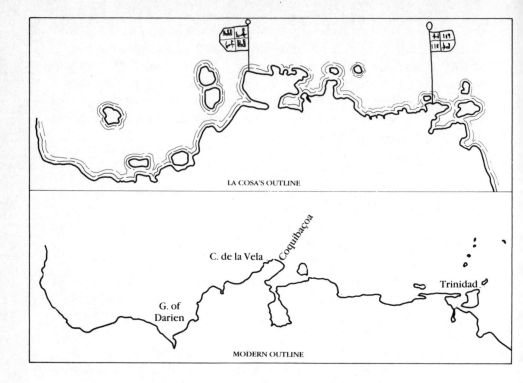

Fig. 21: (above) La Cosa's outline of the Caribbean coastline of South America; compared with (below) the true outline.

source that Hojeda obtained his information about the region's gold, emeralds and pearls?

Only the very occasional scholar, most notably Bernard Hoffman, has gone so far as to assert that the La Cosa map must be an outright fake. Others have suggested the accurate coastline to be just a lucky piece of fancy, pointing out that La Cosa undoubtedly resorted to imagination in his delineation of non-existent islands off Coquibaçoa. Somewhat more serious arguments have been put forward to contest the date that the map bears, some arguing for its having been created in 1509 (Morison), others even as late as 1529, when La Cosa was long dead.

But Dr Williamson, for one, has very steadfastly insisted that it is actually only the map's given date of 1500 that accounts for its maker's ignorance, for instance, of what Vasco da Gama learned from his voyage to India. Maps made after 1502 almost invariably took account of Vasco da Gama's discoveries, but La Cosa's did not. In Williamson's words: 'It was only in 1500 that a Spaniard could have known just so much and so little.'

It is only fair also to point out, however, the well-justified comments on the La Cosa map made by the redoubtable Admiral Samuel Morison:

> Theorists treat it like rubber – they squeeze, stretch, twist, and telescope it to fit anything from a hundred to a thousand miles, and even turn it sideways or upside down.

Indeed, La Cosa's northern coastline has been enthusiastically claimed to 'fit' almost any and every real geographical feature on North America's eastern seaboard such as the Delaware, Cape Cod, Long Island, the Hudson river and Florida. So even if we accept that the map was made in 1500 it is important to be realistic and recognize that in general, and very much in line with the limitations of map-making competence at that time, it is insufficiently accurately drawn for any surefire identifications of this kind to be made.

Yet the extent of the map's anticipation of what we now know to be the actuality of the American continent remains too real and self-evident to be ignored or attributed to pure chance. For instance, its configuration of the North American coastline is hugely superior to that of Portugal's so-called Cantino map of 1502, which shows effectively no North American coastline, and what is undoubtedly Newfoundland as an isolated island thousands of miles out into the Atlantic.

The same coastline configuration is also strikingly similar to that of the true North American seaboard as is shown on substantially later maps such as that made in 1529 by the Florentine pilot Gerolamo da Verrazzano, who under the flag of France had voyaged along the coast in 1524. Indeed, both La Cosa's and Verrazzano's coastlines show much the same mistakenly exaggerated east-west directionality, arising from a declination of the magnetic compass at these latitudes that frequently caused sixteenth-century navigators to err when taking their bearings along this coast.

So do we have in the La Cosa map an echo of a first tracing of the near-entire North American coastline as made by an unknown group of survivors from Cabot's expedition of 1498, survivors who met up with Hojeda and La Cosa at Coquibaçoa, and never lived to get their story back to England?

Strikingly in favour of the map deriving from Cabot's 1498 voyage is the already noted fact that no fewer than five English flags are shown along the 'English' coast. Although five such flags should not necessarily be taken to mean five actual flag-planting landings, nonetheless they strongly suggest a much more significant and thorough English exploration of the coast than could be expected of the timid and perfunctory single landfall made by the Cabot expedition of 1497.

Another argument for the map's derivation from the 1498 voyage is the fact that while some of the place-names marked along the English coastline are difficult to read, none of them seem to bear any relation to those on Newfoundland, such as 'Cape Bonavista', that have been attributed to Cabot's 1497 voyage. While the perpetuation of place-names as given by fifteenth- and sixteenth-century discoverers was always a hit-and-miss affair, nonetheless those on the La Cosa map suggest initiators who never survived to lodge them in the record books back home, precisely as happened to those who sailed with Cabot.

In all this it might be supposed that if men of Cabot's 1498 voyage had found their way all the way south to Coquibaçoa, if they had made a careful geographical record of all they had found, and if this record had been taken from them by Hojeda and his companions, then the latter would scarcely have been able to restrain themselves from boasting about their achievements back in Spain. After all, they could fully justify arguing that the Englishmen, as trespassers, had brought their fate upon themselves.

Yet in fact, while privately Ferdinand and Isabella would have fully endorsed any such 'stopping' of the English, as clearly indicated by their arguably retrospective licence to Hojeda of 8 June, 1501, undoubtedly they would also have been most anxious, particularly around the year 1500, that absolutely nothing of the story should ever be learned in England.

This was because of the very delicate negotiations which at that very time envoy Ayala was bringing to completion to arrange that Ferdinand and Isabella's daughter Catalina (better known to us as Catherine of Aragon) should marry Henry VII's eldest son and heir, the Prince Arthur, thus uniting the kingdoms of England and Spain against their common enemy France. The months of 1500-1 were those of the final intense diplomatic activity preceding Catherine's actual sailing to England in the August of 1501. It would therefore have been absolutely imperative that news of the murder of Englishmen by Spaniards, even as justified by a papally endorsed treaty (i.e the Treaty of Tordesillas), should not be allowed to leak out to the outside world.

There is even some reason for believing that just in case there was any such leak, this very map may well have been prepared to justify the Spanish action, a justification perhaps intended for the privileged eyes of the pope most responsible for the Treaty of Tordesillas, the Borgia Pope Alexander VI. As noticed by the historian Dr James Williamson, the map displays some curious falsifications of latitude, most particularly relating to the Spanish and English areas of discovery. Thus the coast shown as discovered by the English appears at a latitude only a little south of southern England, then immediately to the south of this are shown all the Spanish-discovered islands of the West Indies. But instead of these latter being drawn at anything like their true latitude, they are shown as too far north by some twelve degrees, thus making any English wandering southward appear that much more of a flagrant trespass upon Spanish territory. In Williamson's words:

> La Cosa was a pilot of repute who had been three times to the West Indies, including twice with Columbus. He could not have made such an error in good faith.

Arguably therefore the map was a deliberate 'cooking of the latitudes' to persuade somebody – and although it might just have been Henry VII, the Pope seems to be much the more likely – that any English movement southwards was seriously out of order. And in this latter regard both the date and location of Walckenaer's discovery hold the faintest of clues. In the early nineteenth century the Emperor Napoleon, when he was at the height of his power, had the Vatican's historically priceless collection of 'secret archives' seized from Rome and taken to Paris. On Napoleon's eventual defeat some of this material was returned. But because of high transport costs much else that was judged unimportant was left behind to be sold by weight for wrapping paper and the making of cardboard. Arguably the La Cosa map may well have been among this latter material, thereupon to be saved from wanton destruction by some unknown Parisian attracted by its quaintness. This same Parisian or their heirs may then have sold the map a few years later to the curio shop where it was found by Walckenaer.

But even the La Cosa Map does not provide the last word on that putative murky encounter between Englishmen and Spanish at Coquibaçoa in the year 1499. For it will be recollected that besides Juan de la Cosa, the piratical Hojeda had a third companion on his voyage of 1499–1500, a companion whose very name cries out for some explanation of his place in the story of America's discovery. The name in question: Amerigo Vespucci.

CHAPTER 12

How America Got Its Name?

But these new lands found lately
Be called America, because only
Americus did first them find.

English poem, circa 1519

As already remarked, no known contemporary portrait exists of John Cabot. Of Columbus, too, none of the familiarly reproduced portraits is thought to have been made in his lifetime. But deservedly or otherwise one man associated with the discovery of America has been rather better served by posterity, and in more ways than just the preservation of his likeness.

In 1472 the Florentine artist Domenico Ghirlandaio was commissioned to paint a devotional group portrait of the well-to-do local Vespucci family as one of the frescoes for the family's chapel in what is today Florence's church of S. Salvador d'Ognissanti. One of those whom he duly depicted in the fresco, seen piously looking out from beneath the Virgin Mary's robe, was an oval-faced teenager with dark brown eyes, aquiline nose and prominent lips whom we can identify as Amerigo, son of the thrusting politician Nastagio Vespucci. This same Amerigo went on to have the whole American continent named after him. And how this happened has to be one of the murkiest and most bizarre episodes in the entire history of America's discovery.

Unlike Cabot and Columbus, Amerigo Vespucci even had the luck to have his baptism recorded. In the archives of Florence's Duomo or Cathedral can be consulted the register of the city's famous Baptistry for the years 1450–60. In this, Amerigo's entry, dated 18 March, 1453 (1454 by our New Year reckoning), can be seen specially highlighted by the later addition of a pointing hand and circle proudly inscribed '*Truvatore dell'Indie nuove*' (Discoverer of the New Indies).

151

With regard to Amerigo's background we know that he was educated at a private school in Florence, the Convent of San Marco, where his uncle, Fr. Giorgio Vespucci, was one of the tutors, and the future Florentine *gonfaloniere*, Pier Soderini, a fellow-pupil. We also know that he then pursued a career in banking and commerce, spending twenty years working for Lorenzo de' Medici's banking house in Florence, before moving to Seville in 1491 to head up a Medici merchant banking and ships' supply agency there. It was in this capacity that he fitted and stocked Columbus's ships for the latter's Third Voyage of 1498, and, presumably, also came to meet Alonso de Hojeda and Juan de la Cosa. To the best of available historical information, therefore, his accompaniment of Hojeda 1499 voyage was his first taste of transoceanic adventure, his rôle in this simply that of gentleman companion and perhaps financial backer.

That Vespucci was not too overjoyed by his association with Hojeda and his Spanish desperados during the 1499 voyage is strongly suggested by the fact that once the Hojeda ships had reached Hispaniola after their departure from Coquibaçoa, he declined to accompany them on the slaving mission to the Bahamas, instead taking the first available ship back to Spain. In his subsequent writings he effectively pretended that Hojeda had never even existed. He also very quickly shifted his allegiance from Spain to Portugal.

Nonetheless his accompaniment of the Hojeda expedition must unquestionably have inspired in him enthusiasm for further adventure of this kind, for within a year he enlisted with the Portuguese to return to South America. This came about because in 1500, the very year of Amerigo's return from the Hojeda expedition, the Portuguese captain Pedro Alvares Cabral had discovered Brazil, the true Brazil that we know today, seemingly quite by accident. Cabral appears to have come across it simply because of making too wide a west Atlantic sweep to catch the best winds while trying to repeat Vasco da Gama's round-Africa route to India. The fact that the name 'Brazil' stuck in this instance would seem to have been because the country really was found to have vivid red dye-woods.

The discovery seems not only to have firmly established in Portuguese minds the existence of the huge piece of mainland across the Atlantic, but also caused them to suspect that their newly found true Brazil probably lay sufficiently to the east to fall to them under the Treaty of Tordesillas.

Meanwhile Amerigo Vespucci had of course only recently returned from having explored with Hojeda the Spanish-claimed coast to the north-west, an exploration which, as we have learned, had notably included the finding of gold and gems. It is unclear whether the Portuguese heard of this and approached Amerigo, or whether he, disgusted with the Spanish, offered his acquired knowledge to the Portuguese on his own initiative.

Tending in favour of the latter are signs of Vespuccian influence on Portuguese maps dating from as early as 1502 (notably the previously mentioned Cantino map), suggesting that he had become sufficiently interested in cosmography to make his own charts of those places he had visited, perhaps having learned from Juan de la Cosa during the 1499 voyage. Certainly when in 1501 Portugal's King Manuel deemed it worthwhile to send nobleman Gonçalo Coelho with three caravels to investigate Cabral's new Brazil, Vespucci accompanied this new expedition, just as he had Hojeda's.

We know that Coelho's expedition left Lisbon on May 10, and after two stops along the way, made first landfall on the Brazilian coastline on August 17 of the same year. As usual, the exact spot cannot be determined with any certainty, but it was probably somewhere between the present-day towns of Fortaleza and Recife. It was also apparently cannibal country, for the natives reportedly seized and ate three of Coelho's men before this danger became properly realized.

Duly chastened, the expedition steadily coasted considerably further south, arriving at the natural harbour of Guanabara Bay on January 1, 1502, thus giving birth to the name of Brazil's capital, Rio de Janeiro, which later came to be built at this spot. Coasting some way further south they then set full sail on February 13, but became caught in storms that sent them well out into the Atlantic. During the ensuing weeks they sighted but were unable to land on the mid-Atlantic uninhabited island of Isla Trinidade. When they eventually reached the next land on May 10 it was to find themselves on the coast of West Africa, from which they worked their way northwards to arrive back in Lisbon on September 7, 1502. To the inevitable disappointment of Portugal's King Manuel, they brought back no gold or gems, only logwood, parrots and monkeys.

It should be explained at this point that determining much more about the Coelho voyage is highly difficult, chiefly because Vespucci happens to have been the prime source of information. While this might not seem so unacceptable – after all, Vespucci was well educated, and genuinely did accompany the Coelho expedition – the problem arises when we realise that he wrote about the venture, just as he did about Hojeda's, as if the two captains had never existed, and he had led the expeditions himself.

Even this might not be so bad but for the further complication that in doing so either Vespucci, or else someone else writing in his name, resorted to so much invention, that determining any real and creditable achievements he may have accomplished is more than a little difficult.

At the heart of the major problems in this regard are two documents which, whatever their origin, achieved the widest circulation in Vespucci's name. The first of these is a letter purportedly written by him, and addressed to Lorenzo di Pier Francesco de' Medici, who had succeeded Vespucci's earlier patron Lorenzo de' Medici as head of the Florentine republic. Published under the title *Mundus Novus* (New World) in August 1504, this was seemingly a report of the Coelho 1501–2 voyage, but ascribing outright to Vespucci himself the discovery of:

> [what] we may rightly call a New World . . . For it transcends the view held by the ancients . . . that there was no continent to the south beyond the equator, but only the sea which they named the Atlantic . . . In those southern parts I have found a continent more densely peopled and abounding in animals than our Europe or Asia or Africa.

The second document is a letter purportedly sent by Vespucci on September 4, 1504 to his former schoolmate Pier Soderini, who at just about this time had become Florence's *gonfaloniere* on Lorenzo di Pier Francesco de' Medici's death.

In this letter Vespucci, or whoever was writing in his name, claimed to have made no fewer than four voyages to the New World. The first of these he said he had undertaken under the flag of Spain as early as May 1497, sailing from Cadiz to arrive first at the Canary Islands, then sailing for 37 days on a course 'toward the west, taking one quarter by south-west', whereupon:

> . . . we reached a land which we judged to be continental, which is distant westward from the Canary Islands about one thousand leagues beyond the inhabited region, within the torrid zone

The second voyage, also under the flag of Spain, was described as having taken place in 1499. This was said to have explored from 5S of the equator to 15N, thus roughly approximating the genuine 1499–1500 voyage with Hojeda.

The third voyage was described as having taken place in 1501 under the Portuguese flag, exploring from 5S of the equator, to 52S. This, although it would seem to be a version of Vespucci's actual 1501–2 voyage with Coelho, would mean that he reached as far south as the Falkland islands and Southern Argentina.

The fourth voyage, apparently in 1503, seems to have been a minor one, again with Coelho, simply re-exploring again some of the parts of Brazil that had already been discovered during the 1501–2 expedition.

Now whatever the origin of the two documents, they were laced with vivid and seemingly authoritative detail, as for instance in the Lorenzo di Pier Francesco de' Medici letter's account of the flora and fauna observed in South America:

> This land is very delightful, and covered with an infinite number of green trees and very big ones which never lose their foliage, and throughout the year yield the sweetest aromatic perfumes and produce an infinite variety of fruit ... And what shall I say of the quantity of birds and their plumage and colours, and their songs, and of such variety and beauty? ... How shall I enumerate the infinite variety of wild animals, lions [!], panthers, cats ... such as wolves, stags and monkeys of every sort, and many very big?

In this same letter we hear similarly unstinting minutiae of the new land's human inhabitants;

> We found all the earth inhabited by people completely nude, men as well as women, without covering their shame. They have bodies well proportioned, white in colour with black hair, and little or no beard ... They have among them no private property, because everything is in common ... They live in common houses made like very large cabins; and for people who have no iron or other metal, it is possible to say that their houses are truly wonderful, for I have seen houses which are 200 *passi* long and 30 wide and artfully made by craftsmen, and in one of these houses perhaps 500 or 600 souls. They slept in nets [hammocks] woven of cotton, exposed to the air without any other covering ... The men are accustomed

to bore holes in their lips and cheeks and in these holes they place bones and stones; and don't believe they are little . . . We found much human flesh in their houses, placed in the smoke; and we purchased of them 10 creatures male and female, who had been marked for the sacrifice . . . One of their men confessed to me that he had eaten the flesh of more than 200 bodies, and this I believe for certain . . .

Whether or not these documents actually emanated from Vespucci, they very definitely became wildly popular publications via the age's still novel toy, the printing press. The *Mundus Novus* alone, for instance, was translated into Latin, Italian, French, German, Flemish and Czech in some 40 editions during the next few years. By contrast there did not exist any equivalent publication either for Columbus's last voyages, or, of course, for the voyages of John Cabot, whose achievements had gone virtually unheard of by the European public at large.

From within a few years of the documents' publication, right up to the present day, controversy has raged over just how much of a hand Vespucci had in their authorship, and just how much they should or should not be believed. Particularly crucial in this regard is the claimed first voyage of 1497, one of the same year as Cabot's first landing on the North American mainland, and predating by a year Columbus's touching of the South American mainland at Paria.

That there were serious doubts about Vespucci's claims even in his own time is evident from the fact that they were hotly challenged both by John Cabot's son Sebastian, and by Columbus's biographer Bartolomé de Las Casas. They were further shaken during the last century when the scholar Viscondé de Santarém found among the Spanish archives documents showing that Vespucci was unquestionably working in Seville in 1497 – throughout the very time that, according to the Soderini letter, he was supposed to have been on his first epoch-making voyage of discovery.

Despite this, some modern enthusiasts have continued to insist on the genuineness of the Medici and Soderini letters, and that Vespucci really did reach the American mainland in 1497. Other pro-Vespucci authors, such as Frederick Pohl, have contended that the letters must have been the work of forgers trading on Vespucci's name – even though he himself lived on for some years after the proliferation of these supposedly rogue publications, without apparently making any attempt to stop them. Yet others have noted that even in the documents undisputedly of Vespucci's authorship he made such absurd claims of his navigational skills (for example, his ability to calculate longitude), also of some vast distances that he purportedly covered in times quite impossible for sailing vessels, that his word is scarcely to be trusted on anything.

But whatever the legitimacy of Vespucci's claims for himself as 'discoverer' of the new continent, the very publishing popularity of his 'New World' stories meant there were many quarters that took them seriously in the sixteenth century. And for the future name of the American continent there was no more important supporter of his claims than the small cathedral town of St Dié nestling amidst the wooded Vosges hills of the Lorraine region of north-eastern France.

Today, sadly, St Dié has few surviving vestiges of its historical past. Many of its mediaeval buildings perished in a fire in 1757. It was bombarded by the Germans during the First World War, and deliberately destroyed by them on their retreat from the advancing Allies in November 1944.

But back in the first decade of the sixteenth century the town was the home of a flourishing cosmography and cartography college, the 'Gymnasium Vosagense', or Vosges School, under the patronage of the studious Duke Renaud (René) II of Vaudemon and of Lorraine. In the very year that Vespucci had returned from the Hojeda voyage the college had acquired its own printing press, with the specific intention of producing a new state-of-the-art edition of Ptolemy's *Geography*, updated in the light of Marco Polo, Columbus's voyages and all the yet more recent discoveries, and accompanied by a definitive world map. The title of the project was to be the *Cosmographiae Introductio*, or 'Introduction to Cosmography'.

To make this work as authoritative as possible members of this college seem to have spent some years travelling in search of the latest information. It is evident that they must have gathered some information on the Portuguese voyages to Newfoundland that found the broken sword and ear-rings, for Newfoundland would appear on their map as an island rather incongruously stuck out in mid-Atlantic. They must also have learned of the Portuguese voyages round Africa that had reached India.

It is also quite definite that someone obtained a copy of Amerigo Vespucci's notorious Soderini letter, and that one member of the college particularly impressed by this was the young geographer Martin Waldseemüller. At Waldseemüller's apparent instigation it was decided that the full Latin text of Vespucci's letter should be incorporated into the *Cosmographiae* in the form of an appendix.

Waldseemüller seems also to have had a particular fondness, not uncommon among educated people of the time, for coining fancy names based on classical derivatives. For instance, for his own name, in German literally 'Wood-lake-miller', he conjured 'Hylacomylus', derived from the Greek υλη, or 'wood', the Latin *lacus* or 'lake', and the Greek μυλος, or 'mill'.

It was perhaps inevitable, therefore, that as Waldseemüller became more and more impressed by what he read of Vespucci's achievements as catalogued in the Soderini letter, so he should decide that a new piece of name-coining was required for this as yet unnamed new continent, as 'discovered' by Vespucci. Accordingly, as he explained in the Latin preface to the *Cosmographiae*:

> Toward the South Pole are situated the southern part of Africa, recently discovered, and the islands of Zanzibar, Java Minor and Seula. These regions [Europe, Asia, Africa] have been more extensively explored, and another or fourth part has been discovered by Americus Vespucius, as may be seen by the attached charts; in virtue of which I believe it very just that it should be named Amerige ['ge' in Greek meaning 'land of'] after its discoverer, Americus, a man of sagacious mind; or *let it be America, since both Europa and Asia bear names of feminine form* [author's italics].

If it had perhaps remained thus buried in a Latin text, this suggestion might never have attracted sufficient attention to be adopted. But Waldseemüller was also the member of the St Dié college most responsible for putting together the great wood-engraved map that was to accompany the *Cosmographiae*. Although this was published in 1507 in an edition of 1,000 copies, it was originally thought that no examples had survived. Then in 1901 one came to light in the German castle of Schloss Wolfegg, bound up in an old book which had once belonged to the sixteenth-century German geographer Johann Schöner.

This well-preserved specimen [pl. 10], which remains to this day the only known survivor, consists of 12 sheets taken from woodblocks. As is immediately apparent from this, Waldseemüller accorded Vespucci the extraordinary distinction of depicting his

Fig. 22: Amerigo Vespucci, detail from the Waldseemüller map of 1507.

likeness at the head of the map, accompanied only by an equivalent likeness of Ptolemy himself. By way of identification, the name 'Americi Vespucci' was written in letters twice as large as the equivalent for Ptolemy, indeed as the largest of the whole work. His name was also repeated along with Ptolemy's in the base inscription: 'The Universal Cosmography according to the tradition of Ptolemy and to the explorations of Americo Vespucci', whereas Columbus, by contrast, was relegated to the small print of an insignificant top-left hand corner panel, together with a tiny cartouche referring to his discovery of the Trinidad islands.

But Waldseemüller's greatest accolade of all to Amerigo Vespucci is to be seen in the map's striking rendition of South America. In his delineation of the Old World Waldseemüller was surprisingly old-fashioned, copying almost exactly a world map that had been made as far back as 1489 by the German cartographer Henricus Martellus. But in respect of South America Waldseemüller broke totally new ground even over the La Cosa map, showing this as a land-mass quite emphatically distinct from Asia. And in the midst of this land-mass, in letters only marginally smaller than those for 'Africa', 'Asia' and 'Europa', Waldseemüller set the name 'America', its first ever known appearance in any map.

The name was repeated solo across the whole of South America in another striking depiction of the sub-continent on gores which Waldseemüller made for a terrestrial globe to accompany the *Cosmographiae*. And thus by these few strokes of the pen in the year 1507 an obscure geography professor living in a tiny town in a state that no longer exists set for all time the name of the world's second largest continent, a name that would subsequently be repeated a billion, billion times in word and in print. And all in honour of a man with the most dubious claim ever to deserving this.

Perhaps inevitably, how this perpetuation of the name 'America' came about is almost as tangled as that of its first inception. For in circumstances that are by no means clear Waldseemüller himself seems soon to have recognized that he might have made a serious misjudgment in attaching too much credence to Vespucci, and in over-honouring him. Certainly as early as 1513 he published a new map entitled 'Terre Nove' or 'New World', showing just the newly discovered terrain in relation to the most western parts of Europe and Africa [fig. 24]. Now not only did he now ascribe this to 'The Admiral', i.e. Columbus, he also seemingly deliberately omitted any mention of the name 'America' in his rendition of South America's northern land-mass. Indeed, as if to emphasise this, he wrote in its place in huge letters 'Terra Incognita', 'Unknown Land', accompanied by an inscription ignoring Vespucci and stating that this and the adjacent islands were found by Columbus.

In a second full world map, the *Carta Marina*, published in 1516 (pl. 11), he again omitted any usage of the name 'America', simply entitling northern South America 'Terra Nova'.

Fig. 23: Detail of Waldseemüller's 1507 world map, showing the first-known naming of America's southern continent.

Inevitably in all this there are many questions that abound, without easy answers. Why, for instance, in his original and apparently rash coinage of the name 'America', did Waldseemüller focus on Vespucci's Christian name? Admittedly Vespuccia, rooted in the Latin *vespa* for wasp (the Vespucci emblem), would scarcely have

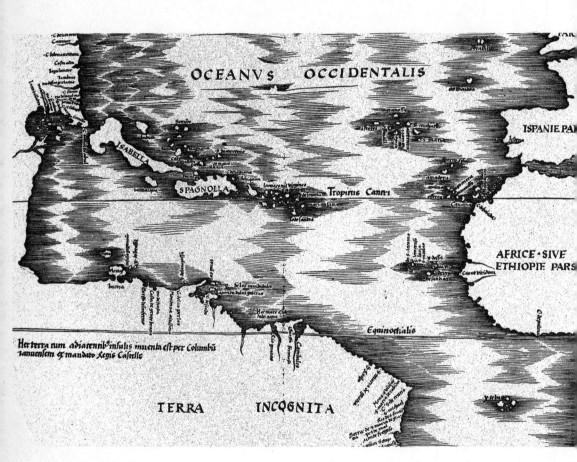

Fig. 24: Waldseemüller's *Terre Nove* map of 1513, showing dropping of the name 'America', and of any concept of ocean between 'America' and Asia.

had the same ring. But it is nonetheless puzzling.

What do we know, also, of any indications that Waldseemüller and Vespucci might have met on some occasion, with Vespucci perhaps having actively canvassed for the 'New World' to be named after him? In fact, there is no direct evidence of this, and modern historians think it unlikely, although others of the sixteenth century were not quite so sure. For instance, in 1543 the German geographer Johann Schöner, the very man known to have owned the surviving copies of Waldseemüller's 1507 and 1516 maps, reportedly claimed that Vespucci had deliberately contrived to get his name on to world charts. Similarly Columbus's biographer Bartolomé de Las Casas, writing in 1559 specifically remarked that:

> He [Amerigo Vespucci] is said to have placed the name America in maps, thus sinfully failing towards the Admiral.

In all this is raised again the possibility, indeed likelihood, that Vespucci had made some chart or charts which influenced Waldseemüller. Here one perhaps significant feature is that in those very same maps of 1513 and 1516 in which Waldseemüller carefully dropped the name 'America', so also he dropped other elements of the 1507 map, even though we know those elements to have been quite reasonably accurate.

Here, even for the uninitiated in the history of map-making, it is quite a revelatory experience to compare the two Waldseemüller world maps, that of 1507 and that of 1516 [pls. 10 and 11]. At first appearance it might seem that there has been a mistake and that the dates ought to be reversed. For that of 1507 actually looks considerably more advanced than that of 1516. It shows 'America' as a new continent quite distinct from Asia, with another ocean to be crossed before the reaching of Cipango and the true Asia (this latter being particularly clear in the vignette next to Amerigo Vespucci's portrait). The 1507 version correctly shows Cuba as an island, just as La Cosa had done, except that it mislabels it 'Isabella'. It even advances on La Cosa by correctly envisaging the southern and northern chunks of mainland as separated by a narrow isthmus, the one we now know as Panama. As to whether this had a strait through to the true Asia, it hedges its bets by showing the isthmus with one on the main map, and without one in the vignette.

By contrast the 1516 map, dating in fact from three years after the Spanish Balboa had made the first historically known European discovery of the Pacific Ocean, completely backtracks even on the idea of '*Terra Nova*' being separate from Asia. Although it shows Cuba as an island, as in the 1507 map, it now gives it no name. And as if to highlight its confusion, one that can be traced right back to Columbus and his Second Voyage's contrived affidavit that Cuba was the Asian mainland, it even labels an apparent chunk of mainland as 'Land of Cuba, *part of Asia*'.

Yet there is no error in the dates of the charts. And the same man, Waldseemüller, was behind both. The one key difference is that in the second chart, either due to pressure from other members of the Vosges School or to his own fresh insights, Waldseemüller made a very vigorous attempt to obliterate a substantial part of the earlier Vespuccian influence. In effect, therefore, in those features of the 1507 chart which were not repeated in 1516, *but which were broadly correct*, we are afforded a tantalising glimpse of the lost contribution (whether by chart or otherwise) that Vespucci had made to the 1507 map.

But now, of course, comes the inevitable twist: was that contribution really Vespucci's, or what in a most important part, at least, he had learned from others? If so, were those others the very same individuals to whom La Cosa's map of 1500 was similarly indebted, the mystery party of Englishmen whom, as we have found reason to believe, Hojeda, La Cosa and Vespucci all met in that still shadowy encounter at Coquibaçoa?

While it would be tempting to 'see' in the Waldseemüller 1507 map some similar influences to La Cosa's, it is important not to press this too hard, for it is all highly speculative, and there are certain respects in which the arguably 'Vespuccian' contributions to Waldseemüller's 1507 map are markedly inferior to the insights of La Cosa's of 1500, even though there are other respects in which they are superior. Furthermore, whatever insights Vespucci may or may not have gained from the any encounter with the English, unlike La Cosa he omitted to show any English flags by way of acknowledgement along what may or may not be the North American coastline.

Nonetheless, even if the Waldseemüller map of 1507 had not survived, there happen to be two other curiosities associated with Vespucci, Cabot and the naming of America that deserve mention, not least because they bring us back again to yet another way in which Bristol may have played its part.

The first of these is that the voyage that Vespucci apparently chose totally to invent in the Soderini letter was the one he claimed as his first, one with a more northerly route than the rest, and specifically dated to May 1497. It is curious therefore that this was not only the same year, but the very same month, as that of the first successful Cabot voyage from Bristol.

Although we might pass this off as mere coincidence if we believed that Vespucci could have known virtually nothing of the Cabot voyage, in fact this is not the case. As already noted, early in 1498 Vespucci was working in Seville arranging supplies for Columbus's Third Voyage. He was therefore mixing in the very circles that at that time were on the receiving end of double-agent John Day/Hugh Say's 'spy' report on Cabot's 1497 voyage. And as we may recall, among the detailed information that Day supplied to Columbus was that Cabot's departure from Bristol had been in the May of 1497. Given Vespucci's unabashed claiming of Hojeda's and Coelho's voyages as his own, it scarcely strains credulity that he might have tried to do exactly the same with Cabot's, neatly blurring his deception by devices such as changing the name of the departure port from Bristol to Cadiz. The importance of claiming Cabot's departure date as his own was that it gave him total priority to claiming for himself the discovery of the mainland of the new continent. And he, more than anyone apart from Hojeda and La Cosa, would have known that John Cabot was unable to refute him.

We therefore have some grounds for believing that Vespucci was quite deliberate and calculating in claiming for himself the discovery of the new continent, however illegitimately. There is even a limited degree of justification for his claims, since he was effectively the first to go on record claiming the new continent as a New World. But even so, could he really have engineered that it should actually be named after him? And if he did, why after his Christian name?

It is at this point that it is relevant to consider our second curiosity, at the very least an extraordinary coincidence, and one which just conceivably may have been responsible for Vespucci's whole cunning idea.

Back in 1897, when Bristol was celebrating the four hundredth anniversary of Cabot's 1497 voyage, someone happened to find among the archives of Westminster Abbey an apparently misplaced, and certainly hitherto unknown roll of accounts prepared by Bristol's two Customs Collectors for the years 1496–9. This was not a full customs account, with ships, cargoes, etc, of the kind preserved in the Public Record Office. Instead it was simply a record of the Customs Collectors' expenses. An important feature was that it included for the years 1498 and '99 entries for the actual payments of John Cabot's £20 per annum pension, which Henry VII had instructed should be paid from Bristol's customs returns by the Customs Collectors [pl. 8].

The real eye-opener of the find, however, was its listing of the names of the two Bristol Customs Collectors, successors of course of the Thomas Croft who had been behind the 'Brasil' voyages. The first of these was Arthur Kemys, of passing interest mainly because, as we noted earlier, Cabot paid his rent to a John Kemys.

But the name of the other collector was Richard Ameryk – and in 1897 this discovery set English, and particularly Bristolian, imaginations leaping. Ameryk ... America ... Was it just conceivable that instead of America having been named after the shady Florentine Amerigo Vespucci, as for so long supposed, it could actually have been named after Cabot's Bristolian paymaster?

Here some considerable interest inevitably pertains to what exactly can be learned of this Richard Ameryk. He is reasonably well attested, his family, although of Welsh origin (as 'Ap Meryk') being well established in late-fifteenth-century Bristol. In the Bristol customs accounts he and a John Ameryk feature as energetic traders with Bordeaux, Spain and Portugal. In the late 1470s he was wealthy enough to lend money to the Canynges family to help them raise a ransom for Thomas Canynges, who had been kidnapped by Breton pirates (and ruthless enough to sue the same family on their failure to repay this debt).

As noted in an earlier chapter, purser John Balsall's accounts of the 1480–1 voyage of the *Trinity* to Huelva and Oran record him as shipping a quantity of cloths along with John Jay, Robert Strange, William Spencer, and others of the Bristol merchant 'mafia'. Bristol property deeds for the early 1490s show him and his wife Lucy purchasing just to the south of Bristol the manor house of Ashton Phillips and extensive surrounding lands, apparently for the benefit of their recently married daughter Joan and her serjeant-at-law husband John Brook, younger son of a Thomas Brook who had purchased William Canynges' mansion in Bristol's Redcliffe Street. The Ashton Phillips manor house, though much altered, is still extant (complete with a chantry chapel built as early as 1230) in what is

Fig.25: Memorial brass of Richard Ameryk's daughter Joan, and her husband John Brook, to be seen virtually alongside that of John Jay in the chancel of Bristol's St Mary Redcliffe church. The Latin inscription reads: 'Here lies the body of that venerable man John Brook, serjeant-at-law to that most illustrious prince of happy memory King Henry VIII and Justice of Assize for the same king in the western parts of England, and chief steward of the honourable house and monastery of the Blessed Mary of Glastonbury in the County of Somerset in which John died on the 25th day of December 1522. And near him rests Joan his wife, one of the daughters and heirs of Richard Amerike, on whose souls may God have mercy, Amen'

now the village of Long Ashton, and is today known as Lower Court Farm, the property of Mr and Mrs Weston.

As already noted, in the late 1490s Ameryk was appointed Customs Collector for Bristol, thus becoming one of the direct successors of the Thomas Croft associated with the first 'Brasil' voyages. We know also that he then became Sheriff of Bristol in 1503, and died in 1504. No known record exists of where he was buried, but his daughter Joan's memorial brass, alongside that of her husband John Brook, can be seen within a few feet of that of our old friends John and Joan Jay in the chancel of Canynges' St Mary Redcliffe church. Since this brass describes Joan as 'one of the daughters and heirs of Richard Ameryk', there is a strong inference that Ameryk had no male heir.

Intriguing in regard to this latter point is the only known merchant mark associated with the Ameryks, recorded in a special study of Bristol merchant marks made nearly a hundred years ago by antiquarian Alfred E. Hudd for the Clifton (Bristol) Antiquarian Club. In line with the lack of standardisation of English spellings before the eighteenth century the Ameryk name appears in different documents in a variety of ways, thus 'Amyreke' in the Balsall accounts, 'Ameryk' and 'Ap Meryke' in the Westminster Abbey Customs Roll; also 'Amerike' in a land conveyance. But on the merchant's seal as published by Hudd the name appears as 'Americ', returning to the initial A . . . a perfect 'America'.

Fig.26: The mysterious Ameryk merchant mark.

It is however at best an insubstantial source of association of Richard Ameryk with the naming of America, for the original seal from which Hudd drew his design has frustratingly proved

Fig.27: The name of Richard Ameryk, detail from the Bristol customs roll found in Westminster Abbey.

untraceable in recent years, and certain stylistic aspects suggest it may date from a later period.

But whatever significance may or may not be attached to Ameryk's merchant mark, quite unquestionably Richard Ameryk himself was a highly important and influential figure in Bristol at just the very time when the continent we now know as America was beginning to be reached. To Cabot, Ameryk and his fellow customs collector would have been particularly significant, directly representing Henry VII and the pension granted by the king. And as we saw earlier, from the letter of Ambassador Soncino, Cabot himself had a tendency to munificent gestures, promising to give his barber and his Burgundian colleague whole islands in the lands awaiting across the Atlantic, and the dignity of counts. So is it not within the bounds of possibility that Cabot on his 1498 expedition, having worked down to what we now know as South America, may have decided to call this impressive new territory after his Bristolian paymaster?

Of course, if he did so, we may duly expect him to have marked this name on one of his charts. But even if so, how could this piece of name-coining have become attributed to Amerigo Vespucci?

There is in fact one simple explanation, and it centres again on that elusive moment when Vespucci, Hojeda, La Cosa and members of the Cabot party may have come together at Coquibaçoa. On studying, perhaps over La Cosa's shoulder, the chart that Cabot had made, might Amerigo Vespucci's eye have happened to alight on Cabot's having given an impressively sized region the name 'America' (or perhaps 'Amerika')? And did this remarkable similarity to his own Christian name fire in him at that very moment the idea that if he claimed the whole new continent as of his own discovery, then the honour could be his? Vespucci was perhaps the one man who was both vain enough to want this, and cunning enough to try to make it happen.

Inevitably, with the paucity of our knowledge of whatever happened at Coquibaçoa, such a scenario can at best be regarded as highly speculative. Certainly Columbus suspected nothing, for as late as February 1505, little more than a year before his death, he wrote of Vespucci: 'He is a very honourable man and always desirous of pleasing me, and is determined to do everything possible for me.' Whether he would have written the same had he known that the name for the whole world of his discovery would be accorded to Vespucci rather than himself must be highly questionable.

Perhaps we may never know exactly how it all happened. And it is equally questionable whether Americans are likely to feel any more comfortable about their continent being named after a Bristol tax collector than a Florentine fraudster. What no one can deny is that, justifiably or otherwise, and despite Waldseemüller's apparent very best efforts to stifle it, the name 'America' somehow did manage to survive – and to a perpetuity that neither Richard Ameryk not the wily Amerigo could even have dared dream of.

CHAPTER 13

Columbus: The Myth Revisited

Now . . . when the day of Columbus's first landfall in the New World
is celebrated throughout the length and breadth of the Americas, his
fame and reputation may be considered secure . . .

Admiral Samuel Morison, 1974

In the light of all that we have learned perhaps it may now seem almost
surprising that the myth of Columbus as 'discoverer of America' should
ever have grown up at all.

Certainly it was a myth that not even Columbus himself believed
in at any point in his life. When, gouty and crippled with arthritis, he
died in Valladolid on May 20, 1506, neither he nor anyone else of his
time had much idea of the exalted place he would subsequently hold
in history. Such was the low esteem to which he had fallen with King
Ferdinand, and such the hollowness of his 'Grand Admiral's' title, that
the Spanish court, even though actually in Valladolid at the time, sent
no great dignitary, either ecclesiastical or lay, to attend his funeral. The
court chronicle similarly did not bother to record his passing. It took
ten years before the historian Peter Martyr set down the first known
public mention of Columbus's death in his book *Second Decade*,
published in 1516.

And as already remarked, Columbus to his very last breath went on
believing that what he had 'discovered' was not any new continent
but simply a new route to the old continent of Asia. His son Fernando
wrote that he died full of sorrow and disappointment, and certainly
what he understood of his achievements could have given him little
joy, because he had so repeatedly failed to find what he expected to
find. This was the case even on his Fourth (and final) Voyage, from
1502–4, when he actually managed to reach and explore a stretch of
true mainland of the kind that he had been seeking for so long. As
we now know, this mainland was the coasts of the Central American
countries of Honduras, Nicaragua, Costa Rica and Panama. But for

Columbus it still raised the question of where exactly were the Great Khan's trading cities of which Marco Polo had written so lavishly? Where was the fabled island of Cipango? And where were the Spice Islands? Columbus's state of mind at the end of his life has been succinctly summed up by University of California historian Dr Carl O. Sauer:

> His [Columbus's] knowledge of geographical position and celestial navigation had not improved . . . [To him] the earth was of such size that the western shores he had found were the eastern shores of Asia. Latitudes were strangely arranged, such as a Caribbean placed halfway between pole and equator. Cathay lay off to the north and west, remaining beyond the horizon as it did on the First Voyage . . . South China he had placed in Cuba and there it stayed, although Cosa and others had represented Cuba as an island . . . The Malay Peninsula – Golden Chersonese, or Aurea, as he called it – he identified with Veragua.

Yet if what we have termed the Columbus myth had not formed even in his own mind at the time of his death, it is important also to stress that it had hardly begun to take root elsewhere either. John Cabot, for instance, even though he would attract his own myth as discoverer of North America, was just as in the dark as Columbus concerning the continent he had reached on his 1497 voyage. Whatever new geographical insights he may or may not have gained from his subsequent fateful 1498 voyage, when he set out he was as convinced as Columbus that he was returning to Asia.

And just as lacking in anything approaching our concept of America was the Venetian map-maker Giovanni Contarini, who in 1506 published a world map that was the first known printed work to show at least something of what we now know as the American continent [fig.28]. Contarini drew Cuba correctly as an island, and under that name. He also correctly placed and delineated other West Indian islands discovered by Columbus. But Cipango ('Zipangu') or Japan he conceived as lying immediately due west of Cuba. To the south he drew South America as a huge island, with not a vestige of any Central American isthmus. And far to the north he indicated a long promontory of land at roughly the latitude of Newfoundland, stretching latitudinally thousands of miles westwards to join the true Asia. Quite evident is that in Contarini's mind, as in Columbus's, there was believed to be continuous ocean all the way to the Asian

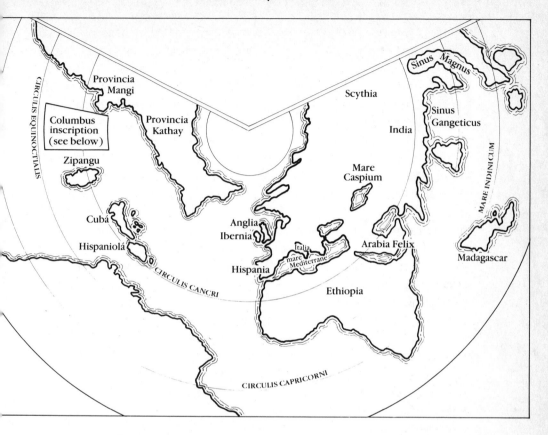

Fig. 28: Outlines of the Contarini map of 1506, after the only surviving example in the British Museum. The first *printed* map to show any part of America, it exhibits very markedly more ignorance than the Waldseemüller map of just a year later.

mainland. His conviction that it was this mainland which Columbus had found on his Fourth Voyage is quite apparent from the inscription he set alongside it:

> Christopher Columbus, Viceroy of Spain, sailing westwards, reached the Spanish islands after many hardships and dangers. Weighing anchor thence he sailed to the province called Ciamba [Marco Polo's 'Champa', today's Indo-China]. Afterwards he betook himself to this place which, as Christopher himself, that most diligent investigator of maritime things asserts, holds a great store of gold.

That Contarini, in his turn, was by no means alone in such misconceptions is evident from the fact that just a year later, in 1507, the Dutchman Johannes Ruysch published from Rome another world map as part of an edition of Ptolemy's *Geography*. In this he repeated many of Contarini's mistakes, differing mainly in omitting Cipango, apparently due to the belief that this and Hispaniola were one and the same. And what cannot be emphasised enough is that both Contarini's and Ruysch's maps actually represented mainstream thinking on the shape of the world as at the first decade of the sixteenth century. Ruysch's map in particular was one of the most influential of its time, yet neither it nor Contarini's had acquired anything approaching a true concept of America.

Ironically, by contrast the one map which did have something of a correct America concept was Waldseemüller's [pl.10], produced in exactly the same year as Ruysch's, but possibly not even circulated. Yet for Waldseemüller, America's discoverer was not Columbus but Amerigo Vespucci! How Waldseemüller with or without Vespucci managed to gain such a broadly accurate idea of America's geography, complete with Central American isthmus and another ocean to be crossed before the reaching of Asia, has to be a mystery that it is quite beyond the scope of the present book to unravel, despite some possible explanations put forward in the last chapter. After all, it was not until 1513 that the Spaniard Balboa, looking westward from a 'peak in Darien' in the midst of the Panamanian jungle, caught the first known European glimpse of the Pacific Ocean. And it was not until 1519 that Magellan actually sailed into the Pacific, after discovering and successfully negotiating the strait that bears his name. Yet Waldseemüller, arguably with Vespucci as his source, had correctly anticipated both.

But the central question still to be addressed is how, given that the very concept of America was still virtually non-existent during the sixteenth century's first decade, what we have termed the Columbus myth actually managed to come into being. It can be said with some confidence that this was already in place at least by the sixteenth century's two concluding decades for this is evident not least from the works of the great Elizabethan chronicler Richard Hakluyt, who in 1582 published *Divers Voyages touching the Discovery of America*, followed in 1589 by his master-work the *Principall Navigations, Voiages and Discoveries of the English Nation*. In the very preface to the first edition of his *Principall Navigations* Hakluyt spoke warmly and admiringly of Columbus as 'that renowned Genoese'. In the second edition of the third volume of the same he specifically introduced his subject as:

> . . . the fourth part of the world, which more commonly than properly is called America: but by the chiefest authors the New World, new, in regard of the new and late discovery thereof made by Christopher Colon, alias Columbus, a Genoese by nation in the year of grace 1492 . . .

It was in Hakluyt's interest to highlight Columbus's achievements, because a major part of his thesis was the contrasting of the Spanish royal patronage of maritime ventures with the neglect that this field had suffered at the hands of England's monarchy, the prime culprit having been Henry VIII, who on Henry VII's death in 1509 effectively abandoned his father's never more than parsimonious support of English transatlantic explorations.

Hakluyt also made quite clear that he had quite definitely read Columbus's published biography as written by his son Fernando, for he quoted several extracts from it. He thus automatically imbibed and then retailed to an English audience some of the exaggerated ideas that the snobbish Fernando had injected into his account of his father's life, along with the important geographical correction that his father had reached the continent subsequently to be known as America. Besides Fernando's biography Hakluyt might have availed himself of the first three volumes of Peter Martyr's history of the New World, complete with an account of Columbus's voyages, that had been available in English since 1555, and in Latin since 1516. He might also have come across Gonzalo de Oviedo's history of the Indies, published in 1535, or some of the early translations of Columbus's First Voyage letter to Ferdinand and Isabella.

It is quite evident then that the prime vehicle for the coming into being of the Columbus myth was the power of the printing press, Columbus not only having been fortunate enough to have been born in the very decade when Gutenberg brought European printing into being, but doubly fortunate in having had around him people who recognised the value of preserving and promulgating his achievements via the new technology.

In the case of the English voyages, by contrast, whatever achievements and human dramas had transpired during these seem scarcely to

Fig. 29: Sebastian Cabot, engraving after a lost contemporary portrait.

have been set in writing at all, let alone committed to publication. It was already far too late in the sixteenth century when Hakluyt specifically devoted himself to trying to rectify this situation. And as he wrote (to England's Lord High Admiral), in the dedicatory epistle to his second edition, some of the documents he had brought to light had:

> long ... lain miserably scattered in musty corners, and [been] carelessly hidden in misty darkness, and would very likely for the greatest part ... have been buried in perpetual oblivion.

Even more lamentable was the huge proportion of potentially highly informative material that was never set into writing at all, one of many notable culprits in this regard having been John Cabot's son Sebastian. In the wake of his father's death Sebastian had his own long and thoroughly interesting career as a navigator, certainly making a journey to Newfoundland under the English flag in the early 1500s, and in 1526 leading an expedition under the Spanish flag to the South American River Plate, followed by living on in England, advising on a variety of projects, well into the late 1550s.

Yet not only did Sebastian fail to set in writing his own adventures, he even stooped so low as to try to pass off his father's achievements as his own. Around the 1530s he went on record as lying to a Mantuan gentleman that his father had died as early as 1492, and that therefore he had led the 1497 voyage himself, purportedly having been specially equipped by Henry VII with 'two caravels' for this purpose. In the light of our earlier, somewhat similar insights with regard to Columbus and Amerigo Vespucci, such an inability to tell the truth seems to have been an almost standard part of the early explorers' psychological make-up.

If only others associated with the Bristolian or other voyages had left even the simplest memorials, such as anything along the lines of the diary kept by the previously mentioned seventeenth-century surgeon James Yonge. But in late-fifteenth/early-sixteenth century England no such vogue appears to have begun to develop.

In this regard, a typical example of the frustratingly slim data that has survived from the years even subsequent to the 'Brasil' voyages and Cabot is a lengthy letters patent document dated March 19, 1501 by which Henry VII granted three Bristol merchants, Richard Warde, Thomas Asshehurst and John Thomas, together with three Portuguese, the 'right to seek out and discover . . . some islands lying in our sphere of influence'. Virtually the only indication that any related voyage ever took place is a chronicle mention from around 1501 of the bringing to Henry VII's court of:

> three men, taken in the New found land . . . [who] were clothed in animal skins, and ate raw flesh, and spoke a language that no one could understand.

Clearly these men must have been either Beothuk Indians or Eskimoes, and they were reported to be still at the Palace of Westminster two years later, now dressed in English clothes, and virtually indistinguishable from Englishmen. Yet we are told nothing of the specific voyages from which they were brought back, nor of the coasts explored, nor the dangers encountered, nor the contacts with native peoples made, just as we have no knowledge of whatever voyage it was, in 1503, from which someone brought back as a present for King Henry VII: 'a brasil bow and 2 red arrows'.

Similarly, while from dry Public Record Office documents we know the earliest officially recorded Bristol cod-fishing voyage to Newfoundland to have been in 1504 in a French-built vessel, the *Gabriel*, again the human minutiae of this expedition and a preceding one in the same vessel in 1502 (but with no record of any cod cargo), have been seemingly totally lost to us. This is all the more regrettable because this 1502 voyage appears to have been personally accompanied by two of the Bristol merchants recorded as backing it, Robert Thorne I and Hugh Elyot. Although these men were arguably literate enough to have kept a journal of their experiences, sadly all we have as even the merest hint that they actually sailed on the venture is a cryptic remark in a letter written as late as 1527 by Robert Thorne's son, Robert Thorne the second. In what was mainly an urging of a search for a North-West Passage through America to Asia, Thorne happened to add, by way of a personal touch:

> this inclination or desire of [discover]ing I inherited from my father, who with an[other] merchant of Bristol named Hugh Elyot [were] the discoverers of the Newfoundland . . .

It should be noted that in the fifteenth and sixteenth centuries the word 'discoverers' did not have its definitive present-day meaning of first finders of a hitherto unknown land, hence the reason for the omission of this quotation from earlier discussion. But the absolutely galling feature of this passage is that Robert Thorne the second (founder of the still extant Bristol Grammar School), did not even bother to put a date to his father's still pioneering voyage. Our main reason for supposing it to have been 1502 is because this is the one year in which documentary sources record a definite voyage associated with Thorne the elder and Elyot, and also allow a gap in their mercantile activities that would be consistent with such a period of absence from Bristol. It is precisely this English lack of concern to set down proper first-person or even third-person narratives of the earliest voyages to America, following on from the initially justifiable secrecy that followed the expulsion from Iceland, that has left us with so few glimpses of what happened, and has thus allowed the Columbus myth to take the hold that it has.

But given that there really were Bristolian voyages before Columbus, is it possible even now that more evidence may yet be found? In this regard there can perhaps be no more encouraging example than recent findings concerning early-sixteenth-century whaling expeditions on the part of the Basques, the enigmatic non-Indo-European people who for many thousands of years have inhabited the environs of the western Pyrenees.

During the thirteenth and fourteenth centuries the Biscayans or Basques are known to have hunted black right whales close to home in the Bay of Biscay, this very bay having actually been named after them. Then when in the fifteenth century the right whales moved much further out into the Atlantic (seemingly as a result of the same oceanic changes which caused herring to move out of the Baltic), the Basques were obliged to follow, giving rise to the question of just how early they, like their Bristolian counterparts, may or may not have reached the shores of America.

During the 1960s this enigma so intrigued a young historical researcher, Selma Barkham, then working for the Canadian government, that she devoted ten years to learning the Basque language and researching old Basque wills, lawsuits and similar legal documents in archives at Oñate in northern Spain. She thereby built up a highly detailed picture of Basque whaling activities, the ships, their owners, their captains and crews, how many whales they killed, etc, and with added guidance from a set of sixteenth-century sailing directions was able to pinpoint no fewer than twelve previously unknown Basque whaling ports on Labrador.

Then it was the turn of the archaeologists, and at one of the designated sites, Red Bay, Labrador, only just across the Belle Isle Strait from L'Anse aux Meadows, a wealth of data corroborative of and complementary to Mrs Barkham's documentary researches soon began to come to light. Working underwater, archaeologists found not only concentrations of whale bones, clear evidence of a one-time whaling port, but also the well-preserved wreck of a Basque ship, identifiable from Selma Barkham's research as the *San Juan*, recorded to have sunk in a storm in 1565, just as it was about to leave for Spain laden with casks of whale oil.

Nearby were the remains of several smaller boats, including a complete *chalupa*, the type of vessel in which teams of up to seven Basques went on the dangerous hunting expeditions for whales. On land the archaeologists found the traces of several shore stations featuring stone-built try works where the whale carcases were reduced to marketable oil, also a cemetery with the skeletons of 140 whalers. Although in the event nothing was found indicative that the Basques had been in Labrador significantly earlier than the mid-sixteenth century, historical understanding of the whole business of early whaling was immensely enriched.

Accordingly it would be a most exciting prospect if something equivalent to Selma Barkham's documentary work with the Basques could as precisely pinpoint any of the actual sites on Newfoundland where the earliest 'Brasil voyage' Bristolians might have set up their cod-fishing stations. And it was in fact thinking along these very lines which prompted the Bristolian maritime engineer and historian Henry Forbes Taylor to scour the late-fifteenth-century Bristol customs records in the hope that appropriate clues might emerge. As mentioned earlier, Taylor was working on the hypothesis that voyages recorded as to 'Ireland' in the accounts were in fact secret cod-fishing expeditions to Newfoundland, but he was prevented from fully developing his researches by his death in 1976.

Unfortunately, however, the customs records which so fascinated Taylor are nowhere near as complete or far-reaching as the Basque documents which proved so helpful to Selma Barkham. From Taylor's notes, as kindly made available to me by his widow Caroline, it is evident that if he had pursued his enquiries to their logical conclusion, he would almost certainly himself have come to realise the weakness of the fragmentary nature of the Bristol customs records, and probably have turned his researches in potentially more profitable directions.

Similarly there are somewhat lesser hopes for quite such illuminating archaeological finds for the Bristolians as for the Basques at Red Bay. Not only are the bones of the cod vastly less conspicuous and long-lasting than those of the whale, on Labrador the Basques used durable stone as a construction material, whereas in the fishing villages of Newfoundland virtually everything, even to this day, is made of more perishable and readily disposable wood.

Nonetheless there are grounds for at least a very mild amount of optimism. Although Newfoundland is nearly as large as the British Isles, and simply riddled with inlets suitable for cod-fishing harbours, Professor James Tuck of the island's Memorial University, who worked on the Basque excavations in Labrador, has already found and begun to investigate some definite surviving remains of early Newfoundland fishery bases, most notably both on land and underwater at Ferryland on Newfoundland's south-eastern or Avallon peninsula. The most permanent materials found so far have been fragments of English West Country pottery, some encouragingly from the late-sixteenth century. But of course the truly fascinating development would be if anything of distinctively earlier date came to light, particularly if this could be matched to wares known to have been in use in late-fifteenth-century Bristol.

Similarly fascinating, indeed spectacular, would be the finding, anywhere off Newfoundland or its environs, of the wreck of an identifiably Bristol-registered ship of the 1480s. The location of such a wreck would of necessity be a needle-in-a-haystack exercise, Newfoundland's surrounding seabed being littered with literally hundreds of wrecks of all periods, their investigation and recording vastly beyond the resources of the island's few specialist underwater archaeologists. But the island does have an enthusiastic underwater team led by former Bristolian biologist and diver, Janette Ginns. And given the finding, as recently as 1978, of the Basque *San Juan*, the dream is by no means an impossible one.

There are also possible sites to investigate further afield, as at Louisbourg on nearby Nova Scotia, where in the last century a bombarda cannon of late-fifteenth/early-sixteenth-century design [fig.30] was fished from the harbour. As yet no one has determined whether this was simply tossed overboard as unwanted ballast, or whether it might have come from an accompanying wreck of an early English ship even now waiting to be retrieved from the mud of Louisbourg's harbour (a harbour perhaps significantly known by its earliest French settlers as the 'Porte aux Anglais', or Port of the English). Light could possibly be shed by the cannon's metal being scientifically analysed and traced to a particular country or perhaps even to a specific town of manufacture – Bristol, it being remembered, having had its own foundry during the fifteenth century. Certainly this somewhat neglected artefact, not even on display in Louisbourg, richly merits some further study.

Further afield still, though certainly no less spectacular, would of course be the finding almost anywhere around America's Caribbean coast (but particularly on Colombia's bleak Guajira peninsula, the

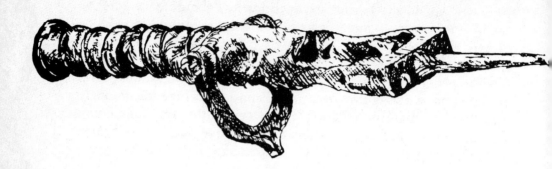

Fig. 30: Cannon of very early type found in the sea off Louisbourg, Nova Scotia.

former Coquibaçoa) of the remains of any ship or ships that could be firmly identified with Cabot's voyage of 1498, perhaps accompanied by the graves of identifiably English fifteenth-century seamen. Something of this kind could provide the real proof that Hojeda, La Cosa and Vespucci genuinely did meet up with that mysterious party of Englishmen, just as Navarrete claimed.

'Dream' discoveries such as these – and other, documentary ones could be mentioned, such as the manuscript from which Navarrete drew his 'certain Englishmen' information, or a copy of the *Inventio Fortunatae,* or a set of Balsall-type accounts for a cod-fishing voyage – are the sort of future finds that would help corroborate so much of what we have been able to glean concerning pre-Columban voyages to America by English mariners. The fact that such discoveries are still needed does of course underline that all that we have found so far admittedly still lacks that degree of proof that was so conclusively provided in the case of the Norse, for instance, by the Ingstads' excavations at L'Anse aux Meadows.

But this is not to downplay the major evidential value of what has been established, and from the most modest and chancily preserved of documentary materials. Thus for instance if John Jay had not happened to have as his brother-in-law the inveterate scribbler William Worcestre, we might never have known that Bristolians had begun westward voyages of discovery at least as early as 1480. If some unknown common informer had not had a grudge against Bristol Customs Collector Thomas Croft, we might never have learned that the *Trinity* of Bristol loaded with salt, as if for cod-fishing purposes, ventured to 'Brasil' as early as the following year. If it were not for the chance preservation of a set of the *Trinity*'s accounts, and Purser Balsall's conscientious noting of a payment to Spain's La Rábida friary, we might never have discovered how easily Columbus could have found out about the Bristolian 'Brasil' voyages. Not least, but for a casual remark by Dr Hayward Keniston to Dr Louis Vigneras at Simancas in 1955, the John Day letter, by far the most important piece of evidence in this book, might very likely still be slumbering on in the Spanish national archives, quite unknown and unrecognised. Indeed, without this single document we would still be lacking the vital corroboration not only that the Bristolians really had reached their 'Brasil', but also that Columbus knew all about their activities, a simple but stunning fact that even on its own puts his voyage of 1492 into a very significantly less heroic and epoch-changing mould.

It deserves repeating that our aim has most emphatically not been to try to destroy the Columbus myth simply to give the Bristolians glory in his place. Not only were they arguably even more ignorant than Columbus concerning what they had found, but as we have earlier established the Norse most definitely preceded them in Newfoundland, and Irish monks may well have preceded the Norse. And, quite deliberately, we have not even attempted to consider certain other alternative 'discoverer' claimants, such as the Welsh Prince Madoc who is very shakily supposed to have voyaged to America in the twelfth century and left behind a tribe of Welsh-speaking American 'Indians'; or the Portuguese Vaz Corte Real, whom Portuguese historians have somewhat more seriously contended to have reached America as early as 1472. Our overriding concern has been to show, even on the basis of the Bristol evidence alone, that Columbus's voyage of 1492 was an altogether less 'out of the blue' affair than has for so long been popularly supposed.

The Columbus myth thereby lies, if not shattered, at least very substantially weakened, in addition to the knocks it had earlier received in the light of the Ingstads' Newfoundland findings. And in the end this raises one final and very topical question: whether, in the light of all we have learned, there is therefore justification for in any way celebrating in 1992 the five hundredth anniversary of Columbus's arrival on the island he called San Salvador? As we are about to see, there are in fact some independent and even more compelling reasons why the world should not.

CHAPTER 14

The True Significance of 1492

While it is to be hoped that we have established beyond reasonable doubt that America had, in Oscar Wilde's phrase, 'often been discovered before' by 1492, nonetheless Columbus's arrival in that year did mark a certain watershed.

Naked as the Arawak Indians were who greeted him,it would be wrong to paint the America at which Columbus had unknowingly arrived as in any way a Garden of Eden. Both on the islands and throughout the continent itself there was a mixture of tribes rarely totally at peace with each other. Even the friendly Arawaks whom Columbus met in the West Indies had comparatively recently dispossessed a people more primitive than themselves, and were in their turn the subject of raids by more war-like neighbours, the Caribs. The Incas had built up their empire by repression. The Aztecs preyed on other peoples to satisfy their religion's seemingly insatiable demands for human sacrifice. On the southern continent cannibalism was also widespread.

Yet despite these human imperfections, in general populations had flourished, and a certain all-American state of order existed that, insofar as we can be sure of anything of pre-Columbian discoveries, had not even begun to be threatened either by St Brendan's Irish monks, or by the would-be Norse settlers, or by the Bristolian cod fishermen.

But there was something altogether different in the wind that day of October 12, 1492 when Christopher Columbus's *Santa Maria*, *Pinta* and *Niña* dropped anchor off the island that he would name San Salvador, and when he and his men rowed to the shore for their first encounter with that island's inhabitants. With hindsight the die for the future was already cast at the moment that Columbus, before even trying to communicate with the islanders, lost no time in proudly planting flags in the name of the Spanish crown.

Certainly his intentions were yet more evident when on the very first day of his arrival he wrote in his Journal, for the benefit of Ferdinand and Isabella back in Spain, that the natives:

> . . . should be good and intelligent servants, for I see that they say very quickly everything that is said to them; and I believe that they would become Christians very easily, for it seemed to me that they had no religion. Our Lord pleasing, at the time of my departure I will take six of them from here to Your Highnesses in order that they may learn to speak.

Two days later he reported further:

> . . . these people are very naive about weapons, as Your Highnesses will see from seven that I caused to be taken in order to carry them away to you and to learn our language and to return them. Except that, whenever Your Highnesses may command, all of them can be taken to Castile or held captive in this same island, because with 50 men all of them could be held in subjection and can be made to do whatever one might wish.

By the time he had arrived on the much larger island of Hispaniola he was even more confident, reporting in his Journal for December 16:

> May Your Highnesses . . . believe that this island and all the others are as much yours as Castile; for nothing is lacking except settlement and ordering the Indians to do whatever Your Highnesses may wish. Because I with the people that I bring with me, who are not many, go about in all these islands without danger, for I have already seen three of these sailors go ashore where there was a crowd of these Indians, and all would flee without the Spaniards wanting to do harm. They do not have arms and they are all naked, and of no skill in arms, and so very cowardly that a thousand would not stand against three. And so they are fit to be ordered about and made to work, plant and do everything that may be needed, and build towns and be taught customs, and to go about clothed.

As some mitigation of this clearly colonial attitude on Columbus's part it is important to realize that for most Europeans of his time it was an essentially universal rule that any who were not Christians needed to be made Christians, and forced if necessary to accept European 'Christian' customs. However unfair and illiberal we might regard this from our near twenty-first-century perspective, it is important to recognize that it was little different from the way that we even now, and for scarce better reasons, would try to impose our 'customs' on anyone who tried to walk around our high streets and into our homes in the same state of nakedness in which Columbus found America's natives.

But what is almost impossible for us today to comprehend is the sheer enormity of the death sentence which this European colonial attitude, combined with the physical diseases which its holders brought with them, spelled for that so diverse and colourful array of peoples which we earlier sketched as inhabiting the American continent at the time of Columbus's arrival in 1492.

The first place to witness this, at least on any scale, was Hispaniola, where the administratively weak Columbus regime, which as we earlier mentioned was terminated by his forced removal in irons in 1500, was followed by that of Nicolás de Ovando, an efficient but oppressive Spaniard who regarded all natives as expendable. From Bartolomé de Las Casas, the Dominican friar to whom, as remarked earlier, we owe the preservation of most of Columbus's First Voyage journal, we learn that Columbus himself was indeed horrified by what happened to Hispaniola's natives following his removal from the island, apparently complaining to King Ferdinand in 1504 that: 'he is informed that six out of seven of its Indians have died since he left the island.'

From his personal observations on Hispaniola Las Casas estimated that between 1494 and 1508, and therefore inclusive of the Columbus brothers' administration, more than three million of the island's natives died of violence, were sent to Castile as slaves, or expired from being forced to work on Spanish mining and agricultural projects. As he exclaimed in all too genuine revulsion:

> Who of those born in future centuries will believe this? I myself who am writing this and saw it and know most about it can hardly believe that such was possible.

Even more horrifying is the fact that what Las Casas saw (and some have had the gall to accuse him of exaggerating), was simply the curtain-raiser to a pattern to be repeated among people after people of America's native inhabitants for centuries to come.

Thus within forty years of the naked and unguarded welcome of Columbus by the Arawak islanders of the West Indies – islanders who in his more grateful moments, as after the *Santa Maria*'s foundering, he described as 'an affectionate people, free from avarice . . . [who] love their neighbours as themselves . . . and are always smiling' — every one of these had been wiped out by enslavement and European diseases, to be replaced in time by hardier black slaves from Africa, who would become known in their turn, with compounded incongruity, as 'West Indians'.

In 1519 Hernán Cortes and his conquistadors marched into the Aztec empire, and seeing only the work of the devil in the Aztec rite of human sacrifice, considered themselves fully justified in near obliterating within little more than two years, virtually the entire rich fabric of the Aztec culture, inclusive of its literature. As recorded in the Annals of Tlatelolco, written in 1528, and one of the few Aztec documents to survive the Spanish destructive zeal:

> . . . all this happened among us. We saw it. We lived through it with an astonishment worthy of tears and of pity for the pain we suffered.
>
> On the roads lie broken shafts and torn hair, houses are roofless, homes are stained red, worms swarm in the streets, walls are splattered with brains,
>
> The water is reddish, like dyed water . . .
>
> The wells are crammed with adobe bricks . . .
>
> We chewed on hard tzompantli wood, brackish zacatl fodder, chunks of adobe, lizards, vermin, dust and worms
>
> We had a single price; there was a standard price for a youth, a priest, a boy and a young girl. The maximum price for a slave amounted to only two handfuls of maize, to only ten tortillas . . .

Further south, in Guatamala the Mayans' religion was much more moderate than that of the Aztecs, yet this did not save them from Cortes's lieutenant Pedro de Alvarado who in 1524 meted upon them the same overwhelming subjugation. In 1531 it was the turn of the Incas of Peru, destroyed by Pizarro and his small contingent of Spanish.

In fairness Pope Paul III in 1537 pontificated that America's natives should at least be considered human, and there were the occasional Europeans who cultivated good relations with native American tribes, as in the case of the seventeenth-century Frenchman Samuel de Champlain, founder of Quebec, who formed an alliance with the Algonquins and Hurons against their more warlike neighbours the Iroquois. Yet in 1665 Champlain's fellow countryman the Marquis de Tracy decimated the Iroquois with the same ferocity that had typified the Spanish. And however much more advanced and 'civilized'

Europeans became during the eighteenth and nineteenth centuries, this did not extend to their treatment of America's native peoples.

Typical was the fate of the handsome and peaceable Beothuks of Newfoundland. Although European fishermen mostly returned to their own countries at the end of each season, and rarely seem to have caused the Beothuks much harm, there were renegade Europeans, often fugitives from justice, who took to the woods in Newfoundland's north, living from hunting and trapping. For these any Beothuks they came across, women and children inclusive, were regarded as good for little better than target practice.

Nor, to the shame of Newfoundland's British administration, was there even any law to stop such practices. A manuscript preserved in Newfoundland's archives records the last years of settlers' wanton butchery of the Beothuks, sometimes involving the massacre of 400 at a time, so that by 1823 there were only 17 left throughout the whole island. Even in that year, in one typical incident a Beothuk father and daughter were gunned down by two unprovoked trappers. By 1829 the entire tribe passed into extinction when the last woman survivor, Shananditti, died of tuberculosis in a St John's hospital.

No better were attitudes on the mainland United States, even on the part of its newly independent and supposedly egalitarian government. In general native Americans had no concept of land as personal property. This belonged to the Great Spirit, and was shared in common. Those fruits they took from it were regarded with reverence, rather than with any sense of exploitation. But land acquisition and exploitation were very much the preoccupations of those Europeans who began to spread across the continent with increasing vigour during the late-eighteenth and early-nineteenth centuries.

So when these Europeans and their white 'American' descendants began to cast covetous eyes on the good cotton-producing country of the Mississippi delta, those native tribes camped on it simply had to go. With the utmost despatch the backwoodsman president Andrew Jackson pushed through Congress a bill requiring the Choctaws, the Creeks, the Chickasaws and the Cherokees all to be forced off their ancestral lands and moved westwards, creating a 'trail of tears' during which more than a quarter of all Cherokees died along the way.

When in the 1860s the white 'Americans' wanted lands in the environs of Arizona, the United States government simply sent an army under the Kentucky frontiersman Kit Carson to terrorize the

Navajo, and to force them to move elsewhere. After the destruction of their homes, sheep and crops, 8,000 Navajo were forcibly marched into Mexico on what has passed into tribal memory as the 'Long Walk'.

Then it was the turn of the Sioux. To move them away from their traditional lands it was government-approved policy to exterminate the huge herds of bison that grazed the Great Plains, thus robbing the Sioux of their main food supply. Although they were granted a title to Dakota's Black Hills by a treaty of 1868, no sooner had gold been found in these hills than this treaty was nullified nine years later. Understandable resistance by the Sioux was finally and most ruthlessly crushed in 1890 when the US Seventh Cavalry massacred 200 Sioux men, women and children in what was euphemistically known as the 'Battle' of Wounded Knee.

All this – and a similar catalogue could be recounted of South America – offers but a small sampling of the heavy burden of crime against humanity that began with the inception of Columbus's colonial attitudes in 1492. From America's native peoples Europeans not only looted all gold, silver, gems and usable land they could lay their hands on, they also gained corn, chocolate, coffee, tomatoes, potatoes, lima beans, cassava, guava, papaya, avocado, alpaca wool, mahogany and other valuable woods, the turkey, quinine, tobacco and rubber. In return they began centuries of genocide on a scale altogether more vast, and little less brutal, than the Nazi holocaust. It has to be doubtful whether any discoverer, even Columbus, Cabot or Vespucci, vain and gold-seeking though they all undoubtedly were, would have wished to claim such a title if they could have known even a fraction of its terrible legacy.

The tragedy is that even today the lessons have still not been learned. One continual reminder, during the writing of this book, has been pleas for justice on the part of the present-day native tribes of Canada. In the United States the native peoples are still second-class citizens, often forced to live far from their ancestral lands, amidst a society with values alien to theirs, as mere side-show freaks for the stares of the people who robbed their ancestors of all they held sacred. Even worse, in the rainforests of Brazil the old destructive process goes on, as Brazil's last substantial surviving native tribe, the Yanomami, culturally strikingly close to the island Arawaks met by Columbus, struggle for survival against hordes of incoming gold-miners, while the very environment that has given them shelter and sustenance is wantonly hacked down around them.

If this book has a message, it is therefore that not only was Columbus most certainly *not* the first European to arrive on American shores, there is actually very little justification for anyone to celebrate his arrival even if he was. All too soon the fragile near-Eden that he discovered tasted the bitterest fruits of the European experience. The only true cause for celebration in 1992 would be if this horrifying and five-centuries-long rape of the American continent and its native peoples could at last be brought finally and utterly to a halt.

Notes & References

For full publishing details of all books mentioned in the Notes & References, see the Bibliography

Introduction

p.1 '. . . the Bahaman island he named San Salvador'. This phraseology is deliberate, because the San Salvador or Watlings Island shown in present-day maps of the West Indies (and featuring no fewer than four historic sites claimed as those of Columbus's first landfall), is not necessarily the true island at which Columbus first arrived on October 12, 1492. Several candidates have been suggested, including Grand Turk, Conception, Plana Cays, Egg, East Caicos, Cat Island, etc. Whichever island it was, Columbus reported that its natives knew it as Guanahani. In 1882 Captain Gustavus Vasa Fox, assistant secretary to the US Navy at the time of President Abraham Lincoln, suggested the now uninhabited and rarely visited Samana Cay, some 70 miles south-east of San Salvador, as the true Guanahani (G.V.Fox 'An Attempt to Solve the Problem of the First Landing Place of Columbus in the New World', United States of America, *Coast and Geodetic Survey Report for 1880*, Appendix no.18). Fox's theory has recently been very cogently revived by two *National Geographic* specialists, Joseph Judge and Luis Marden. See Joseph Judge, 'Our Search for the True Columbus Landfall', *National Geographic*, vol. 170, no.5, November 1986. Even more recently, however, a strong argument in favour of Grand Turk has been advanced by Josiah Marvel and Robert H.Power, 'In Quest of Where America Began: The Case for Grand Turk', in *American History Illustrated*, Jan/Feb 1991, pp.48–69.

p.2 Columbus's Journal. For the most authoritative and accurate English language translation, with accompanying original Spanish text, see Oliver Dunn and James E.Kelley, Jr, *The Diario of Christopher Columbus's First Voyage to America 1492–1493*. All quotations from the Journal, as given later in this book, derive from Dunn & Kelley.

p.3 Fernando Columbus's biography. For an English language edition, see Benjamin Keen (trans.), *The Life of the Admiral Christopher Columbus by his son Ferdinand*.

p.5 Journal quotations. In making his transcriptions, Las Casas set these in the third person, and this is the way they appear in Dunn & Kelley's translation,

191

op.cit. I have, however, returned them to the original first person to suit the context in which they are used here.

p.5   Compass card story. This derives from a now lost letter which Columbus wrote to Ferdinand and Isabella from Hispaniola in January 1495. This is quoted by Fernando Columbus in the fourth chapter of his biography. For a commentary see Admiral Samuel E.Morison, *Admiral of the Ocean Sea*, p.17. How Columbus doctored the compass is not entirely clear.

Chapter 1

p.8   American Indian anthropology. For an excellent introduction to the anthropology of native Americans, see particularly Robert F.Spencer, Jesse D.Jennings et al., *The Native Americans*.

p.10   Human entry to America as early as 32,000 years ago? Professor Niède Guidon's findings are reported in N.Guidon & G.Delibrias, 'Carbon-14 dates point to man in the Americas 32,000 years ago', *Nature* vol.321, 19 June 1986, pp.769–71.

p.11   Isolation or Diffusion? For the arguments of Thor Heyerdahl, see his *Early Man and the Ocean*; also his contribution to Geoffrey Ashe et al., *The Quest for America*.

p.12   The *Ra II* voyage. The full background story of this voyage is told in Thor Heyerdahl's *The Ra Expeditions*.

p.12   The Phoenician circumnavigation of Africa. See Herodotus, *The Histories*, A.de Selincourt (trans.), p.255 ff.:

> As for Libya [i.e.Africa], we know that it is washed on all sides by the sea except where it joins Asia, as was first demonstrated, so far as our knowledge goes, by the Egyptian king Necho, who after calling off the construction of the canal between the Nile and the Arabian gulf, sent out a fleet manned by a Phoenician crew with orders to sail west-about and return to Egypt and the Mediterranean by way of the Straits of Gibraltar. The Phoenicians sailed from the Arabian gulf into the southern ocean, and every autumn put in at some convenient spot on the Libyan [i.e.African] coast, sowed a patch of ground, and waited for next year's harvest. Then, having got their grain, they put to sea again, and after two full years rounded the Pillars of Hercules in the course of the third, and returned to Egypt.

The Necho referred to seems to have been the twenty-sixth dynasty Pharaoh Necho II, who reigned 610–595 BC, and therefore not overly long before Herodotus's own time. He is known to have attempted to build a canal between the Nile and the Red Sea, indicative of his serious interest in maritime matters, and the fact that the voyage is described as over two years long, inclusive of protracted stops, certainly has credibility for the 15,000-mile round trip that would be required of a circumnavigation of Africa.

p.13 Pinzón and the Vatican Library document. After both Pinzón and Columbus were dead there took place various lawsuits in Spain, at one of which, held in Seville in 1515, several witnesses answered in the affirmative when asked if they knew of Pinzón and the Vatican Library document. For background and documentary sources, see William Giles Nash, *America: The True History of its Discovery*.

p.13 The Parahyba inscription. This was an inscribed stone tablet supposedly unearthed by a slave at Ouso Alto in north-east Brazil during the early 1870s. The original, if it ever existed, has never been made available to scholars. According to Professor Cyrus H.Gordon's translation of the transcription:

> We are sons of Canaan from Sidon, the city of the king. Commerce has cast us on this distant shore, a land of mountains. We set [sacrificed] a youth for the exalted gods and goddesses in the eighteenth year of Hiram, our mighty king. We embarked from Ezion-Geber into the Red Sea and voyaged with ten ships. We were at sea together for two years around the land belonging to Ham [Africa] but were separated by a storm [literal translation: 'from the hand of Baal'] and we were no longer with our companions. So we have come here, twelve men and three women, on a new shore which I, the Admiral, control. But auspiciously may the exalted gods and goddesses favour us!

Gordon has argued that the inscription is in a form of Canaanite writing no forger could have known about in the 1870s. But his interpretation has been vigorously contested by Professor Frank M.Cross of Harvard University. There was a lively correspondence on the subject in the *New York Times* and *Washington Post*, 16–19 May, 1968.

p.13 Chaco canyon astronomical clock. See: 'The Anasazi: Riddles in the Ruins', *National Geographic*, vol.162, no.5, November 1982, pp.580–1.

p.14 Parallels between Mongolian peoples and those of north-west America. See F. Boas, 'Relationships between North-West America and North-East Asia' in D. Jenness (ed.), *The American Aborigines: Their Origin and Antiquity*.

p.14 Hwui Shan. See E.P.Vining, *An Inglorious Columbus, or Evidence that Hwui Shan and a Party of Buddhist Monks from Afghanistan Discovered America in the Fifth Century AD*; also C.G. Leland, *Fusang, or the Discovery of America by Chinese Buddhist Priests in the Fifth Century*.

p.15 Mexican chronicler Tezozomoc. This is from the *Cronica Mexicana*, Chapter 108, as translated in D.G. Brinton, *Hero Myths . . .*, p.138.

p.15 Cortès, *Carta Segunda*. This is also quoted in Brinton, op.cit., p.140.

p.16 Written books of the Aztecs. For a detailed account of what has been lost of the literature of the native peoples of Mexico and the Yucatan, see Leo Deuel, *Testaments of Time*, Chapters XXIII-XXV.

Chapter 2

p.18 Translation from *Landnámabók*. This derives from Gwyn Jones, *The Norse Atlantic Saga*.

p.19 Irish monks' house on Greenland. For the best account of this, see Farley Mowat, *West Viking*, pp.48ff. There is an extensive literature relating to artefacts and inscriptions thought to be of early Irish travellers to America. See for instance James Tuck and Robert McGhee, 'Did the medieval Irish visit Newfoundland?'; also Warren E.Duliere, 'Did Irishmen discover America?' in *Wonderful West Virginia*, June 1986

p.21 Translation from the *Navigatio Sancti Brendani*. This and subsequent translations are derived from the synthesis of the Brendan narratives given in Appendix I of Tim Severin's *The Brendan Voyage*. This same work also, of course, provides full details of the Severin *Brendan* voyage of 1976–7.

p.25 Archaeology of the early Norse settlements on Greenland. The most authoritative work is K. Fischer-Møller, *The Mediaeval Norse Settlements in Greenland*, but for an excellent popular account see Helge Ingstad, *Land under the Pole Star*.

p.25 The Greenlanders' Saga (*Grœnlendinga Saga*). This was set in writing c.1190, and is included in the famous codex *Flateyjarbók* compiled in the late 1380s. There is an excellent translation of this and other sagas into modern English by Jones, op.cit.; also Magnus Magnusson and Hermann Pálsson's, *The Vinland Sagas*.

p.28 Journal of James Yonge. This provides some fascinating insights into sailing voyages to Newfoundland in the seventeenth century. For an excellent edited version of this, see *The Journal of James Yonge, Plymouth Surgeon (1647–1721)*, F.N.L. Poynter (ed.). The reference to wild grapes occurs on p.58 of this edition.

p.28 Newfoundland's flora. For pollen analyses showing that wild grapes have never grown in Newfoundland during at least the last 2,500 years, see Anthony M.Davis, 'Modern pollen spectra from the tundra-boreal forest transition in northern Newfoundland, Canada', *Boreas* 9, 1980, pp.89–100. Also relevant is F.K. Hare, 'The climate of the island of Newfoundland: a geographical analysis', *Geographical Bulletin* 3, 36–88. I am indebted to Dr Birgitta Wallace, staff archaeologist, Canadian Parks Service, for much helpful information on this point.

p.28 Vinland Map. For the scholarly arguments in favour of the map's authenticity, see R.A. Skelton, Thomas E. Marston & George D. Painter, *The Vinland Map and the Tartar Relation*.

p.29 Dr McCrone and the Vinland Map. See, W.C. McCrone, 'Chemical Study of the Vinland Map'; Report to Yale University Library; Yale University,

Newhaven, Connecticut, 1974. The Crocker Nuclear Laboratory's refutation of this, by T.A. Cahill, R.N. Schwab et al., 'The Vinland Map Revisited: New Compositional Evidence on its Inks and Parchment', was published in *Analytical Chemistry* 1987, 59, pp.829–33. McCrone's response 'The Vinland Map' followed in *Analytical Chemistry* 1988, pp.1009–18.

p.30 Ingstad excavations at L'Anse aux Meadows. See Helge and Anne Stine Ingstad, *The Norse Discovery of America* in two volumes.

p.31 Post-Ingstad excavations at L'Anse aux Meadows. See Birgitta Wallace 'The L'Anse aux Meadows Site', appendix VII, in Jones, op.cit., pp.285–304. In answer to a personal enquiry by the author on the subject of the butternuts, Dr Wallace responded in a letter dated December 12, 1990: 'Concerning butternuts (*Juglans cinerea*) found at L'Anse aux Meadows, three such nuts were found in the sedge peat fen bordering the terrace with the Norse buildings. The nuts occured in three separate locations, but in all three cases they were associated with the Norse deposits of worked wood.'

p.32 Skraelings. Erik the Red's saga described these as 'small (dark) ill-favoured men . . . [who] had ugly hair on their heads. They had big eyes and were broad in the cheeks.' This information is too sparse to identify with any certainty who they may have been. Since the Beothuks of Newfoundland were tall, handsome and mainly peaceable, the Skraelings may have been Dorset Eskimoes.

p.32 Latest radiocarbon dating of L'Anse aux Meadows charcoal. See Reidar Nydal, 'A Critical Review of Radiocarbon dating of a Norse settlement at L'Anse aux Meadows, Newfoundland, Canada', *Radiocarbon*, 31, no.3, 1989, pp.976–85. I am indebted to Dr Sheridan Bowman, Research Laboratory, British Museum for bringing to my attention this recently updated information.

p.33 Icelandic Annals. This quotation derives from the *Skálholt Annals* as published in Gustav Storm, *Islandske Annaler indtil 1578*, Cristiania, 1888, quotation translated into English in Ingstad, *The Norse Discovery of America*, vol. 2, p.358.

p.33 *Inventio Fortunatae*. For the most authoritative article on this lost work, see E.G.R.Taylor, 'A Letter Dated 1577 from Mercator to John Dee', *Imago Mundi* 13, 1956, pp.56–68.

Chapter 3

p.39 Fra Mauro map. The original of this as made for Portugal has not survived, but a copy made for Venice at the same time is preserved in the Biblioteca Nazionale Marciana, Venice. For an excellent colour reproduction, see Kenneth Nebenzahl, *Maps from the Age of Discovery*, p.13.

p.39 John Cabot's grant of Venetian citizenship. The documents are in the Venice Archivio di Stato: first, the grant made on March 29, 1476, in Senato Terra, Reg.VII, fol.109v; second, the terms of this same grant, in Privilegi,

Reg. II, fol.53. The Italian texts are printed in Henry Percival Biggar, *The Precursors of Jacques Cartier*, pp.1–6, with English translation.

p.40 Brasil/Brazil. With regard to the naming of the present-day South American country, the name first appears in this context on the Jerónimo Marini map of 1511, reproduced in *Hist. Col. Port. Brasil*, II, 332. See Morison, *The European Discovery of America: Vol.II, The Southern Voyages*, p.299.

p.40 Columbus's lack of interest in the mythical islands during his First Voyage. This is evident from his journal entry for September 19, 1492.

p.40 Ivar Bárdarson. Bárdarson was a Bergen priest, issued with a passport to Greenland in 1341, and seems to have spent some years there. According to the *Description of Greenland* quoted, with sources, in Ingstad, *The Norse Discovery of America*, vol 2, '. . . now the Skraelings possess the whole Western Settlement; there are indeed horses, goats, cattle and sheep, all wild, and no people either Christian or heathen – all this is said above was told us by Ivar Bárdarson, a Greenlander, who was steward of the bishop's residence at Gardum in Greenland for many years, that . . . when they came there [the Western Settlement] they found no man, either Christian or heathen, but some wild cattle and sheep, and ate of them, and took as much as the ships could carry and sailed home [i.e. to the Eastern Settlement], and the said Ivar was among them.'

p.41 Excavations in the churchyard at Herjolfnes. These were carried out in 1921 by the eminent Danish archaeologist Dr Poul Norlund. He dug up some 200 graves. The clothing represents virtually the only substantial costumes of common people from the Middle Ages to have been preserved, and is today in the National Museum of Copenhagen. See Poul Norlund, 'Buried Norsemen at Herjolfness', *Meddleleser om Gronland*, vol.LXVII, 1924.

p.41 English trade with Iceland, early-fifteenth century. For full background on this and later trade, see Eleanora Carus-Wilson, 'The Iceland Trade' in Eileen Power and M.M. Postan (eds.), *Studies in English Trade in the Fifteenth Century*.

p.42 Letter of the Icelanders to King Eric. Quotation from Carus-Wilson, op.cit., p.163.

p.43 'By needle and stone'. This refers to the Bristolians using a fairly primitive form of lodestone compass. The full quotation, as first printed by Richard Hakluyt, runs:

> Of Island to write is little nede,
> Save of stock-fish: Yet forsooth in deed
> Out of Bristowe, and costes many one,
> Men have practised by nedle and by stone
> Thider wardes within a litle while
> Within twelve yere, and without perill
> Gon and come, as men were wont of old
> Of Scarborough unto the costes cold.

Chapter 4

p.44   Norse place-names at the approaches to Bristol. According to Henry Lyon, *The Vikings in Wales*: 'Scandinavian seamen were active in the Bristol Channel. They made a strong enough impression to leave their names on most of the principal navigation points on the north shore of the channel, and it is probable that they were the first to open up the trade route from Ireland deep into the Severn estuary to regular and continuous port-to-port navigation.'

p.45   Quotation from Alexander Pope. This derives from his *Letters to Martha Blount*, 1732. For further details of Bristol's unusual tides, and the problems these posed for the port during the days of sail, see Alan F.Williams, 'Bristol Port Plans and Improvement Schemes of the 18th century', *Transactions of the Bristol and Gloucestershire Archaeological Society*, 1962, pp.138ff.

p.45   Bristol in the reign of King Stephen. For this quotation and much of the further background concerning Bristol in mediaeval times, I am particularly indebted to Carus-Wilson, op.cit., p.183 ff.

p.47   Two very fine funeral effigies of William Canynges are to be seen in St Mary Redcliffe church, Bristol.

p.48   Alice Chester's crane. See J.W. Sherborne, *The Port of Bristol in the Middle Ages*, p.17. The crane cost the then very substantial sum of £41.

p.48   Salmon of Bann. The original reads 'salmon of Bame' but Professor D.B. Quinn has kindly informed me that this refers to the River Bann salmon fishery, which still exists. Apparently this fishery was farmed out to Bristol and Chester merchants in the fifteenth and sixteenth centuries.

p.49   The main source for the tunnages of Canynges'ships is the *Itineraries* of the Bristol-born fifteenth-century antiquarian William Worcestre. See John H. Harvey's translation of this, *William Worcestre, Itineraries*.

p.49   Robert Sturmy. For details see Carus-Wilson, op.cit., pp.225–9.

p.50   Dried cod. For useful background on the traditional methods used, see Harold Horwood, *Newfoundland*, especially p.82.

p.52   For detailed transcriptions from a substantial cross-section of Bristol's late mediaeval customs records, see Eleanora Carus-Wilson, *The Overseas Trade of Bristol in the Later Middle Ages*.

p.53–4   Catalan chart showing Iceland. The quotation derives from Hermannsson, *The Cartography of Iceland*, p.121. For further discussion see Skelton, Marston & Painter, op.cit., pp.166–7

p.54 Trade war with the Hanseatics. For full background and sources, see Carus-Wilson, 'The Iceland Trade', pp.180–1.

Chapter 5

p.57 John Jay funeral brass. See Sally Stevens and Tim Tiley, *A Few Notes on Monumental Brasses from the West Country*, p.18.

p.58 John Jay in Bristol customs records. See several references in Carus-Wilson, *The Overseas Trade . . .*, e.g. p.130, 131, 133, etc.

p.59 Notebook of William Worcestre. See Harvey, op.cit.

Worcestre's death notice of John Jay the second. The original text, which appears on p.195, is in Worcestre's typically poor and heavily abbreviated Latin, as follows: 'Johes Jay seds maritus Johane sororis mee obijt die.15 mes maij a° xri' (Abbreviation marks not included). It is worthy of note that immediately before this passage occurs a mention of Ireland's 'Brandon Hill', or Mount Brandon, the second highest mountain in Ireland, though Worcestre says it is the highest.

p.59 Date of Worcestre's death. Scholarly opinion on this varies between 1482 and 1485

p.59 'Brasil' voyage of 1480. The original text reads: '1480 die. 15. jullij Navis . . . et Johis Jay junioris ponderis. 80. dolior/jnceper/t viagu apd. portum Bristollie de Kyngrode vsqz ad insulam de Brasylle in occidetli pte hibernie sulcando maria per . . . et . . . Thloyde est magist^r navis. scientificus marinarius tocius Anglie. et nova vener/t Bristollie die lue.18. die septebris qd dicta navis velauer/t maria p c^{r}ca.9. mses nec jnvener/t jnsulam sed p tempestas maris reuersi sut vsqz. portum in hibernia reposicoe navis & marinarior' (Abbreviation marks not included)

p.59 'Lloyd was master of the ship' A John Lloyd was recorded in 1466 (Feb. 28) as master of the *Mary Grace* of Bristol, sailing on behalf of merchant John Gaywood, who traded chiefly with Portugal.

p.60 Islands mentioned by Worcestre. See Harvey, op.cit., p. 375.

p.60 Licence of 18 June, 1480. This is Public Record Office Treaty Roll C76/164, m.10.

Thomas Croft. A brief biography appears in J.C. Wedgewood and A.E. Holt, *History of Parliament: Biographies of the members of Commons' House, 1439–1509*. For background details on the Croft family, see O.G.S. Croft, *The House of Croft at Croft Castle*.

p.61 Mayor-making ceremony of 1479. The illustration referred to is part of the original manuscript of Robert Ricart's *Kalendar*, as preserved in the Bristol Record Office.

p.61 Foundation of the Guild of the Holy Cross by Spencer, Strange and others. See Hirst, *History of the Church of St John the Baptist, Bristol*, pp. 8, 27.

p.61 William de la Fount is recorded in the Customs Accounts for 1479 as having shipped nine barrels of herring from Ireland in the *Christopher* of Bristol. Other mentions of him occur in the accounts for February 24 and 26, 1480.

p.62 Charge of 1481 against Thomas Croft. This appears in the Bristol customs records in the Public Record Office, London as E.122/19, 16. The translation is from James A. Williamson (ed.), *The Cabot Voyages and Bristol Discovery under Henry VII*, pp. 188–9.

p.62 Another *Trinity* of Bristol. For discussion on the possible confusion of names, see Quinn, *England and the Discovery of America*, p.54.

p.66 Quotation from Captain John Mason. This derives from his *A brief discourse of Newfoundland* published from Edinburgh in 1620.

p.68 Quotation from James Yonge. This derives from his Journal, as edited by Poynter, op.cit., p.56ff.

p.69 Quotation from Lord Burghley. This is published in D.W. Prowse, *A History of Newfoundland*, p.33.

p.69 Henry Forbes Taylor. For an introduction to his hypothesis, one that acted as an initial spur to this whole book, see the article by Philip Howard, 'A fishy secret about who found America' in *The Times*, April 15, 1976. Further discussion of Forbes Taylor's argument follows in Chapter 13.

p.60–70 Professor Quinn on the non-trading nature of the Bristol cod voyages. This opinion derives from private correspondence with Professor Quinn.

p.70–71 Icelandic servants in Bristol, 1484. The manuscript is preserved in the Public Record Office as E.179, 270,54. For detailed discussion, see Quinn, *England and the Discovery of America*, pp.49–51. I am indebted to Mary Williams, former Bristol city archivist, for a careful transcription from the Latin.

p.71 Henry VII told Bristol's trade is bad, due to loss of business with Iceland. See R.L. Storey, *Henry VII*, after John Leland, *De Rebus Britannicis Collectanea*, Thomas Hearne (ed.), London, 1774, vol 4, p.200.

p.71 Painting by Tom Mostyn. This is displayed with several other modern works depicting episodes from Bristol's history in an upstairs court room of the Old Council House, Corn Street, Bristol.

Chapter 6

p.73 Quotation regarding Thule. The translation is from Keen, op. cit., p.11. I have however corrected two translation errors made by Keen as pointed out by Dr Ruddock in her important paper 'Columbus and Iceland: New Light on an Old Problem' *Geographical Journal*, 1970, pp177–89. Keen's 'northern' has been replaced by 'southern', and '26 fathoms' by 50 feet. I am similarly indebted to Dr Ruddock for much of the arguments concerning Columbus and Iceland.

p.75 Quotation from Morison. This derives from his *Admiral of the Ocean Sea*, p.52.

p.75 Quotation from Toscanelli's letter. This translation, from the original Latin in a book owned by Columbus, derives from Bjorn Landström's *Columbus*, p.19.

p.75 Henry Vignaud on the Toscanelli letter. See Vignaud's dated but still valuable study, *Toscanelli and Columbus, The Letter and Chart of Toscanelli*, first published 1902.

p.76 Quotation from Fuson, op. cit., p.29.

p.76 Story of the Portuguese pilot. This derives from Bartolomé de las Casas, *Historia de las Indias*, lib.1, cap.xiii, first printed 1552, as translated in Williamson, *The Cabot Voyages . . .*, p.179. The story of the two dead men found on Flores derives from the same source, p.180.

p.77 Columbus's serious miscalculations of the circumference of the earth. For detailed discussion of these, see Morison, *Admiral of the Ocean Sea*, pp.62–3.

p.77 Quotations from Pierre d'Ailly's *Imago Mundi*. The translations derive from Morison, *Admiral of the Ocean Sea*, pp.86–7.

p.78 Columbus's wife. She was Doña Felipa Moniz de Perestrello, who seems to have died in childbirth circa 1481.

p.79 Antonio de Marchena. According to Morison 'a man of spirit and intelligence, and of high repute as an *astrólogo* (astronomer)'; *Admiral of the Ocean Sea*, p.74.

p.80 Accounts of the *Trinity*. These were found in a general record book of the Company of Mercers, Drapers and Ironmongers for the town of Bridgnorth, Shropshire, dating 1497–1691. This volume was made up of a number of smaller books sewn together, the shipping accounts in question forming part of the records of the Bridgnorth Company for the reign of Henry VII. The book is in the archives of the Mercers' Company in the Mercers' Hall, London, and I was kindly allowed to inspect the original by the archivist, Anne Sutton. The crucial paper elucidating the accounts in question is T.F. Reddaway and Alwyn Ruddock, 'The Accounts of John Balsall, Purser of the *Trinity of Bristol*, 1480–1'. *Camden Miscellany XXIII*, Royal Historical Society, 1969, pp.1–28.

p.81 Quotation regarding La Rábida. The original of this reads, on fol.9 of the manuscript, 'to the ffryres at our lady of Rebedewe to pray ffor us'.

p.82 Portolan sea chart of c.1490, Paris. For excellent colour reproductions of this map, and accompanying background information, see Nebenzahl, op. cit., pp.22–5. Nebenzahl dates the map to circa 1492–1500, basing his argument on the Spanish flag flying over Granada. See however Quinn's *England and the Discovery of America*, p.60ff., for the map dating ca.1490.

p.84 Charles de la Roncière. For his arguments, see his *La Carte de Christophe Colomb*.

Chapter 7

p.87 Globe of Martin Behaim. For an excellent clarified colour rendition of this, see the Joseph Judge *National Geographic* article, op. cit., pp.564–5.

p.89 John Cabot Montecalunya in Valencia. The original documents are in the Archivo Regional de Valencia, Archivo del Real, Epistolarum vol.496. Translations from the Aragonese are printed in Williamson, *The Cabot Voyages* . . ., pp.196–9. For the abandoning of the harbour project, see Manuel Ballestrero-Gailbrois, 'Juan Caboto en Espana', *Revista de Indias*, XIV, 1943, p.610.

p.90 Letter of the Milanese Ambassador. This letter, from Raimondo de Raimondi de Soncino to the Duke of Milan, sent December 18, 1497, is in the Milan Archives, Potenze Estere: Inghilterra. An English translation is reproduced in Williamson, *The Cabot Voyages* . . ., pp.209–10.

p.91 Letter of Ferdinand and Isabella to Ambassador Gonzalez de Puebla. This is in the Archivo General de Simancas, Estado Tratados con Inglaterra, leg.2, fol.16. An English translation from the Spanish, after Dr Biggar, is printed in Williamson, *The Cabot Voyages* . . ., pp.202–3.

p.91 Licence of Henry VII to John Cabot and his sons. The original, in Latin, is preserved in the Public Record Office, London as Treaty Roll 178, membr.8. An English translation is given in Biggar, op.cit., pp.7–10; also Williamson, *The Cabot Voyages* . . ., pp.204–5.

p.92 Bristol Rent Book. For the full text of this, see St Clair Baddeley 'A Bristol Rental 1498–9. The property of Mrs Chester-Master', *Transactions of the Bristol and Gloucestershire Archaeological Society*, vol.47, 1925, pp.123–9.

p.94 Bristol customs records for 1503–4. These are preserved in the Public Record Office, London as E.122/199, 1. Account, 19–20 Hen.VII. A transcription of the references to the *Matthew* is printed in Williamson, *The Cabot Voyages* . . ., p.206.

p.94 Quotation from Williamson, *The Cabot Voyages* . . ., p.61.

p.94–5 Letter of Venetian merchant Lorenzo Pasqualigo. This derives from the MS *Diarii* of Marin Sanuto, Venice, Biblioteca Marciana MSS Ital. Cl.VII,

Cod.417 (vol.1), fol.374v. The translation is from Biggar, op.cit., pp.13–15.

p.96   Quotation from Horwood, op. cit., p.7.

p.98   Sixteenth-century Bristol chronicle. This was the so-called Fust manuscript, and has an interesting story in its own right. The manuscript was originally in the collection of the Fust family of Hill Court, Gloucestershire, then was sold in the early-nineteenth century to a Bristol bookseller who sold it to a Mr John Hugh Smyth-Pigott of Brockley Hall, a few miles south of Bristol. When Smyth-Piggott's effects were put up for auction in 1849, the manuscript was listed in the sale catalogue as 'Lot 1554. "A Brief Chronicle, conteyning the accompe of the Reignes of all the Kings in the Realme of Englande, from the entering of Brutus untill this present yeere, with 11 the notable acts done by the dyvers of them, and wherein is also conteyned the names of all the Mayors, Stewardes, Bayliffes and Sheriffes, of the laudable town of Bristowe . . . from the first yeere of King Henry ye 3rd, AD 1217 until the present yeere, 1565", a very curious MS containing many facts not recorded by the historians of Bristol, from Sir Francis Fust's library, folio.' The manuscript was purchased by the Bristol bookseller Thomas Kerslake, but sadly was destroyed when Kerslake's shop in Bristol's Park Street was burnt out by fire on February 14, 1860. Some excerpts had, however, previously been copied from the chronicle, and one of these read as follows:

> 1496. John Drewes [Mayor]. Thomas Vaughan.
>   Hugh Johnes [Sheriff] John Elyott   (Bailiffs)

> This year, on St John the Baptist's Day [24 June] the land of America was found by the Merchants of Bristow in a shippe of Bristowe, called the *Mathew*; the which said ship departed from the port of Bristowe, the second day of May, and came home again the 6th. of August the next following.

It is to be noted that the civic year went from 29 September to 28 September, and that therefore any events from January to September of 1497 (by our reckoning), would be listed in their reckoning as occurring in 1496. The Fust manuscript would seem to have been assembled about 1565 by a Maurice Toby from earlier, untraceable sources. According to J.A.Williamson: 'Toby is the prime authority for the three dates [of the Cabot voyage] and the ship's name, all of which receive partial corroboration from sources which, except for that of June 24, could not have been known to him. We must conclude that he represents a genuine documentary authority.' (Williamson, *The Cabot Voyages* p. 57). One curiosity is Toby's seemingly anachronistic reference to the 'land of America'.

p.98–99   The notarised statement. These quotations derive from Frederick Pohl's *Amerigo Vespucci*, p.42. For discussion, see Morison, *Admiral of the Ocean Sea*, p.458 ff.

p.99   The name Newfoundland first appears, as 'the newe founde launde' in an entry of September 30, 1502 in the Daybooks of King Henry VII, Public Record Office E 101/415 3 [1 October 1499–30 September 1502].

p.100 Cape Bonavista. The great Newfoundland historian Judge D.W. Prowse remarked: ' "Bonavista! Oh good sight!" is the natural exclamation the old Italian [i.e.Cabot] might make as after his long voyage he first caught sight of land, bright and green with the springing grass of June. There is no other cape with the same name on the eastern shore of America.' From Prowse, op.cit., p.10, notes.

p.100 Grates Cove inscription. The inscription purportedly carried the letters IO CABOTO SANCCIUS SAINMALIA but nothing of this can be discerned today. For deservedly sceptical discussion, see Morison, *The European Discovery of America: Vol.I, The Northern Voyages*, pp.202–3.

Chapter 8

p.101 The quotation from Dr Alwyn Ruddock derives from her article 'John Day of Bristol and the English Voyages . . .', *Geographical Journal*, 1966, p. 227.

p.101 Dr Louis André Vigneras. For background to Dr Vigneras's discovery, see his article 'New Light on the 1497 Cabot Voyage to America', *Hispanic American Historical Review*, 36, 1956, pp.503–9. This reproduces the Spanish text of the letter.

p.102 English translation of the John Day letter. This derives from Dr Vigneras's 'The Cape Breton landfall: 1494 or 1497?', in *Canadian Historical Review* 38, 1957, pp. 226–8.

p.106 '*en otros tiempos*'. Vigneras remarked on p. 224 of his 'The Cape Breton Landfall' article: 'I have been conducting a sort of Gallup poll in Madrid, among archivists and historians, to try to ascertain the exact meaning of "*en otros tiempos*", but I have failed to find unanimity of opinion. Most of those I have consulted believe it refers to the distant past, to "*muchos años*" rather than to "*pocos años*", to at least one generation back or a quarter of a century. There is however a small minority who are of the opinion that "*en otros tiempos*" might apply to three or four years, as well as to three or four centuries.'

p.106 Grant of Henry VII to Cabot. This is in the Public Record Office among Privy Seals, 13 Henry VII, December. The English text is given in Biggar, op. cit., p.16 and Williamson, *The Cabot Voyages* . . . p. 217.

p.107 Identification of the 'Grand Admiral' with Columbus. Vigneras's remarks on this appear as note 26 in his 'The Cape Breton Landfall . . .'

p.109 Document of 20 December, 1500 mentioning John Day. This was discovered by Vigneras in the Archivo General de Simancas, Cédulas de la Camara, leg 4, f.252,2. See Williamson, *The Cabot Voyages* . . ., p. 56, n.1.

p.109 John Day as an importer of wine from Lisbon. See Ruddock, 'John Day of Bristol . . .', p. 225.

p.109   Researches of Dr Alwyn Ruddock. Dr Ruddock's masterly article on this subject is the already quoted 'John Day of Bristol . . .'. Much of the rest of my chapter is heavily dependent on this article, in which will be found all necessary sources.

p.113   Columbus's copy of Marco Polo. See, Vigneras's 'The Cape Breton Landfall . . .', p. 226, note 29. In note 27 Vigneras remarks of the *Inventio Fortunatae* mentioned by Day: 'This work is mentioned by Fernando Colón [i.e.Columbus's son Fernando] *Historia del S.D. Fernando Colón*, (Venetia, 1571), cap.ix, 21, and by Bartolomé de Las Casas, *Historia de las Indias*, (Mexico, Buenos Aires, 1951), I, 67, as having influenced Columbus.'

Chapter 9

p.118   Letter of Pedro de Ayala, July 25, 1498. The original is in the Archivo General de Simancas, Estado Tratados con Inglaterra, leg.2, fol.196. There have been some inaccurate decodings of the cipher in which it is written. The translation as given derives from Biggar, op.cit., pp. 27–9. It is also given in Williamson *The Cabot Voyages . . .*, pp. 228–9.

p.121   *The Great Chronicle of London*. For a modern published edition, see that of A.H.Thomas and I.D. Thornley, published from London in 1939. The quotation, in the original English, appears on pp. 287–8, and has been modernised by me.

p.122   Henry VII's Household Books for Spring 1498. The extracts as given derive from Public Record Office documents E101/414, 16, and are published in Williamson *The Cabot Voyages . . .* pp. 214–15. The spellings have been modernised by me.

p.123   Letter of Agostino de Spinula. This derives from the Milan Archives (Potenze Estere: Inghilterra). The translation is from the *Calendar of State Papers, Milan*, vol.I, no.571.

p.123   Carbonariis as royal messenger. For discussion of this individual, and appropriate sources, see Williamson, *The Cabot Voyages . . .*

p.123   Survival of Lancelot Thirkill. He is referred to in British Museum Additional MS. 21480. f.35b.

p.124   Payment of Cabot's pension. The record of the payment is preserved in Public Record Office manuscript Exchequer 122, 20/11 (View of Account, Bristol Customs, Michaelmas-Easter 13 Hen VII). For text, see Biggar, op. cit., pp. 25–7 and Williamson, *The Cabot Voyages . . .*, pp.218–19.

p.124   Polydore Vergil. See *The Anglica Historia of Polydore Vergil*, Denys Hay (ed. and trans.), *Camden Series*, vol. XXIV (Royal Historical Society 1950), pp. 116–7.

p.124   Quote from Williamson, *The Cabot Voyages . . .*, p.105.

p.127 Manuel of Portugal's letters patent to João Fernandes. For English translation, see Biggar, op. cit., pp. 31–2; also Williamson, *The Cabot Voyages* . . ., p.235.

p.128 Letter of Pietro Pasqualigo, October 19, 1501. The original is in *Paesi nouamente retrouati* (Vicenza, 1507), lib VI, cap. cxxvi. For English translation, see Williamson, *The Cabot Voyages* . . ., p.229.

Chapter 10

p.131 Quotation from Columbus's diary of his Third Voyage. The translation derives from Landström, op. cit., p. 144.

p.134 Alonso de Hojeda (also referred to as Ojeda). For general background, see Morison, *The European Discovery of America: Vol II, The Southern Voyages*, pp. 185ff; also Carl O. Sauer, *The Early Spanish Main*, pp.106 ff.

p.136–7 Quotation from Martin Fernández de Navarrete. This derives from his *Colección de los viages y descubriementos*, vol III, Madrid 1829, p.41. The Spanish text reads: '*Lo cierto es que Hojeda en su primer viage halló á ciertos ingleses por las immediaciones de Coquibaçoa*'.

p.138 Hojeda's licence from Ferdinand and Isabella. This is in the Archivo General de Simancas, Cédulas, no.5. The Spanish text is published in Navarrete's *Collección*, op.cit., vol III, pp.85–8. The English translation is from Williamson, *The Cabot Voyages* . . ., pp.233–4.

p.139 For the sources of the gold, pearls, etc. see Sauer, op.cit., p.114.

Chapter 11

p.141 The La Cosa Map. For the best available reproduction in colour, see Nebenzahl, op.cit., pp.30–3; also the *National Geographic*, November 1975, p.605. There is also a considerable scholarly literature. An important, though dated, introduction to the issues is G.E. Nunn's *The Mappemonde of Juan de la Cosa*. Some lively remarks by Morison are to be found in his *European Discovery of America: Vol I, The Northern Voyages*, pp.239–242.

p.142 Capitán de Corbeta Roberto Barreiro-Meiro. His arguments are given in his pamphlet *Juan de la Cosa y su Doble Personalidad*, Instituto Histórico de Marina, 1970. The Spanish scholar Antonio Ballesteros y Beretta accepted the view that there were two different Juan de la Cosas in his *Historia de América y de los pueblos americanos*. But in his posthumously published book *La marina cántabra y Juan de la Cosa*, he finally concluded there was only one.

p.145 'Seems to be called Cavo Descubierto'. The decipherment of place-names on the La Cosa map's 'English' coastline is a ticklish problem in its own right. In 1929 the Canadian W.F. Ganong, working from good reproductions, made what at that date was considered the best possible transcription. Then in 1951 the Spanish Admiral J.F. Guillén y Tato, working from the original, and aided by infra red, published some rather different readings in his contribution to the atlas *Mapas Españoles de América*, published at Madrid by the Real Academia de la Historia. The two lists are given below, the names being shown as running from west to east, and therefore theoretically in 'discovery' order:

Ganong	Guillén
mar descubierta por inglese	mar descubierta por inglese
cauo descubierto	C° . . . s
co. de S:jorge	C° de S:Jorge
lago fori	lago so . . .
ansto or austo	gosfica
co. de s. luzia	C°: de S luzia
requilea or r. conilia	. . . tias
jusquei or insquei	los sep . . .
s:luzia	s. luys
co.de lisarte	C° de lisarte
meniste	meniste
argare	. . . .
forte	fo.te
ro. longo	.longo
isla de la trenidat	illa de la trenidat
s.nicolas	S Matias
cauo de s.iohan	cauo de s.iohan
agron	opon
c.fastanatre	c . . . slin
cauo de ynglaterra	cauo de ynglaterra
s.grigor	C:grago
y.berde or verde	y: verde

On my own visit to the Naval Museum in Madrid, I spent some while studying what appeared to be the La Cosa map, finding my own reading corresponding curiously easily with Ganong's. I was particularly gratified to read 's.nicolas', Cabot seemingly honouring his Bristol parish church. Then the penny dropped: what was being shown as the La Cosa original, complete with antique frame, was in actuality a hand-made facsimile.

Despite the frustration, therefore, of having been unable to examine the original, nonetheless an early nineteenth century transcription of the 'English' coastline, also displayed in the Naval Museum, shows 'Cauo descubierto' and other readings closely corresponding to Ganong's. Study of modern colour transparencies of the map suggests likewise.

My overall impression is that the place-names shown on the map's 'North American' coast derive from Cabot's 1497 voyage, and that the remaining coastline, extending southwards all around the Caribbean to South America, and shown without placenames, derives from Cabot's 1498 voyage.

p.146 Argument of Bernard Hoffman. This appears in his *Cabot to Cartier* . . ., pp.93–6. The only other alternative he offers is that the map was made after 1529, but even Morison does not accept this.

p.146 Quotation from Williamson, *The Cabot Voyages* . . ., p.77.

p.147 Quotation from Morison, *European Discovery of America: Vol I, The Northern Voyages*, pp.238–39.
   Cantino Map. For excellent reproductions of this, see Nebenzahl, op.cit., pp.34–7.

p.147 Verrazzano's Map. For excellent reproductions from this, see Nebenzahl, op.cit., pp.88–91.

p.148 Place-names on the English coastline. For the variant readings of these as elucidated by W.F.Ganong (1929), and by the Spanish Admiral G.H.Guillén y Tato, see Williamson, *The Cabot Voyages* . . ., pp.77–9.

p.149 La Cosa's deliberate falsifications of latitudes. See Williamson, 'The early falsifications of Western Indian latitudes', *Geographical Journal*, March 1930.

p.149 Vatican archives. For background to the fate of the Vatican Secret Archives brought by Napoleon to Paris, see Maria Luisa Ambrosini & Mary Willis, *The Secret Archives of the Vatican*, pp.324–31.

Chapter 12

p.151 Poem of circa 1519. This derives from 'A new Interlude of the IV Elements. Printed 1519–20', British Museum Press-mark C39.6.17.

p.151 Portrait of Amerigo Vespucci as a teenager. See Morison, *The European Discovery of America: Vol II, The Southern Voyages*, pp.278–9.

p.151–2 Amerigo Vespucci's early years. For general background I have followed Pohl, op.cit.

p.153 Coelho voyage. For detailed background, see Morison, *The European Discovery of America: Vol II, The Southern Voyages*, op.cit., p.280ff.

p.154 Text of Vespucci's letter to Lorenzo di Pier Francesco de' Medici. The translation is from Pohl, op.cit., p.148.

p.000 The Soderini letter. For detailed background on this, see Pohl, op.cit., p.150ff.

p.155 Quotation from the letter to Pier Francesco de' Medici. The translation is from Morison, *The European Discovery of America: Vol II The Southern Voyages*, pp.284–6, made by Morison with the aid of Dr Gino Corti.

p.156 Doubts concerning Vespucci's claims. For background to these, from Sebastian Cabot on, see Morison, *The European Discovery of America: Vol II, The Southern Voyages*, pp.306–11.

p.158 Waldseemüller map of 1507. For a large-scale reproduction and useful background, see Nebenzahl, op.cit., pp.52–5.

p.159 Map of Henricus Martellus. For reproduction, see Nebenzahl, op.cit., p.15.

p.163 Quote from Las Casas. This derives from his *Historia General de las Indias, AD 1527–59*, published in 1559.

p.165 Bristol customs roll. This is reproduced and discussed in Edward Scott (trans.), *The Cabot Roll, The Customs Roll of the Port of Bristol AD 1496–9*.

p.166 Ameryk and America. See the article by Alfred E. Hudd, 'Richard Ameryk and the name America', *Proceedings of the Clifton Antiquarian Club*, vol VII, pt.I, 1909–10, pp.1–9.

p.167–8 Joan and John Brook memorial brass. See Stevens & Tiley, op.cit., p.22.

p.169 The Ameryk merchant mark. See Alfred E. Hudd, 'Bristol Merchant Marks'.

p.170 Christopher Columbus on Vespucci. From a letter of Columbus of February 25, 1505, forwarded to Segovia by Vespucci, as quoted in Morison, *Admiral of the Ocean Sea*, p.648.

Chapter 13

p.171 Quote from Morison, *The European Discovery of America: Vol II, The Southern Voyages*, pp.266–7.

p.172 Quote from Sauer, op.cit., p.142.

p.174 Quote from inscription on the Contarini map. The translation from the Latin derives from Nebenzahl, op.cit., p.44.

p.174 Ruysch map. For an excellent reproduction, see Nebenzahl, op.cit., pp.48–9.

p.174 Balboa. For the dramatic story of Balboa's first sighting of the Pacific, see Morison, *The European Discovery of America: Vol II, The Southern Voyages*, pp.199–204.

p.175 Hakluyt. For the quote from the second edition of the third volume of his *Principall Navigations*, see the readily available Everyman edition, Hakluyt *Voyages*, vol 1, p.47.

p.175 Hakluyt's quotations from Columbus's son Fernando, op.cit., vol 5, pp.80–2.

p.176 Hakluyt's dedicatory epistle to his second edition, op.cit., vol 1, pp.13–14.

p.176 Sebastian Cabot's conversation with the Mantuan gentleman. The account of this appears in Giovanni Battista Ramusio's *Primo Volume delle Navigationi et Viaggi*, Venice 1550, ff.398–403. An English translation is published in Williamson, *The Cabot Voyages . . .*, pp.270–3.

p.177 'Three men, taken in the New found land'. This account derives from *The Great Chronicle of London*, Thomas & Thornley (eds.), op.cit., p.320.

p.178 '[A] brasil bow and 2 red arrows'. The original reads: 'a brasell bowe and ij Rede arowez', and derives from the Phillipps Manuscript 4104, folio 32v, 15–20 September, 1503. The manuscript belongs to the Robinson Trust. See Quinn, *England and the Discovery of America*, p.123.

p.178 1504 voyage of the *Gabriel*. The *Gabriel*'s return, with 20 lasts of salted fish and 7 tons 1 pipe fish livers from the 'Newe Found Iland' is recorded in P.R.O., E 122/199/I; also E 356/24, m.2. Thorne and Elyot were allowed to bring in this cargo free of customs duty and subsidy. For discussion, see Ruddock, 'The Reputation of Sebastian Cabot', p.98. Dr Ruddock believes the route to 'Brasil' as found during the 1480s became lost by the Bristolians, and that this particular document records the first true fishing voyage, since otherwise 'we might have expected to find either some record of payment or a claim for exemption from payment of this subsidy on salt fish much earlier than 1502 and 1504.' First, assuming that the Bristolians actually found Newfoundland in the 1480s (with which Dr Ruddock fully agrees), the subsequent losing of the route seems somewhat improbable. Second, it seems more than coincidental that this recording of a Newfoundland dried cod cargo (only for the duty to be immediately waived), should occur just after Customs Controller Richard Ameryk's death in 1503. Arguably, under Ameryk and his predecessors, such as Croft, Newfoundland dried fish cargoes simply went through 'on the nod'.

p.178 1502 voyage of the *Gabriel*. This is recorded in P.R.O., E 368/276 *stasus et visus*, Easter term 18 Hen. VII, m.11d.

p.178 Quotation from Robert Thorne the second. The original reads:

> I reason that as some sicknes[ses are] hereditarious and come [from the Father] to the Sonne: So this Inclynation or desyre of [discover]ing I inherited from my father, which with an [other] Marchaunt of Brystow named hughe Elliot [were] the discoverers of the Newfound Landes, of the w[hich] there is no dowt, (as now plainly appeareth) yf [the] mariners wolde then have bene ruled and followed the[ir] Pilots mynde, the Land of the Indians from wh[ence] all the Gold commeth had been ours: for all is one Coast, as by the Carde appeareth, and is afores[aid].

This derives from a letter written by Robert Thorne the second in Seville in 1527, and addressed to Dr Edward Lee, English Ambassador in Spain (British Museum, Cotton MS, Vit c.vii, ff 329–45). For further discussion, see Williamson, *The Cabot Voyages . . .*, pp.26–8, and 202. As Williamson shows, in 1578 Dr John Dee wrote on the back of a map an inscription that 'Mr Robert Thorn his father, and Mr Eliot of Bristow' had discovered Newfoundland in 1494, three years before 'Sebastian' (sic) Cabot in 1497 (pp.202–12). But this would appear to be one of the all too common muddles caused by the misinformation spread by Sebastian Cabot and others.

In our own time even the redoubtable Admiral Samuel Morison has succumbed to confusion over the Thornes. On p.237 of his *The European Discovery of America: Vol I, The Northern Voyages* he gives Robert Thorne's date of death as 1527, seemingly referring to Robert Thorne the second. In fact Robert Thorne the first died sometime before July 1519, when his will was proved in London, while Robert Thorne the second died at the age of 40 in London in 1532, being buried in the church of St Christopher in the Stocks. For particularly authoritative background on the Thornes, see C.P.Hill, *The History of Bristol Grammar School*, Chapter 1.

p.179   Selma Barkham and the Basque Whalers. For an introduction to the story of Selma Barkham's research, see 'Sixteenth-century Basque Whaling in America', *National Geographic*, vol 168, no.1., July 1985.

p.179   Archaeology at Red Bay, Labrador. See James A.Tuck & Robert Grenier, *Red Bay, Labrador, World Whaling Capital AD 1550–1600*; also reports in *Archaeology in Newfoundland and Labrador*, publication of the Newfoundland Museum, Historic Resources Division, Government of Newfoundland and Labrador.

p.181   James A. Tuck's excavations at Ferryland, Newfoundland. See his article 'Excavations at Ferryland, Newfoundland, 1986', *Archaeology in Newfoundland & Labrador*, op.cit., pp.296–307.

p.181   Early cannon found at Louisbourg. For a description of this, see J.G.Bourinot, *Historical and Descriptive Account of the Island of Cape Breton*, Montreal, Foster Brown, 1892, p.284 ff. I am grateful to Jim Campbell, Archaeology Collection Supervisor, Canadian Parks Service, for much helpful information concerning this cannon.

p.183   Discovery of America by the Welsh prince Madoc. There is an extensive literature on Madoc. See for example Gwyn A. Williams, *Madoc, The Making of a Myth*; also *Dictionary of Canadian Biography*, I, 1965, appendix; and David Williams, 'John Evans' Strange Journey', *American Historical Review*, LIV 1949, pp.271–95; 508–29.

p.183   Portuguese pre-Columbian discovery of America. See the Introduction to Morison's *Portuguese Voyages to America in the Fifteenth Century*. Morison quotes as the best résumé of the Portuguese literature on this subject, with bibliography, Manuel Heleno, *O Descobrimento da América*, Lisbon, 1933.

Chapter 14

p.185   Quotations from Columbus's Journal. These derive from Dunn & Kelley, op.cit., pp.67–9; 75; and 235–7 respectively.

p.186   Quote from Las Casas regarding Columbus's concern at the death of Hispaniola's native population. This derives from Las Casas *Historia General*, Book II, Chapter 37. For much detailed information concerning the decimation of the islands' native populations see Sauer, op.cit., especially pp.155–6. I am also indebted to Sauer for the quotation from Las Casas 'Who of those born . . .?'

p.187   Quotation '. . . all this happened among us.' This derives from the Annals of Tlatelolco, part 5, (§§103–394), as reproduced in Brotherston, *Image of the New World*, pp.34–5.

p.188   The fate of the Beothuks of Newfoundland. The manuscript recording the Beothuks' last years is the 'Liverpool Manuscript' preserved in the Newfoundland Archives at Memorial University, St John's, Newfoundland. For a harrowing introduction to the atrocities committed, see Horwood, op.cit., pp.75–7.

Chronology

BC (all dates of necessity approximations only)

30,000 First arrival into the South American continent of native peoples, according to the archaeological findings of Professor Nième Guidon.

12,000 First arrival into the North American continent of big game-hunting native peoples who had crossed the Bering land-bridge from Siberia, according to the general consensus of present-day archaeologists.

3,000 First pottery appears among native American peoples.

1,200 Beginning of Olmec civilisation in central America.

AD

c.500 Rise of Toltec civilisation of Mexico. Voyage eastwards from China of Buddhist missionary Hwui Shan, possibly reaching Toltec Mexico, which he called Fusang.

c.550 Voyage or voyages westwards from Ireland by St Brendan and fellow monks into waters with whales and icebergs, reaching fog-shrouded 'Promised Land' which may have been Newfoundland.

c.795 Irish monks settle in Iceland.

c.860 First arrival of Norse on Iceland, displacing Irish monks, some of these latter possibly fleeing to western Greenland.

c.870 Norse begin colonisation of Iceland, this latter rapidly becoming over-grazed by the sheep and cattle the Norse bring with them.

c.900 *Navigatio Sancti Brendani*, the popular form of the St Brendan story, set into written Latin.

c.950 Icelandic Norse discover Greenland.

982 Icelandic Norse sentence Eirik the Red to three years' exile, during which he explores ice-free western coast of Greenland.

985 Encouraged by Eirik the Red, a migration of hundreds of colonists leaves Iceland to set up new homes on Greenland.

Late summer. Bjarni Herjolfsson sails from Iceland to join the colonists but is driven too far west by storms. He sights what seem to be Newfoundland and Labrador before reaching Greenland.

c.995   Eirik the Red's son Leif Eiriksson determines to visit the southernmost land that Bjarni had sighted. He buys Bjarni's ship and departs in early summer, reaching what he calls 'Vinland' where he builds houses for shelter over winter.

c.1000   Icelandic Norse converted to Christianity.

c.1004   Associated with Thorfinn Karlsefni and Thorvald Eiriksson, short-lived attempts to establish permanent settlement on 'Vinland', foiled by 'Skraelings'.

c.1075   The somewhat unreliable German Adam of Bremen writes of Vinland in his *Adamii Gesta Hammaburgensis ecclesiae pontificum*:

> Moreover he also mentioned another island which many have found in that great ocean, which is called Vinland, since there grow wild grapes and they give the best wine. That place has also an abundance of self-sown wheat, and we know this, not from legend but from the reliable report of the Danes . . . Beyond this island there is to be found no habitable land in that great ocean, but everything else beyond is filled with intolerable ice and terrible mist.

1124   According to the *Annals of Morgan*, 'The people of the Norwegians came in the autumn and wintered in Bristol'. *Annales Monastici 1*, Rolls series vol.36/1.

c.1190   *Grœnlendinga Saga (Greenlanders' Saga)* written.

c.1260   *Eirik's Saga* written.

1261   Greenland voluntarily accepts rule of Norway.

1291   **May.** Two Genoese, Ugolino and Vadimo Vivaldi, sail with two ships from Genoa through Gibraltar towards the west (*'directione di Ponente'*) to attain 'through the ocean the Indies'. A certain Thedisio d'Oria goes with them. According to Moorish records one ship was wrecked on the west African coast; the other sailed on. Apparently the Vivaldi brothers did not continue to follow the African coast, but when almost opposite the Canaries they turned westward to attempt the ocean. Thereafter – no one knows.

     Sometime in this same decade Lancellotto Malocelli of Genoa sights the Canary Islands.

1347   Icelandic Annals record: 'There came also [to Iceland] a ship from Greenland . . . There were 17 men on board, and they had sailed to Markland, but were afterwards driven hither.' This seems to have been a ship blown off course on her homeward voyage from a timber-gathering run to Markland or Labrador, inadvertently landing in Iceland.

1349   Icelandic Annals:

At that time a cog sailed out of England with many folk aboard and laid in off Bergen-bay but was little unladen when all the folk died on board and as soon as the goods came into the town off the ship the townsfolk straightway began to die. Then the sickness went all over Norway and laid it so waste that there did not survive one-third part of the people of the land. English cog sunk with nigh all the goods and the dead and it was not unladen . . .

c.1350 Ivar Bardarson, priest at the bishop's palace in Greenland's Eastern Settlement, sails to the Western Settlement, to find it mysteriously deserted, with not a single Norseman, only untended cattle and sheep. If the people of the Western Settlement had emigrated, clearly they had not gone to the Eastern Settlement.

1360 According to the now lost *Inventio Fortunatae*, a mathematically inclined Franciscan friar from Oxford (identified by some as Nicholas of Lynn, by others as Hugh of Ireland) journeys to Greenland, and appears to accompany a timber-gathering expedition to Labrador.

1410 Pierre d'Ailly, Cardinal of Cambrai, writes *Imago Mundi*, a comprehensive world geography compiled before Ptolemy's *Geography* had been rediscovered.

1412 Icelandic Annals record: 'No news from Norway to Iceland'. 'A ship came from England east of Deerholmsey [Dyrholm]; they rowed out to them, and they were fishermen out of England . . .'

1424 The Venetian Zuane Pizzigano draws map with islands of Brasil, Ventura, Saya, Satanazes, Antillia and Ymana. Saganazes and Antillia are shown as large and rectangular. This is the first time that the island of Antillia appears on a map.

1436 Proceedings in the Court of Exchequer arising from the *Christopher* of Bristol having been caught illegally fishing in Iceland, claiming this as Ireland. [P.R.O. Exchequer Memoranda Rolls, Hilary, 14 Henry VI. m. 12]

c.1436 Political poem *The Libelle of Englyshe Polycye* refers to Bristol mariners finding their way to Iceland 'by needle and by stone'.

c.1440 John Wyche, a Bristol surveyor of customs, is suspected of illegal practices. A commission is appointed to inquire into his behaviour. His ship, the *Mary*, is arrested by his successor in office, John Maryot, on her return from Iceland laden with fish. The ingenious Wyche, however, forestalls the surveyor, hands over all the fish to the Mayor in payment of debts, and sells the ship. The surveyor appeals to Chancery. [Calendar of Patent Rolls 1436–41, p.572; 1441–6, p.274; Early Chancery Proceedings 19/316]

1448 Papal letter tells of foreign ships that came to the Greenland settlement, where 'the barbarians ravaged with fire and swords, and destroyed the sacred buildings.' [Dipl.Norv.VI no.527]

1451 Birth of Christopher Columbus in Genoa, the son of a family of wool-weavers.

1454   **9 March.** Birth of Amerigo Vespucci in Florence, the son of a prominent local politician.

1457   John Jay the first a Bailiff of Bristol.

1460   Death of Henry the Navigator. Reports of Portuguese discoveries now become a state secret.

1461   Edward IV visits Bristol. A brilliant pageant is staged for him, and he is entertained to a banquet by William Canynges.

1464   **30 May.** John Shipward, William Bird, Gilbert Smyth, John Jay and William Wodyngton, all Bristol merchants, are granted a royal licence to trade in the *Trinity* of Bristol, described as a ship of 300 tuns or less, to any parts of Acquitaine in the next four months.

1468   John Jay the first dies, leaving to his son John Jay the second his share in the ship *Trinity*. He also leaves 20 shillings to be buried in the choir of St Mary Redcliffe.

1471   **14 February.** Bristol merchants William Spencer, Robert Strange and John Poweke granted licence to trade for one year to any parts except Iceland. [Carus-Wilson, *Overseas Trade*, p.137, no.180; P.R.O. Treaty Roll 144 m.6]

1471–3 First known documentary reference to John Cabot – a grant of Venetian citizenship, to which he was apparently eligible having resided in Venice for 15 years.

1473   Truce signed with Denmark in this year, renewed in 1476 and 1478. But English still not allowed to visit Iceland without permission.
       John Jay Sheriff of Bristol; William Spencer Mayor.

1474   **1 November.** Edward IV grants John Jay the second, William Wodyngton and William Bird, apparent owners of the *Trinity*, privilege of sending their ship on one voyage to Seville or any other Spanish or Portuguese ports, free of all customs payments. Similar licences are also granted in respect of the *Mary Redcliffe*, the *Mary Grace*, and the *James*. Robert Strange elected Mayor this year. Death this year of the great William Canynges: 'the richest and wisest merchant of Bristol'.

1475   British (and particularly Bristolian) fishing rights off Iceland severely challenged by the Hanseatic League, with armed clashes on the high seas.

1479   Richard Ameryk sues the family of William Canynges, nephew of the famous one, William having borrowed money from Ameryk to pay a ransom for Thomas Canynges, who had been captured by Breton pirates.
       First printed edition (text only) of the *Cosmographia* of Claudius Ptolemy published at Vicenza.

c.1476 Joint Scandinavian-Portuguese expedition to the western lands under Pilning and Pothorst, accompanied by Joa Vaz Corte-Real and piloted by Johannes Scolvuss.

1477 Second printed edition of Ptolemy published at Bologna, with 26 maps of Europe and the known parts of Asia and Africa.

1478–9 William Spencer again Mayor of Bristol, for his third and last time.

1479 **29 September**. Beginning of particularly well-preserved Bristol customs account for the Exchequer year September 29, 1479 – July 3, 1480, showing Thomas Croft as collector of customs, together with John Wildegris.

4 March. *Trinity* returns to Bristol with 76 tuns wine, 182 tuns oil, 53½ cwt sugar, 59½ cwt wax and other produce of Iberian peninsular. Ninety-nine different shippers, including John Jay II (salt and wax), Richard Ameryk (sugar), William Bird (oil and wax), Robert Strange, John Esterfeld (oil and wine), and William Wodyngton (oil, sugar and wine). Also several women are listed as having shares in this large cargo. [Carus-Wilson, *Overseas Trade*, p. 260]

4 May. *Trinity* leaves Bristol for Lisbon, with more than 400 cloths on board, with William Wodyngton, William Bird and John Jay the second among the 30 shippers. [Carus-Wilson, *Overseas Trade*, pp. 281–2]

18 June. Thomas Croft, collector of customs at Bristol, together with Bristol merchants William Spencer, Robert Strange, and William de la Fount, is granted three-year licence to trade in any parts, with any except staple goods, with two or three ships, each of 60 tuns or less.

3 July. Bristol accounts end, without return of the *Trinity*.

15 July. According to William Worcestre, an unnamed 80-ton vessel part-owned by Bristol merchant John Jay, and captained by one Lloyd 'the [most] knowledgeable seaman of the whole of England', sets out from Bristol in search of 'the island of Brasil to the west of Ireland'. After nine weeks the vessel arrives storm-battered back in Ireland, ostensibly not having found anything.

18 October. *Trinity*, with Richard Parker as master, commences voyage from Bristol, carrying cargo of cloths and quantity of cheap cotton russetts being shipped by the prominent Bristol merchants Edmund Westcott, John Jay, William Bird, William Spencer, Robert Strange, John Esterfeld and Richard Ameryk. In addition to captain Parker, his mate, purser John Balsall and three cabin boys, the *Trinity* also carries a complement of some 28 others, including at least eight soldiers, and two gunners. The *Trinity* calls first at Milford Haven, then Kinsale, then she sails on to Huelva in southern Spain, where she stays for four or five weeks while the cargo is sold or exchanged. Here a donation is made to the Franciscan friary of Santa Maria de la Rábida. Here also gunpowder is purchased, brought specially from Seville, also brimstone, oakum, pitch and vinegar for the gunners, pots for wildfire, a gunhammer, fittings for the guns, and for the soldiers' crossbows. The *George* also seems to have been with the *Trinity* at this point, for some of the purchase of gunpowder is allotted to it. *Trinity* then goes on to Puerto de Santa Maria.

1481   **January**. *Trinity* goes on to Gilbraltar, and then, after taking on board
        a pilot, into notoriously pirate-infested North African waters to berth
        at the Moorish port of Oran. Since the Spanish are known to have
        occupied nearby Melilla and Kasserès, in an endeavour to check
        Moorish corsairs, it is possible that *Trinity* took some part in this
        action, it being significant that the ship needed beaching, mizzen mast
        and topmast replacement, sail repairs, and other major refurbishment
        at Puerto de Santa Maria on her return.

        End April. *Trinity* sets sail back to Bristol, calling for revictualling at
        Berlingas, Portugal, then Kinsale, Ireland, en route.

        6 July. *Trinity* and *George* are apparently loaded with salt by Thomas
        Croft.

        3 September. Thomas Croft is cleared of having, on 6 July, loaded with
        salt two ships, the *Trinity* and the *George*, allegedly for the purpose of
        trading, which as a customs man was forbidden to him. In his defence
        Croft apparently claimed the salt was 'for the repair, equipment and
        maintenance' of the ship for the purpose of 'examining and finding a
        certain island called the Isle of Brasile'.
            In this same year Pope Sixtus IV, by the bull *Aeterni Regis*, assigns to
        Portugal sovereignty 'over whatever islands shall be found or acquired
        from beyond [south of] the Canaries, and on the side [west] of and in
        the vicinity of Guinea'.

1484   Fierce storm hits Bristol. Cellars flooded and much merchandise
        spoilt. The *Antony* and a ship of Bilbao run aground. Sebastian
        Cabot born before or about this time. Alien subsidy roll of this
        year shows 48 Icelandic men and boys as employed as servants in
        Bristol households.

1485   Columbus arrives at Palos, with the idea of offering his 'Enterprise of
        the Indies' to Ferdinand and Isabella. His wife Doña Felipa having died
        not long before, he is accompanied by his five-year-old son Diego and
        takes the young boy to the Franciscan friary of La Rábida in the hope
        that he can be cared for while he makes contacts in Spain. He is helped
        on this occasion by Antonio de Marchena, custodio of the Franciscan
        sub-province of Seville.

        22 August. Battle of Bosworth, in which Henry Tudor wrests the
        English crown from Richard III, becoming Henry VII.

1486   **Summer**. Henry VII visits Bristol for several days, making a pilgrimage
        to Brislington's shrine of St Anne, and meeting the mayor and other
        prominent townsmen. He is told that trade is bad, apparently due to
        a decline in the Iceland connection, but notes that the women look
        suspiciously well dressed.

1489   In or just before this year Bartholomew Columbus, brother of
        Christopher, visits Henry VII and presents him with a world map in

an attempt to persuade him to back the 'Enterprise of the Indies'. On the advice of his councillors Henry prevaricates and Bartholomew goes to France on a similar mission, where he is employed as a map-maker up to the time of Christopher's successful commissioning and voyage. Robert Strange again Mayor of Bristol, for the last time (1489–90).

1490   On a return visit to Bristol, Henry VII notes that the merchants' wives look even more richly gowned and bejewelled than on his last visit. He demands of the Mayor £500 as a benevolence to the royal coffers, together with £1 from every man who was worth £200 'because men's wives went so sumptuously apparelled'. In this same year the Bristolians decline the opportunity to renew their old trade with Iceland. Also in this year a 'Venetian' named John Cabot Montecalunya is described in documents in Valencian archives as having arrived there.

1491   According to Spanish Envoy Pedro de Ayala's letter of 25 July, 1498, commencement of seven years of Bristol expeditions in search of 'Brasille'.

Summer. Columbus visits La Rábida to call for his son Diego, now ten or eleven, with a view to the boy's staying with his mother's sister at nearby Huelva, while Columbus himself, seemingly defeated in his efforts to interest Spain, departs intending to go to France to offer himself to Charles VIII. But at La Rábida, Fray Juan Pérez, the head of the friary, deplores this intention. A message is sent to Queen Isabella (then at Santa Fe, preparing the siege of Granada) who replies favourably, even to the extent of sending money for Columbus to appear at court in a respectable suit of clothes.

Autumn. Columbus appears before the Queen to renew his argument.

1492   A John Cabot Montecalunya is described in this year as proposing certain improvements to the harbour at Valencia, as having 'designed and painted' plans of these, and as offering to supervise the constructional work involved.

January 2. Granada capitulates and Columbus enters among the victors. But a few days later he is told that his scheme for the Indies is rejected (this is the third occasion), probably because of his exorbitant demands for honours, titles, etc. He leaves with the faithful Fray Juan, but Luis de Santangel, keeper of the privy purse, whom Columbus has befriended, persuades Isabella to change her mind. A messenger is sent post haste after Columbus and Fray Juan, overtaking them only four miles from Santa Fe, where the court was residing.

17 April. Articles of agreement are drawn up for Columbus.

30 April. Columbus is given his 'Commission' and letters for foreign potentates. Also on this date orders are given for the fitting out of the ships for Columbus's expedition. Very curiously, the documents say nothing about any route to the Indies; only of discovering and acquiring 'islands and mainlands of the Ocean Sea'.

22 May. Columbus arrives back in Palos to commence preparations for the voyage.

July. In Bristol Richard Ameryk buys manor house and lands of Ashton Phillips, part of the parish of Long Ashton to the south of Bristol.

3 August. The *Santa Maria, Pinta,* and *Niña* sail from Palos on Columbus's First Voyage.

September. In Spain Cabot has interview with King Ferdinand, explaining his ideas for the Valencia harbour works.

12 October. Columbus sets foot on Bahaman island which he names San Salvador.

15 October. Columbus expedition sails on to visit further islands, named Santa Maria de la Concepción, Fernandina, and Isabela.

24 October. Columbus writes in his log 'on the globes which I saw, and in the paintings of *mappamundis*, it [Japan] is in the vicinity'.

26 October. Diego de la Torre, chief Bailiff, or Governor-General of Valencia, replies to a letter from King Ferdinand regarding Cabot's harbour project, declaring the whole scheme feasible.

28 October. Columbus drops anchor in harbour on Cuba.

November. Bristol customs account shows John Day importing wine in a Portuguese ship from Lisbon.
   In this same month Cabot again has an interview with King Ferdinand, explaining his ideas for the Valencia harbour project.

6 December. Columbus arrives at Haiti.

24 December. Columbus's *Santa Maria* runs aground and founders.

1493 **26–27 February**. King Ferdinand sends instructions to Diego de la Torre, and the *jurats,* or aldermen, of Valencia, regarding the carrying out of Cabot's Valencia harbour works scheme.

4 March. The *Niña* anchors at Rastelo, the outer harbour of Lisbon. Columbus despatches a letter to Ferdinand and Isabella describing the results of his First Voyage.

13 March. The *Niña* leaves Lisbon.

15 March. The *Niña* drops anchor at Palos. The *Pinta* arrives a few hours later.

28 March. The aldermen of Valencia refuse to appropriate the necessary funds for Cabot's harbour project, and the scheme falls through.

April. Bristol customs account shows John Day importing wine and oil from Lisbon in an English ship, the *Nicolas of the Tower*.

Early April. Columbus, having arrived in Seville, is bidden to attend Ferdinand and Isabella at Barcelona. He passes through Valencia en route in a triumphal procession with his captured natives, etc, claiming to have reached 'Asia' by an unprecedented new route. Here, as argued by Williamson, it is almost inevitable that Cabot would have seen the procession and with his knowledge, drawn the shrewd deduction that Columbus had not reached Asia as he had claimed, and that the proper mainland of this was still to be found.

Newly elected Spanish Pope Alexander VI (Rodrigo Borgia) issues bull recognising Spanish sovereignty of all that Columbus has found.

25 September. Columbus sets out on his Second Voyage to the West Indies, sailing from Cadiz with 17 ships.

1494 **2 January.** Columbus anchors in a bay in what is today the Dominican Republic.

6 January. Alonso de Hojeda and Gines de Gorbalán are sent inland with about 40 men and two Indian guides to explore for gold. Columbus sends 12 of the fleet back to Spain with a quantity of Indian captives, 26 of whom, including 3 man-eating cannibals, eventually arrive back in Cadiz.

10 May. Bristol's Tolzey Court records admission of John Day of London, merchant, as member of the Bristol Staple by payment of a 'fine' or fee of £6.13.4d, a considerable sum.

7 June. Spain and Portugal sign Treaty of Tordesillas whereby Ferdinand and Isabella consent that the line of demarcation be moved to the meridian 370 leagues west of the Cape Verde Islands. East of this meridian all discoveries, even if made by Spanish ships, should belong to Portugal; west of it all discoveries, even if made by the Portuguese, should belong to Spain.

12 June. Columbus's ships anchor in the modern Bahia Cortés, Cuba. The crews are pressed to sign a statement that they believe Juana (Cuba) to be mainland.

September. Columbus seriously ill. Decision is made to stay at Isabela on Hispaniola (present-day Dominican Republic).

1495 **June.** Three Columbus ships lost in hurricane while at Isabela.

1496 **5 March.** Henry VII grants Cabot and his sons patent 'to find, discover, and investigate whatsoever islands, countries, regions or provinces . . . which before this time were unknown to all Christians.'

10 March. Columbus leaves Hispaniola for Spain with the *Niña*.

11 June. *Niña* and companion ship anchor at Cadiz.

Late summer? Preliminary, unsuccessful expedition by John Cabot. According to John Day (see 1497 – winter) 'he went with one ship, his crew confused him, he was short of supplies and ran into bad weather, and he decided to turn back'.

12 August. Henry VII in Bristol, according to an entry in the Household Book. (P.R.O., E 101.414.6)

1497   **Circa 20 May.** John Cabot in the *Matthew* with 18 crew sails from Bristol.

24 June. Cabot sights land and goes ashore. He plants a crucifix, the English banner, and the arms of Venice and of Pope Alexander VI. Cautious exploration inland reveals various signs of human habitation, but there is no clear sighting of any natives. Cabot then explores along the coast for about a month.

8 July. Vasco da Gama leaves Lisbon with four ships, intending to sail round Cape of Good Hope to India.

August. With the aid of favourable winds and good weather, Cabot makes landfall in Brittany 15 days after leaving the American coast, having been diverted too far south at the insistence of his crew. By about 6 August he is back in Bristol, and by 10 August he arrives in London, where according to the Household Book he has an audience with Henry VII.

   Columbus is in Spain, spending most of his time at the monastery of Las Cuevas, Seville.

13 December. Henry VII grants John Cabot an annual pension of £20, to be paid from Bristol customs receipts. Customs Roll for the port of Bristol, discovered at Westminster Abbey in 1897, shows payment of £20 to John Cabot from these customs receipts. This reveals Cabot's direct paymasters as Arthur Kemys and Richard Ameryk, 'collectors of the king's customs'.

18 December. Milanese Ambassador Raimondo de Soncino, reporting from London to the Duke of Milan, describes the recent Cabot expedition. He remarks that Cabot has personally told him that Henry VII intends 'before very long' to equip a new expedition with several ships. Significantly, he notes Cabot's generosity with favours. He tells how Cabot had apparently given one of his companions an island, and 'He has given another to his barber, a Genoese by birth, and both consider themselves counts . . . I also believe that some poor Italian friars will go on this voyage, who have the promise of bishoprics.'

1498   **January–March.** English merchant/spy John Day, alias Hugh Say, then in Puerto de Santa Maria, Andalusia, writes to Spanish Grand Admiral (almost certainly Columbus), giving a clearly well-informed report of John Cabot's expedition, and remarking: 'It is considered certain that the Cape of the said land was found and discovered in the past (*en otros tiempos*) by the men from Bristol who found Brasil, as your lordship knows. It . . . is assumed and believed to be the mainland that the men from Bristol found.'

May. Third expedition by Cabot, with five ships, equipped still in the belief that it was Asia that lay across the Atlantic, and with the avowed intention of reaching the empire of the Great Khan and the riches of Cipango

25 July. Pedro de Ayala, Spanish envoy in London, reporting on Cabot to his royal masters, tells them: 'For the last seven years the people of Bristol have equipped two, three [and] four caravels to go in search of the island of Brazil and the Seven Cities according to the fancy of this Genoese. The king made up his mind to send thither, because last year sure proof was brought him they had found land.' He says: 'I have seen the map made by the discoverer, who is another Genoese like Columbus.' He goes on to say that the location of Cabot's discoveries was 'at the cape which fell to Your Highnesses by the convention with Portugal', and reports of Cabot's 1498 expedition that five vessels had set out 'provisioned for a year', but that one of the ships had returned 'badly damaged' to Ireland.

1 August. Columbus's Third Voyage sights American mainland for the first time, at the modern Punta Bombeador, but does not realise that it is mainland.

Sunday 4 August. Men from Columbus's Third Voyage land on the Paria peninsula of what is now Venezuela. But Columbus is seriously ill, and so far as can be determined, does not step ashore. Shortly after, he hastens the fleet to Hispaniola.

1499 May. Spaniard Alonso de Hojeda, together with map-maker Juan de la Cosa and Florentine Amerigo Vespucci, sail westwards from Cadiz, reaching the New World somewhere in the region of the Guianas. They then coast northwards where a 'Little Venice' - type Indian village is seen, giving rise to the name Venezuela. On reaching Cabo de la Vela, this expedition then heads out to sea northwards, first to Hispaniola, then to the Bahamas. According to the very authoritative Spanish historian Fernández de Navarrete, writing in 1829, 'It is certain that Ojeda in his first voyage [1499] encountered certain Englishmen in the vicinity of Coquibaçoa [a little to the east of Cabo de la Vela].' At this date these can only have been men from Cabot's 1498 expedition that had set out from Bristol.

September. John Cabot's pension is paid for the last time, but seems to have been collected by a member of his family.

9 September. Vasco da Gama returns to Lisbon, having sailed successfully to India. Columbus, faced with mutiny at the settlement on Hispaniola, comes to terms with Roldán, the leader of the mutineers, by the end of the month. Towards the end of the year Vicente Yáñez Pinzón sails from Palos and discovers the coast of the true Brazil.

1500 9 March. Pedro Alvares Cabral leaves Lisbon for the Indies. Sailing too far west in order to catch the best winds, he arrives by accident at a part of Brazil and calls it Terra de Santa Cruz.

May. Gaspar Corte-Real sails from Lisbon, 'discovering' at about latitude 50°N 'a land that was very cool, and with big trees' which he names Terra Verde.

Early summer. Hojeda's two caravels, with 200 slaves, arrive back in Spain.

Map of this year, drawn by Juan de la Cosa, shows a portion of the North American coast marked with English flags. La Cosa verbally attributes discovery of this territory to the English. His is also the first to show Cuba as an island, and he also shows a remarkably accurate coastline for Venezuela from Trinidad westwards to the northern side of the Isthmus of Panama even though he himself had only sailed along this no further than Cabo de la Vela, and no other European is known to have sailed further west up to that time. The inference is that La Cosa may have incorporated information gleaned from Cabot's 1498 voyage.

1501 **19 March.** Three Bristol merchants, Richard Warde, Thomas Asshehurst and John Thomas, together with three Portuguese, João Fernandes, Francisco Fernandes and João Gonsalves (described as squires of the Azores), petition Henry VII for the right to 'seek out and discover some islands lying in our sphere of influence.' A patent is granted the same day, giving permission to sail in all seas, southern and northen, eastern, western and Arctic, in order to discover or recover in any part of the world heathen lands 'which before this time were and at present are unknown to all Christians.' Subsequent evidence (see 7 January, 1502) suggests that an expedition left Bristol later on in this same year. Also in this same year a second Bristol syndicate, subsequently known as the 'Company Adventurers into the new Found Lands', with Hugh Eliot among its members, is granted letters patent for voyages of discovery and annexation.

10 May. Having mysteriously changed his allegiance from Spain to Portugal, Amerigo Vespucci sails from Lisbon with Portuguese explorer Gonçalo Coelho on expedition to Brazil, making landfall on 17 August, 1501, and exploring an uncertain distance south.

Mid-May. Portugal's Gaspar Corte Real sets out on new expedition to Newfoundland with three ships.

8 June. Alonso de Hojeda receives exploration licence from Ferdinand and Isabella of Spain specifically worded:

[G]o and follow that coast which you have discovered, which runs east and west, as it appears, because it goes towards the region where it has been learned that the English were making discoveries; and that you go setting up marks with the arms of their Majesties . . . in order that it be known that you have discovered that land, so that you may stop the exploration of the English in that direction . . . likewise their majesties make you gift in the island of Española of six leagues of land . . . for what you shall discover on the coast of the mainland for the stopping of the English, and the said six leagues of land shall be yours forever.'

August. Ferdinand and Isabella's daughter Catherine, the future Catherine of Aragon, sets sail for England as the intended bride of Henry VII's son Prince Arthur.

19 October. Pietro Pasqualigo, Venetian Ambassador in Portugal, reports to Venice that two caravels under the command of Captain Gaspar Corte Real had returned earlier that month from an exploratory transatlantic expedition 'to discover lands towards the north'. He says that they found land and 'examined the coast of the same for perhaps six to seven hundred miles and never found the end, which leads them to think it a mainland. This continues to another land which was discovered last year in the north. The caravels were not able to arrive there on account of the sea being frozen and the great quantity of snow.' He reports of the just returned expedition that 57 of the natives had been brought back with them and that 'these men have brought from there a piece of broken gilt sword, which certainly seems to have been made in Italy. One of the boys was wearing in his ears two silver rings which without doubt seem to have been made in Venice, which makes me think it to be mainland, because it is not likely that ships would have gone there without their being heard of.' Pasqualigo goes on: 'They have great quantity of salmon, herring, cod and similar fish. They have also great store of wood and above all of pines for making masts and yards of ships.'

According to the crews of the two ships who returned, Corte Real himself was continuing to explore southwards. But he was never heard of again, and seems like Cabot to have been lost with all hands.

Sometime in this same year Bristol merchants Robert and William Thorne and Hugh Elyot purchase in Dieppe a ship of 120 tons, the *Gabriel*.

1502 **7 January**. Household Book of Henry VII records 'Item to men of bristoll that founde thisle, Cs'. This is a key indication that the 1501 expedition took place and had returned successfully. On the same day Henry VII grants a £20 bounty to Robert and William Thorne and Hugh Elyot for their purchase of the *Gabriel*. [P.R.O. Exchequer, Warrants for Issues, E. 404/84] Later this same year the *Gabriel* of Robert and William Thorne and Hugh Elyot seems to make the first officially recognised fishing voyage to Newfoundland, with a John a Mayne (or Amayne), who was related to the Thornes, as master. This voyage seems to have been an exploratory expedition on which Robert Thorne and Hugh Elyot sailed in person (see entry for 1527), since Thorne could not have accompanied the one in 1504.

Miguel Corte Real, Gaspar's brother, sets out on new voyage to Newfoundland with two ships. Again the flagship, with Miguel, is lost with all hands, only the companion ship returning.

7 September. After leaving the South American coast in April, the Coelho expedition, still accompanied by Amerigo Vespucci, calls at Sierra Leone on 10 May, before returning to Lisbon on 7 September.

25–30 September. Daybooks of Henry VII record 'Item to the merchauntes of bristoll that have bene in the newe founde launde' xx li.

26 September. Henry VII grants Francisco Fernandes and João Gonsalves pensions of £10 each 'in consideration of the true service they have doon unto us, to our singular pleasure, as Capitaignes into the newe founde lande.' From about this same time chronicles report on the bringing to Henry VII's court of 'three savage men . . . taken in the new found Iland . . .'

Autumn. Amerigo Vespucci writes vivid letter of his travels (subsequently to be known as the Bartolozzi Letter) to his former employer Pier Francesco de' Medici.

19 November. Secret agent Alberto Cantino sends from Lisbon to his patron Ercole d'Este, Duke of Ferrara, a map (made by an unknown cartographer) of what he had been able to learn of the latest world discoveries. This has a surprisingly accurate east coast of Newfoundland.

9 December. Henry VII grants patent to João Gonsalves, Francisco Fernandes, Thomas Asshehurst and Hugh Elyot, their heirs and deputies to sail all the seas and 'to find, recover, discover and search out' any heathen lands in any part of the world, and to annex in the King's name any such places by them found. Significantly this omits the phrase 'lands hitherto unknown to Christians' of earlier patents. The patent also acknowledges respect to be accorded to any prior claims by the King of Portugal.

1503 Richard Ameryk elected Sheriff of Bristol, only to die during his year of office.

10 May. Again with Coelho, Vespucci accompanies an expedition which sails from Lisbon, and after a detour via Africa, and the loss of the flagship, reaches Brazil in the November.

15 September. Daybook of Henry VII records payment of 6s 8d to servant of Sir Walter Herbert for bringing to the King 'a brasil bow and two red arrows'. This and the entry of 17 November strongly suggests a voyage in this year.

17 November. Daybook of Henry VII records payment of 20s 'To one that brought haukes from the Newfounded Island.' (Williamson, p. 216)

29 December. The *Matthew*, with Edmund Griffeth as master, sails from Bristol for Ireland with cargo chiefly for Hugh Elyot.

1504 **8 April.** Daybooks of Henry VII, as transcribed by Craven Ord c. 1829, record payment of 4s 'To a preste that goth to the new Ilande'. This suggests that some form of settlement had already been established (Williamson, p. 136). Bristol customs account book for period from Michaelmas of 1503 shows absence of business activity on the part of Hugh Elyot (no entry from 22 February to 16 August); William Thorne (no entry from 16 January to 28 August); William Clerk (a Londoner who traded at Bristol, no entry from 9 February to 12

August); and Thomas Asshehurst (no entry at all until 12 August). The *Gabriel* must have left Bristol with at least some of these men on board this spring, but its departure is unrecorded in the customs accounts. Robert Thorne could not have been away on this occasion, since the accounts entries name him about once a month throughout the summer, engaged in short-distance trade.

Between 29 September and 12 December. The *Gabriel*, together with the *Jesus*, vessels fitted out by Robert Thorne and Hugh Elyot, bring back the first officially recorded cargo of 20 lasts of salted fish and 7 tons 1 pipe fish livers (value £207.10s) from the 'Newe Found Iland'. [P.R.O. E 356/24, m.2 (enrolled customs return for between Michaelmas and 12 December)]. The Thornes and Elyot have previously been granted an exclusive licence for this and it arrives back free of customs duties. Researches by Alwyn Ruddock strongly suggest that Sebastian Cabot was chief navigator in charge of charting and exploration on the Newfoundland voyage of this year.

28 June. The Coelho/Vespucci expedition returns to Lisbon.

4 September. Amerigo Vespucci writes a colourful letter to his old school friend the Florentine Soderini, grossly exaggerating his rôle in the recent explorations, and, even worse, blatantly lying that he had reached the mainland of the New World as early as 1497. This letter, together with a shorter tract *Mundus Novus* is published in Florence 1504–6. Full of sexual titillation, it achieved a wide circulation, before anything equivalent had appeared relating to Columbus.

1505 **3 April.** Henry VII grants pension to Sebastian Cabot 'in consideracion of the diligent seruice and attendaunce that oure wellbeloued Sebastian Caboot, Venician, hath doon unto us in and aboute the fyndynge of the newe founde landes to oure full good pleaasur and for that he shall doo hereafter in and aboute the same'.

1506 **20 May.** With a priest in attendance and a small group of friends and relatives at his bedside, death of Columbus in Valladolid, Spain, convinced to the last that he had reached Asia.

1507 Martin Waldseemüller, a young professor of geography at St Dié in Lorraine, publishes an *Introduction to Cosmography*. Clearly totally deceived by Vespucci's false claims, he includes in this an appendix with Vespucci's notorious Soderini letter, accompanied by the remark: '. . . [Since] another or fourth part [of the world] has been discovered by Americus Vespucius, as may be seen by the attached charts . . . I believe it very just that it should be named Amerige after its discover Americus, a man of sagacious mind, or let it be America, since both Europa and Asia bear names of feminine form . . .'

In this same year Waldseemüller publishes a big wood-engraved map, on the South American part of which he sets AMERICA in capitals, the first appearance of the name in any known map.

1508–9 Ocampo completes first known circumnavigation of Cuba, establishing it to be an island.

Sebastian Cabot makes a disastrous transatlantic voyage, concerning which he will claim, in old age, that he was compelled to turn back through the faint heart and cowardice of Thomas Spert. According to a report made to the Venetian state in 1536 (and which appears to have been more accurate than others), Cabot had had two ships from Henry VII, and with 300 men had sailed into the frozen sea. He had turned back without accomplishing what he had intended, with a resolve to resume the project at a better season. When he reached England he found that Henry VII was dead.

1509   **21 April.** Death of Henry VII.

1510   **28 February.** Death of Juan de La Cosa at Cartagena, killed by a poison arrow while with a Spanish raiding party trying to capture South American Indians.

1511   **October.** Spanish government in Castile gives instructions to a captain named Juan de Agramonte to explore and colonise the New Land south-west of the fishing region. No expedition actually carries this out. The name Brasil first appears on a map this year, the Jerónimo Marini map. [*Hist.Col.Port.Brasil*, II, 332]

1512   **22 February.** Amerigo Vespucci dies in Seville. This same year Sebastian Cabot, apparently on the strength of his knowledge of Newfoundland, is invited to join the Spanish service.

1513   Ponce de León 'discovers' Florida. In this same year Martin Waldseemüller publishes from Strasbourg '*Terre Nove*', a map in which the name 'America' is now deleted and Columbus accredited as the 'new land's discoverer'.

1515   First printed account of Cabot's voyage in Peter Martyr's *Decades*.

1516   Ferdinand of Aragon dies. In this same year Martin Waldseemüller publishes from Strasbourg a *Carta Marina*, made up of 12 woodcut sheets, as in the map of 1507, but in respect of the American continent showing the same retrograde geographical misconceptions as on the map of 1513.

1519   Death of Robert Thorne the first (will proved at the Prerogative Court of Canterbury, Lambeth, 8 July).

1519–22   Magellan leads expedition to discover a South West Passage to the Spice Islands via the southern tip of South America. Cortés in this same period conquers the Aztec civilisation of Mexico.

1522   **September.** Surviving ship of Magellan's expedition arrives back, having crossed the Pacific and become the first to circumnavigate the world. Magellan himself has died during the voyage. The spices brought back more than pay for the ships lost.

1524   **January.** Florentine Gerolamo da Verrazzano, sailing under the flag of France, crosses the Atlantic to explore and map the eastern seaboard of North America. In this same year Cortés's lieutenant Pedro de Alvarado conquers those of the already much declined Mayan civilisation who were now in Guatamala.

1526   Sebastian Cabot heads expedition to South America, where he discovers and names the Rio de la Plata. He spends three years in an unsuccessful attempt to find large silver deposits near this river.

1527   From Seville, where he has been residing and prospering as a merchant, Robert Thorne the second writes a 'Booke' to Dr Edmund Lee, English Ambassador at Lisbon. He tells Lee that there being 'no land uninhabitable, nor sea innevigable', nothing prevented 'sayling Northward and passing the Pole', the concept of a North-West passage that would occupy English adventurers well into the nineteenth century. Thorne also remarks in his letter: 'As some sicknesses are hereditarious, and come from the father to the sonne, so this inclination or desire of this discoverie I inherited of my father, with another marchant of Bristow named Hugh Eliot, were the discoverers of the New found lands.' In the sixteenth century, 'discovery' did not have such a strict meaning as today. The passage seems to refer to the Thorne-Eliot expedition of 1504.

1531   Robert Thorne the second returns to England. He founds Bristol Grammar School. In Peru Francisco Pizarro, after deceiving and killing the Inca leader Atahualpa, overwhelms and destroys the Inca empire.

1532   **Summer**. Robert Thorne the second dies, aged 40, and is buried in the church of St Christopher in the Stocks in London.

1537   Pope Paul III decrees that native American 'Indians' should be considered human.

1541   First English Act of Parliament relating to America – 3 Henry VIII c.II 'The Bill concernyng bying of fisshe upon the see this Acte ... shall not extende to any person whiche shall bye eny fisshe in any partes of Iseland Scotlands Orkeney, Shotlande, Irelande, or Newland [Newfoundland]'.

1546   Last of the Maya in the Yucatan surrender to conquistador Francisco de Montejo.

1557   Death of Sebastian Cabot.

(This chronology was drawn up principally for the author's rough-and-ready reference, and as such is neither fully polished, nor totally comprehensive. Along with the Notes & References, it is appended mainly to help the student follow up further lines of enquiry)

Bibliography

Ambrosini, Maria Luisa, & Mary Willis, *The Secret Archives of the Vatican*, London, Eyre & Spottiswoode, 1970

Andrews, K.R., N.P. Canny & P.E. Hair, *The Westward Enterprise*, Liverpool University Press, 1978

Ashe, Geoffrey et al., *Quest for America*, London, Pall Mall, 1971

Axtel, James, 'Europeans, Indians and the Age of Discovery in American History Textbooks', *American History Review*, 92, 1987, pp. 621ff

Baddely, St Clair, 'A Bristol Rental, 1498–9', *Transactions of the Bristol & Gloucestershire Archaeological Society.* vol XLVII, 1925, pp. 123–9

Ballesteros y Beterra, Antonio, *Historia de América y de los pueblos americanos*, Barcelona, 1936 and later

Ballesteros y Beterra, Antonio, *La marina cántabra y Juan de la Cosa*, Santander, 1954

Ballesteros-Gailbrois, Manuel, 'Juan Caboto en España', *Revista de Indias*, XIV, 1943, pp. 607–27

Bettey, Joseph, 'Two Tudor Visits to Bristol', in *A Bristol Miscellany*, Patrick McGrath (ed.), Bristol Record Society 1985, pp. 3–6

Biggar, Henry Percival, *The Precursors of Jacques Cartier, 1497–1534*, A collection of Documents Relating to the Early History of the Dominion of Canada, Ottawa, 1911

Brinton, D.G., *Hero Myths. A Study of the Native Religion of the Western Continent*, Philadelphia, 1882

Burman, Edward, *The World before Columbus, 1100–1492*, London, W.H. Allen, 1989

Caraci, Giuseppe, 'The Vespuccian Problems – What Point Have They Reached?', *Imago Mundi*, vol XVIII

Carus-Wilson, Eleanora, M., 'The Iceland Trade' in Eileen Power & M.M. Postan (eds.) *Studies in English Trade in the Fifteenth Century*, London, Routledge & Kegan Paul, second impression, 1951, pp. 155–182

Carus-Wilson, Eleanora, M., 'The Overseas Trade of Bristol' in Eileen Power & M.M. Postan, op cit., pp. 183–246

Carus-Wilson, Eleanora, M., *The Overseas Trade of Bristol in the later Middle Ages*, Bristol, The Bristol Record Society, 1937; reprinted London, Merlin Press, 1967

Cortesào, Jaime, 'The Pre-Columbian Discovery of America', *Geographical Journal*, vol 89, 1937, pp. 29ff

Croft, O.G.S., *The House of Croft of Croft Castle*, Hereford, 1949

Crone, G.R., *The Discovery of America*, London, Hamish Hamilton, 1969

Crosby, Alfred W., *The Columbian Exchange, Biological and Cultural Consequences of 1492*, Wesport, Connecticut, Greenwood Press, 1972

Cumming, W.P., R.A.Skelton and D.B.Quinn, *The Discovery of North America*, London, Elek, 1971

Deuel, Leo, *Testaments of Time, The Story of the Scholar Adventurers and the Search for Lost Manuscripts*, London, Secker and Warburg, 1966

Dunn, Oliver, and James E.Kelly, Jr, *The Diario of Christopher Columbus's First Voyage to America, 1492–1493*, Norman and London, University of Oklahoma Press, 1989

Dunning, Brian, 'The man who gave America its name', *Country Life*, June 20, 1963, pp. 1507–8

Elliott, J.H., *The Old World and the New 1492–1650* Cambridge University Press, 1972

Fernandez de Navarrete, Martin, *Collección de los viajes y descubrimientos que hicieron por mar los Españoles*, Madrid, 1825–37

Fernandez de Navarrete, Martin, *Viajes de Américo Vespucio*, Madrid, 1941

Fingergerhut, Eugene R., *Who First Discovered America? A Critique of Writings on Pre-Columbian Voyages*, Claremont, California, Regina Books, 1984

Fischer, J., & F. Von Wieser, *The Oldest Map with the name America of the year 1507 and the Carta Marina of the year 1516 by Martin Waldseemüller*, Innsbruck, 1903; reprinted Amsterdam 1968

Fischer-Møller, K., *The Mediaeval Norse Settlements in Greenland*, Copenhagen, 1942

Fox, Gustavus, 'An attempt to solve the problem of the first landing place of Columbus in the New World', *Report of the Superintendent of the U.S. Coast and Geodetic Survey* (Appendix no. 18, June 1880), Washington: Government Printing Office, 1882

Fuson, Robert H., (trans.), *The Log of Christopher Columbus*, Southampton, Ashford Press, 1987

Ganong, W.F., 'Crucial maps in the early cartography and place-nomenclature of the Atlantic coast of Canada', *Transactions of the Royal Society of Canada*, ser.III, vol xxiii, 1929

Guidon, N., & G. Delibrias, 'Carbon-14 dates point to man in the Americas 32,000 years ago', *Nature*, 19 June 1986, pp. 769–71

Hakluyt, Richard, *Voyages*, 8-volume Everyman edition, with introduction by John Masefield, London, Dent, 1907

Hale, J.R., 'A World Elsewhere', *The Age of the Renaissance*, D. Hay (ed.) London, Thames & Hudson, 1967

Harden, D.B., *The Phoenicians*, London, Thames & Hudson, 1962

Harrison, W.E.C., 'An Early Voyage of Discovery', *Mariner's Mirror*, XVI, 198–9

Harrisse, Henry, *The Discovery of North America*, London, 3 vols, 1892

Harvey, John H., *William Worcestre, Itineraries*, Oxford, Clarendon, 1969

Hemming, J., *The Conquest of the Incas*, London, Macmillan, 1970

Hermannsson, Hálldor, *The Cartography of Iceland*, Ithaca, New York, 1931

Herodotus, *The Histories*, A. de Selincourt (trans.), Harmondsworth, Penguin, 1954

Heyerdahl, Thor, *American Indians in the Pacific*, London, Allen & Unwin, 1952

Heyerdahl, Thor, *The Ra Expeditions*, London, Allen & Unwin, 1971

Heyerdahl, Thor, *Early Man and the Ocean*, London, Allen & Unwin, 1978

Hill, C.P., *The History of Bristol Grammar School*, London, Pitman, 1951

Hirst, H.C.M., *History of the Church of St John the Baptist, Bristol*, Bristol, Arrowsmith, 1921.

Hoffman, Bernard, *Cabot to Cartier, Sources for a Historical Ethnography of Northeastern North America, 1497–1550*, University of Toronto Press, 1961

Horwood, Harold, *Newfoundland*, Toronto, Macmillan, 1969

Howard, Philip, 'A fishy secret about who found America' *The Times*, 15 April, 1976.

Howley, James P., *The Beothucs or Red Indians: The Aboriginal Inhabitants of Newfoundland*, Cambridge, Mass., 1915

Hudd, Alfred E., *Bristol Merchant Marks*, reprinted from the *Proceedings of the Clifton Antiquarian Club*, vol VII, pt. II

Ingstad, Helge, *Land under the Pole Star*, trans. Naomi Walford, London, Cape, 1966

Ingstad, Helge, *Westward to Vinland*, Erik J. Friis (trans.), London, Cape, 1969

Ingstad, Anne Stine & Helge, *The Norse Discovery of America*, Oxford University Press, 2 vols, 1985

Jenness, J. (ed.), *The American Aborigines: Their Origin in Antiquity*, University of Toronto Press, 1933

Jones, Gwyn, *The Norse Atlantic Saga*, Oxford University Press, 1986

Judge, Joseph & Luis Marden, 'Our search for the true Columbus landfall' *National Geographic*, vol 70, no. 5, Nov 1986

Keen, Benjamin, *The Life of the Admiral Christopher Columbus by his son Ferdinand*, translated and annotated by B. Keen, New Brunswick, New Jersey, 1959

Landström, Bjorn, *Columbus*, London, Allen & Unwin, 1967

Leland, C.G., *Fusang, or the Discovery of America by Chinese Buddhist Priests in the Fifth Century*, New York, J.W.Bouton, 1875

Longfield, A.K., *Anglo-Irish Trade in the Sixteenth Century*, London, 1929

Lyon, Henry, *The Vikings in Wales*, Viking Society for Northern Research, London, 1976

McGrath, Patrick, 'Bristol and America, 1480–1631', in Andrews, Canny & Hair, op.cit., pp. 81–102

Magnusson, Magnus, & Hermann Pálsson, *The Vinland Sagas*, Harmondsworth, Penguin, 1965

Markham, Sir Clements, *Amerigo Vespucci; Letters and Other Documents Illustrative of his Career*, London, Hakluyt Society, vol. no. XC, 1894

Marvell, Josiah, & Robert H. Power, 'In Quest of Where America began: the Case for Grand Turk', *American History Illustrated*, Jan/Feb 1991, pp. 48–69

Morison, Samuel. E., *Admiral of the Ocean Sea*, 2 vols, Boston, 1942 [page references in this book refer to the New York, Time Incorporated paperback edition produced in the same year]

Morison, Samuel. E., *Portuguese Voyages to America in the Fifteenth Century*, Cambridge, Massachusetts, 1940; reprinted New York, 1965

Morison, Samuel. E., *The European Discovery of America: Vol I, The Northern Voyages, AD 500–1600*, Oxford University Press, 1971
Vol II, *The Southern Voyages 1492–1616*, Oxford University Press, 1974

Morison, Samuel. E., *Journals and Other Documents on the Life and Voyages of Christopher Columbus*, New York, 1963

Mowat, Farley, *West Viking: The Ancient Norse in Greenland and N.America*, London, Secker & Warburg, 1966

Munn, W.A., *Wineland Voyages, Location of Helluland, Markland and Vinland*, St Johns, 1919

Nansen, Fridtjof, *In Northern Mists*, 2 vols, London, 1911

Nash, William Giles, *America: The True History of its Discovery*, London, Grant Richards, 1924

Nebenzahl, Kenneth, *Maps from the Age of Discovery, Columbus to Mercator*, London Times Books, 1990

Nunn, G.E., *The Mappemonde of Juan de la Cosa, A Critical Investigation of its Date*, Jenkintown, George H.Beans Library, 1934

Oleson, Trygvi J., *Early Voyages and Northern Approaches 1000-1632*, London & New York, McLelland and Stewart/Oxford University Press, 1964

Parry, J.H., *The Age of Reconnaissance 1450-1650*, London, Weidenfeld 1963

Pohl, Frederick J., *Amerigo Vespucci, Pilot Major*, New York, Columbia University Press, 1944

Power, Eileen & M.M. Postan, (eds.), *Studies in English Trade in the Fifteenth Century*, London, Routledge & Kegan Paul, second impression 1951

Poynter, F.N.L. (ed.), *The Journal of James Yonge, Plymouth Surgeon (1647-1721)*, London, Longmans, 1963

Proulx, Jean-Pierre, *Whaling in the North Atlantic from Earliest Times to the Mid-19th Century*, Ottawa, Parks Canada, 1986

Prowse, D.W., *A History of Newfoundland*, London, Macmillan, 1895

Quinn, D.B., 'The Argument for the English Discovery of America between 1480 and 1494', *Geographical Journal* CXXVII pt.3, 1961, 277ff.

Quinn, D.B., 'Did Bristol sailors discover America?', Letter to *The Times*, 30 April, 1976

Quinn, D.B., 'Edward IV and Exploration', *Mariner's Mirror*, XXI, 1935, pp. 277–80

Quinn, D.B., *England and the Discovery of America*, London, Allen & Unwin, 1974

Quinn, D.B., *New American World*, 5 vols, New York, Macmillan, 1979

Ravenstein, E.G., *Martin Behaim: His Life and his Globe*, Philip London, 1908

Reddaway, T.F., & Alwyn A., Ruddock, 'The Accounts of John Balsall, Purser of the *Trinity of Bristol* 1480–1; *Camden Miscellany XXIII*, Royal Historical Society, 1969

Ricart, Robert, *The Maire of Bristowe his Kalendar*, Lucy Toulmin Smith (ed.), Camden Society, 1872

Roncière, Charles de la, *La Carte de Christophe Colomb*, Paris, 1924

Roukema, E., 'The Mythical "First Voyage" of the Soderini Letter', *Imago Mundi*, vol XVI

Roukema, E.A., 'Some Remarks on the La Cosa Map', *Imago Mundi*, vol XIV

Ruddock, Alwyn A., 'Columbus and Iceland, New Light on an Old Problem', *Geographical Journal*, 1970, pp. 177–89

Ruddock, Alwyn A., 'John Day of Bristol and the English Voyages across the Atlantic before 1497', *Geographical Journal*, 132, 1966, 225–33

[G1.R.801]

Ruddock, Alwyn A., 'The Reputation of Sebastian Cabot', *Bulletin of the Institute of Historical Research*, vol 47, 1974, pp. 95–9

Sauer, Carl O., *The Early Spanish Main*, Cambridge University Press, 1966

Scott, Edward (trans.), *The Cabot Roll. The Customs Roll of the Port of Bristol AD 1496–9*, with introduction by Alfred E.Hudd, Bristol, William George's, 1897

Seary, E.R., *Placenames of the Avalon Peninsula of the Isle of Newfoundland*, University of Toronto, 1971

Severin, Tim, *The Brendan Voyage*, London, Hutchinson, 1978

Sherborne, J.W., *The Port of Bristol in the Middle Ages*, pamphlet, Bristol Branch of the Historical Association, 1965

Shirley, Rodney. W., *The Mapping of the World, Early Printed World Maps 1472–1700*, Holland Press Cartographia, 1988

Skelton, R.A., Thomas E.Marston, & George. D.Painter, *The Vinland Map and the Tartar Relation*, New Haven & London, Yale University Press, 1965

Soulsby, B.H., 'The First Map containing the name America', *Geographical Journal*, London, 1902

Spencer, Robert F., & Jesse D.Jennings, *The Native Americans*, New York, Harper & Row, 1977

Stevens, Sally, & Tim Tiley, *A Few Notes on Monumental Brasses from the West Country*, Bristol, Tim Tiley, 1979

Storey, Robin L., The reign of *Henry VII*, London, Blandford, 1967

Storm, Gustav, *Islandske Annaler indtil 1578*, Christiania, 1888

Taylor, E.G.R., *The Haven-Finding Art*, London, Hollis & Carter (new edition), 1971

Thomas, A.H., & Thornley, I.D. (eds.), *The Great Chronicle of London*, London, 1939

Thomson, J.Callum & Jane Sproull Thomson (eds.), *Archaeology in Newfoundland and Labrador 1985, Annual Report No. 6*, also *Archaeology in Newfoundland and Labrador 1986, Annual Report No. 7*, Newfoundland Museum and Historic Resources Division, Department of Municipal and Provincial Affairs, Government of Newfoundland and Labrador

Tuck, James A. & Robert McGhee, 'Did the medieval Irish visit Newfoundland?' *Canadian Geographical Journal* 92(3), 1977, pp. 66–73

Tuck, James A., & Robert Grenier, *Red Bay, Labrador, World Whaling Capital AD 1550–1600*, St. John's Newfoundland, Atlantic Archaeology, 1989

Tuck, James A., & Robert Grenier, 'Sixteenth-Century Basque Whalers in America', *National Geographic*, July 1985, pp. 40–71

Vignaud, Henry, *Toscanelli and Columbus*, Freeport, New York, Books for Libraries Press, 1971 (reprinted from original edition of 1902)

Vigneras, Louis André, 'The Cape Breton landfall', *Canadian Historical Review*, 38, 1957, pp. 219–28

Vigneras, Louis André, 'New Light on the 1497 Cabot Voyage to America', *Hispanic American Historical Review*, 36, 1956, pp. 503–9

Vining, E.P., *An Inglorious Columbus, or Evidence that Hwui Shan and a Party of Buddhist Monks from Afghanistan Discovered America in the Fifth Century AD*, New York, D.Appleton, 1885

Wedgwood, J.C., & Holt, A.E., *History of Parliament: Biographies of the*

Members of the Commons House, 1439–1509, London, 1936

Williams, A.E., 'Bristol Port Plans and Improvement Schemes of the Eighteenth Century', *Transactions of the Bristol & Gloucestershire Archaeological Society*, 1962, p. 142

Williams, Gwyn A., *Madoc, The Making of a Myth*, London, Eyre & Spottiswoode, 1979

Williamson, James A., 'The Early Falsifications of Western Indian Latitudes', *Geographical Journal*, March 1930

Williamson, James A. (ed.), *The Cabot Voyages and Bristol Discovery under Henry VII*, Cambridge University Press for the Hakluyt Society, second series no.CXX, 1962

Yonge, James, *The Journal of James Yonge, Plymouth Surgeon (1647–1721)*, F.N.L.Poynter (ed.), London, Longmans, 1963

Index

(Numbers in bold indicate page for relevant text figure)